"Best Practice"?

Insights on Literacy Instruction From an Elementary Classroom

Margaret Taylor Stewart
Louisiana State University
Baton Rouge, Louisiana, USA

T 78267

INTERNATIONAL
Reading
Association

800 Barksdale Road,
PO Box 8139
Newark, Delaware 19714-8139, USA
www.reading.org

NATIONAL READING CONFERENCE

National Reading Conference
122 South Michigan Avenue
Suite 1100
Chicago, Illinois 60603, USA

Director of Publications   Joan M. Irwin
Editorial Director, Books and Special Projects   Matthew W. Baker
Senior Editor, Books and Special Projects   Tori Mello Bachman
Permissions Editor   Janet S. Parrack
Production Editor   Shannon Benner
Assistant Editor   Corinne M. Mooney
Editorial Assistant   Tyanna L. Collins
Publications Manager   Beth Doughty
Production Department Manager   Iona Sauscermen
Supervisor, Electronic Publishing   Anette Schütz
Senior Electronic Publishing Specialist   Cheryl J. Strum
Electronic Publishing Specialist   R. Lynn Harrison
Proofreader   Charlene M. Nichols

Project Editor   Corinne M. Mooney

Library of Congress Cataloging in Publication Data
Stewart, Margaret Taylor.
    "Best practice"? : insights on literacy instruction from an elementary classroom / Margaret Taylor Stewart.
        p.   cm. -- (Literacy studies series)
    Includes bibliographical references and indexes.
ISBN 0-87207-344-0
    1. Language arts (Elementary)   I. Title: Insights on literacy instruction from an elementary classroom.   II. Title.   III. Series.
LB1576.S796   2002
372.6044—dc21

"Best Practice"?

Insights on Literacy Instruction
From an Elementary Classroom

To my loves—George, Virginia, Amy, and Ginna—who have supported and challenged me in all good ways.

Contents

Note From the Series Editors

French philosopher Michael Foucault described language and discourse as fractured, prismatic reflections of reality that work to construct us as much as we use them to construct our perceptions of reality. This idea of a fractured reflection applies particularly to the terms *best practices* and *research*. Although these terms seem innocuous enough, literacy teachers and teacher educators grasp the complexity of their interrelationship and the various nuances denoted with each term. Daily, we explicitly and implicitly contend with the questions of what counts as best practice, for whom and in what contexts, and what role research, in all its varying formats, plays in our pedagogical beliefs and practices.

In this book, Margaret Taylor Stewart openly and honestly explores these issues and provides us with a window into best practices and research through one of the most interesting prisms: that of the teacher-researcher. Through her intensive exploration and description of her 26th year of teaching children, we are powerfully reminded of our individual and collective responsibilities of negotiating what counts as best practice.

Thomas W. Bean
University of Nevada, Las Vegas
Las Vegas, Nevada, USA

Lisa Patel Stevens
State Department of Education
Honolulu, Hawaii, USA

Series Editors

Review Board

Allan Luke
University of Queensland
Brisbane, Queensland,
    Australia

Jamie Myers
Pennsylvania State University
University Park, Pennsylvania

Victoria Purcell-Gates
Michigan State University
East Lansing, Michigan

John E. Readence
University of Nevada,
    Las Vegas
Las Vegas, Nevada

Terri Rogers
State Road School
Webster, New York

Marjorie Siegel
Columbia University
    Teachers College
New York, New York

Margaret M. Smith
Clark County School District
Las Vegas, Nevada

Sharon Vaughn
University of Texas at Austin
Austin, Texas

Josephine Peyton Young
Arizona State University
Tempe, Arizona

Acknowledgments

I am indebted to the many individuals who have contributed to this work. A special thank you goes to the many children from whom I have learned over the years, especially those whose voices are reflected in this book. Their ways of knowing have broadened my own. Thank you to fellow teachers from whom I also have learned and with whom I have shared experiences daily. I especially thank Mary Catrett, Gloria Wood, Maggie Murphy, Brenda Sanders, and Marie Remson for their support as a community of peers. Thank you to administrators who allowed me to create classrooms built on my beliefs about sound ways of working with children, especially to Becky Robinson, who also invited me into the world of professional development and pushed me to share my ideas on a broader level. Thank you to academicians who have challenged my thinking, supported my efforts, expanded my horizons, and welcomed me as a peer, especially Maryann Manning, Jerry Aldridge, Cecilia Pierce, Ed Ort, Gary Manning, Lois Christensen, and JoAnn Portalupi. Thank you to Nancy Nelson for her willingness to critique my writing so that my expression of ideas was strengthened and to Avril Font for insightful conversations about literacy. Thank you to Tom Bean and Bonnie Konopak for encouraging the development and completion of this book. I especially thank Matt Baker and Corinne Mooney for their patience and vision as they worked with me to translate my cumbersome manuscript into a finished text. I also thank my friends and family who have been so supportive of the time and effort necessary to complete this book. And thank you to George, Ginna, Amy, and Virginia for encouraging me to keep writing and for being willing to give me time and space to do just that.

Introduction

What Is "Best Practice"?

Teachers, parents, and politicians who are interested in reading to find out what type of instruction is best for teaching children to read, write, spell, or build other forms of literacy may well expect to spend hours looking through references in the "best practice" literature. They may end that search having more questions than they had at the beginning, because there are literally thousands of resources that claim to be best practices in the field of literacy. A keyword search of *best practices* on the Library of Congress Online Catalog generated this response: "Your search retrieved more records than can be displayed. Only the first 10,000 will be shown" (Stewart, 2001). I examined the first 1,000 entries of the first 10,000 and found that, especially in the 1990s, we have become obsessed with using the term *best practices* in almost every aspect of our lives—from best practices in banking to best practices in mental health, Internet usage, medicine, 9-1-1 services, and divorce agreements, among many others. Obviously, anyone can say they are putting forth the best practices. Regrettably, many readers accept what they read as truth simply because it appears in print form. And thus emerges a problem for people who are conscientiously trying to find what is really best practice in literacy instruction, especially for those who are charged with making decisions about that process. Who are they to believe?

When I narrowed my search to *reading best practice*, I was forced to limit my examination yet again to the first 1,000 entries of the first 10,000 given. Again I found seeming obsession with the term *best practices*, which was sometimes included in the title, sometimes

1

implied. The more recent manuscripts with this term were published from the late 1990s until the present, but there were entries that were published as far back as the 1800s. This search for *the* best method is not restricted to the present time in educational history, nor is it restricted to one particular worldview. And therein lies another problem: One's view of the world and of the purposes of education presupposes what one will advocate as best practices. What liberals conceive as best practice obviously is not what conservatives value, and vice versa. How can teachers, parents, or politicians make sense of what has been learned so far about classroom literacy instruction? Do we limit our examination to only "scientifically reliable, replicable research studies" (Reading Excellence Act, 1999), as is being currently advocated by conservatives in government and education (c.f., National Institute of Child Health and Human Development, 2000; National Reading Panel, 2000; Ravitch, 2000), or do we include often currently overlooked classroom-based literacy studies, such as those that taught us about the processes and products of writing, connections between reading and writing, and connections between literacy and community in classrooms (e.g., Calkins, 1983, 1986; Dyson, 1989, 1993; Fisher, 1991; Fraser & Skolnick, 1994; Graves, 1983)? Do we include other qualitative methodologies, such as those that taught us the importance of early detection of reading difficulties (e.g., Clay, 1979, 1998), the importance of helping children make connections between literacy at home and in school (e.g., Bissex, 1980; Heath, 1982, 1983), and those that taught us to value approximations, particularly constructive errors, as a way in which children move forward in their use of language (e.g., Ferreiro & Teberosky, 1979/1994)? Do we include the work of well-respected literacy authorities who provide clear literacy learning mandates built on years of classroom-based research (e.g., Allington, 2001; Gambrell, Morrow, Neuman, & Pressley, 1999; Strickland & Morrow, 2000; Weaver, 1998a, 1998b)? Who decides?

Literacy best practice is currently discussed, debated, strongly suggested, even mandated from many directions in the United States (e.g., Adams, 1990; Children's Literacy, 1997; Dahl, Scharer, Lawson, & Grogan, 2001; Flippo, 1999; Lyon, 1997, 1998b; McQuillan, 1998; Reading Excellence Act, 1999; Snow, Burns, & Griffin, 1998; Taylor, 1998; Zemelman, Daniels, & Hyde, 1998). The impact of this debate is immediate and far-reaching. It behooves every U.S. citizen to give careful consideration to an issue that so profoundly affects the most vital resource of the United States—children.

The Search for "Best Practice": Whose Perspective Is Valued?

The effective-practices literature continues to gain momentum as educators and others persevere in looking at what is working in schools (e.g., Brandt, 1989; Darling-Hammond, 1997; Fine, 1994; Hill & Weaver, 1994; Purkey & Novak, 1996; Taylor, 1990; Whitford & Gaus, 1995) and as researchers examine the practice of teachers who are deemed exemplary in their practice (e.g., Collinson, 1999; Ladson-Billings, 1994; Pressley et al., 1998; Wharton-McDonald, Pressley, & Hampston, 1998). The quest of effective practices is to discover what is best in terms of *actual children* in *actual classrooms*. Teacher research is another way to establish high-quality research within the classroom. Instead of investigating the teaching practices of another culture, teacher-researchers investigate their own teaching practices.

The renewal of interest in teacher research in the United States during the 1980s and 1990s came in part through efforts of qualitative researchers, such as Calkins (1983, 1986) and Graves (1983), who investigated writing. These qualitative researchers had the foresight to study real classrooms, real teachers, and real students to understand the process of writing within the classroom and to document growth in students' writing processes and products. Because of the interest of those researchers and others of the same era (e.g., Bissex, 1980; Harste, Woodward, & Burke, 1984; Newkirk, 1989), other researchers and teachers began paying attention to the importance of *how* young writers and thinkers go about their work in the classroom. A generation of teacher-researchers began writing about their close and careful examinations of their own practices, particularly in the field of literacy. Many of these teacher-researchers (e.g., Atwell, 1987; Fisher, 1991; Fraser & Skolnick, 1994; Giacobbe, 1986) gave readers an insider's look at their classrooms and children, as they showed the power of connection in classrooms and bridged the gap that often existed (and often still exists) between theory and practice. The connections in this research (and my own) are many: connections between students

3

and teachers, connections to learning, to literature, and to the world of school and the world beyond school. Many teachers and university researchers (e.g., Anderson, Herr, & Nihlen, 1994; Cochran-Smith & Lytle, 1993; Dyson, 1989, 1993; Goswami & Stillman, 1987; Hubbard & Power, 1993, 1999) continue to bridge that gap as they work together to support, guide, and encourage today's teacher-researchers.

Unfortunately, during this time of emphasis on high-stakes testing and calls for back-to-the-basics, high-caliber, classroom-based research (e.g., Cambourne & Turbill, 1991; Clay, 1993; Edwards, Gandini, & Forman, 1979/1994; Goodman, Smith, Meredith, & Goodman, 1987; Holdaway, 1979) is being either ignored or negated in the call for "the strongest of objective scientific evidence" (Lyon, 1998a, p. 5), "scientifically based reading research" (Reading Excellence Act, 1999, Section 2252, Definitions [5], p. 2), or "scientifically based research" about reading (Carnine & Meeder, 1997, p. 2). Often in the search for the silver bullet to fight against the long-standing reading and writing problems that some children face, the mass media has led parents, legislators, and the general public to either forget or question the importance of lessons learned from teacher research (e.g., Colvin, 1996; Manzo, 1997, 1998; Zemelman, Daniels, & Bizar, 1999). We must gather evidence from many angles in studying the complex issue of best practice. We must continue to value academic research that enters the debate from an authoritarian stance (e.g., Allington, 2001; Calkins, 2001; Flippo, 1999; Gambrell et al., 1999; Graves, 1994; Pearson, 1984, 1993). We must continue to call for publicly and privately funded research to deliberate about this important issue (e.g., Coles, 1998b, 2000; Marzano, Pickering, & Pollock, 2001; Ohanian, 1999; Reading Excellence Act, 1999; Snow et al., 1998). Most important, we must continue to value research from teachers who conduct investigations into their own practices (e.g., Bigelow, Christensen, Karp, Miner, & Peterson, 1994; Donoahue, Van Tassell, & Patterson, 1996; Genishi, Yung-Chan, & Stires, 2000; MacLean & Mohr, 1999; Paley, 1979/1990, 1995, 1997).

Why Look at One Classroom?

The main emphasis of this book is a sustained look at my own second-grade classroom, during my 26th year of teaching. What can we possibly learn about best practice from one teacher's presentation of her own classroom? How can a teacher think that she has the answer to so large an issue when many of the best minds in the United States cannot agree? My point is just that: We do not agree. Issues of exemplary practice are not simple, and whether called "best practices," "researched-based practices," or practices by any other name, there can be no one set of prescribed practices to fit all teachers and all children in all settings.

This book is similar to *Children Achieving: Best Practices in Early Literacy* (Neuman & Roskos, 1998) and *Children's Writing: Perspectives From Research* (Dahl & Farnan, 1998), although those books are organized differently. Neuman and Roskos's text is made up of essays written by several authors on a variety of literacy topics in order to illustrate early literacy best practices. Dahl and Farnan's book is a synthesis of a broad range of research studies that deal with elementary and middle school children's development as writers in the classroom and examine the students' processes of writing. *"Best Practice"? Insights on Literacy Instruction From an Elementary Classroom* focuses on one classroom to illustrate that what emerges as "best practice" for the students in that classroom grows out of complex interactions across time and through a variety of situations.

The book's main focus is on what can be learned about exemplary practice in schools by looking carefully at the work, words, actions, interactions, and reflections of the *people* involved. This text examines praxis, or reflection on practice, through a systematic investigation of a series of *critical incidents* that occurred in my teaching during this study. I use the term *critical incidents* in the sense that Tripp (1993) describes; that is,

> [I]ncidents [that] appear to be "typical" rather than "critical" at first sight, but are rendered critical through analysis.... [Or] an incident which passed entirely unnoticed when it occurred, but which was made into a critical incident by what was subsequently seen in and written about it.... The critical incident is created by seeing the incident as an example of a category in a wider, usually social, context. (p. 25)

The two stages of a critical incident as explained by Tripp are observation of the incident and notation of the incident (respectively, *production* and *explanation* of the incident—the "what" and "why"). I have presented my interpretation of reality in the text through the voices I chose to share, the stories I chose to tell, and the data I chose to use.

I am not satisfied that *everything* has been said that needs to be said on the subject of best practice; therefore, I find myself eager to enter the current dialogue from the perspective of both teacher and learner in the world of children's literacy education and to bring my students along as contributors to the discourse. I offer my reflections on practice and examples of my students' work to contribute to the broader examination of classroom literacy issues (pseudonyms have been used in place of students' real names).

Conducting research in my own classrooms has nudged my thinking—about students as individuals and groups; students' processing in writing, reading, and oral language; and the power of classroom community—to a different level. My teacher research has challenged my ideas about my role in the classroom, about the place for practitioner research in the overall scheme of educational research, and about ways to help preservice and inservice teachers incorporate practitioner research into their own classrooms. I believe reflective practice is the direction in which classroom teachers should be moving, and I am pleased to see U.S. national teaching standards supporting reflective practice, particularly in standards documents for educators of preservice teachers (e.g., Interstate New Teacher Assessment and Support Consortium [INTASC], 1992; National Council for Accreditation of Teacher Education [NCATE], 2000).

Organization of the Text

The first two chapters provide a framework for the study, so readers may better understand the structures underlying the practitioner research study on which the text is based. Chapter 1 sets forth 10 issues that have an impact on best practice and discusses how these issues pressure classroom life. The chapter concludes with the promise of possibilities brought by *people within the classroom* as they influence classroom practice. Chapter 2 sets the foundation, looks at the theoretical beliefs and philosophy of the teacher-researcher, and presents the methodology of the study. Chapters 3 through 6 give specific details of the study through the collected data. These chapters attempt to *show* how the students and I influenced our classroom community through our complementary roles as artists and architects. Chapter 7 identifies and examines the study's themes. It reflects on the scenes of classroom life presented throughout the text to point out what works and what does not in the reality of *this* classroom. Then, it relates what this classroom-based study means to *all* teachers and learners. The chapters are followed by two appendixes, which provide time frames.

Conclusion

This book attempts to heighten readers' awareness of many issues underlying the current educational debate of literacy best practice in the United States and urges readers to make informed opinions. I challenge readers to become researchers themselves, by finding at least one child who needs their mentoring. By observing children, looking for children's personal strengths, and finding ways to build on those strengths, these readers, who have become researchers, will discover many new things about what is *best for those children*. What will they learn? How can they share that learning? How can such knowledge contribute to understandings of excellent practice in settings in which teachers must work with many and diverse children?

I ask readers to search for understandings that translate from this particular setting to other settings, with other students, in other places, and at other times. This book also celebrates children and their work. It discusses themes that emerged from my study of children within an elementary classroom that support both language literacy and classroom community. Although this is a book with a seemingly narrow focus, it provides readers with an insider's look at how the *people* within the classroom—the students and the teacher—learn and grow in complex and powerful ways.

CHAPTER 1

Pondering Classroom Pressures, Celebrating Possibilities

The general public assumes that teachers are the decision makers in their own classrooms, although the reality has been that forces outside the classroom have tried to take on this role. Hoffman (1998) interprets educational attitudes and gives what he calls his "highly impressionistic" interpretation—not a synthesis—of shifts in educational focus during the 20th century in the United States. I find his interpretation helpful to view the changes I experienced during my teaching career, as I was a student during the end of what Hoffman terms Phase 1 and a teacher during Phases 2–4. An abbreviated version of his phases of educational focus open this chapter, which centers on the pressures that many classrooms and teachers have faced and continue to face.

Shifts in Educational Focus During the 20th Century

Phase 1 (Early 1900s–Mid-1960s): "If we tell them, they will come (along)" (Hoffman, 1998, p. 106)

The scholarly/academic community (university faculty), primarily in control of education during this period, regarded practicing teachers as capable but "woefully undertrained" (Hoffman, 1998, p. 106) products of a self-perpetuating educational system. Most major educational theorists of the time were not directly responsible for teacher education, and laboratory schools and clinics were not even part of mainstream teacher education. In his analysis of this phase, Cremin (as cited in Hoffman, 1998) attributed lack of wide implementation of progressive-type reforms to the following factors: (a) Those practices required teachers who were infinitely skilled; (b) the number of such teachers was insufficient to sustain the complex teaching and schooling that would be required; (c) beginning teachers adapted to the contexts into which they entered rather than change them; and (d) experienced teachers seemed little inclined to investigate or use new educational ideas.

Phase 2 (Mid-1960s–Mid-1970s): "Change the materials, change the teaching" (Hoffman, 1998, p. 106)

Because university ideas did not have a smooth transition into classrooms, new ideas began to be directly communicated to practicing teachers, primarily through changes to curriculum materials used in schools. Numerous curriculum reform initiatives occurred because educational professionals and the general public acknowledged the need for changes in the quality of teaching, and because there was a huge influx of federal money to support educational innovation. Primary criticisms of the reforms were abstractness, radical change from existing practice, and limited success as measured by test results (Dow, as cited in Hoffman, 1998). The educational establishment—primarily university faculty and system administrators—blamed teachers for the failure of reform efforts, presuming that most teachers did not understand effective teaching practices, were too busy with teaching demands to spend sufficient time on in-depth planning and curriculum development, and often did not teach to the basics.

Phase 3 (Mid-1970s–Mid-1980s): "Keep it simple, stupid" (Hoffman, 1998, p. 107)

Hoffman contends that the mindset of Phase 3 grew out of the failures of Phase 2: "Change is more likely to occur if (a) the innovation itself is quite explicit in terms of its features and procedures, (b) the implementation process is carefully monitored, and (c) expectations and accountability for change are clear" (p. 107). According to Englemann and Carnine (as cited in Hoffman, 1998), programs such as Direct Instructional System of Teaching Arithmetic and Reading (DISTAR) focused on explicit, intensive training, with careful monitoring of implementation. Initiatives such as Project Follow Through—a social-action program, originally designed to extend Head Start into primary grades, that explored effective methods for educating disadvantaged children—included direct instruction, monitoring, and accountability (Meyer, as cited in Hoffman, 1998; Stallings & Kaskowitz, as cited in Hoffman, 1998). Systematic study of change revealed that even apparently successful innovations required continuous supervision to survive; innovations that were somewhat flexible and adaptable to the context seemed most likely to survive at the classroom level (Berman & McLaughlin, as cited in Hoffman, 1998).

Phase 4 (Mid-1980s–Mid-1990s): "Forget the teachers; fix the system and you fix instruction" (Hoffman, 1998, p. 108)

The most recent perspectives of educational change are school-reform initiatives, which surfaced in response to the report titled *A Nation at Risk: The Imperative for Educational Reform* (National Commission on Excellence in Education, 1983). Hoffman suggests that the prevailing attitude toward teachers shifted, with teachers now viewed as "pawns within a system. They are neither inherently bad nor good; they simply respond to the conditions (rewards, punishment, constraints, accountability structures, resources, opportunities, etc.) that surround them" (p. 108). School reformers hope to bring about meaningful change by adjusting contexts of schools. Hoffman concludes, "At best, we can argue that the 'systemic' reform may set the stage for innovations in practice, but does not assure them" (p. 108).

Pressures Within the Classroom

For years, the general public seemed to respect teachers and entrusted teachers with knowing what and how to teach students. Teachers as a generic group within the United States are often portrayed by mass media, thus perceived by the general public, as inefficient. Schools and classrooms have become less isolated and autonomous and are more *public* than ever before, which means that outside factors are affecting schools and classrooms more than ever before. Those factors often appear as pressures that directly and indirectly influence teachers' practice. The following sections set forth 10 pressures that influence what may be perceived as "best practice" within those classrooms: paradigms and politics, pedagogy and pragmatics, programs and professionalism, processes and products, and prerequisites and praxis.

Paradigms and Politics

A *paradigm*, which is commonly thought of as an example, is also defined as " a philosophical and theoretical framework of a scientific school or discipline... " (Merriam-Webster's Online, 2001). In this context, *paradigm* refers to an overarching belief system or worldview held by individuals or groups (Aldridge, 1991).

Two competing views of the purposes of schooling are the traditional and liberal perspectives, which form ends of a continuum on which numerous educational beliefs and practices rest. The traditional perspective sees schooling in the United States as a way to

- prepare for the future (especially future education, future occupation, and the elusive, much coveted success of the individual, which is possible through the traditional capitalist system of the United States);
- maintain the economic, social, and political status quo;
- transmit a core curriculum of classical knowledge, for which individuals are held accountable through high-stakes testing; and
- maintain the mainstream U.S. culture and values.

Generally, the traditional perspective is held by conservatives in business, politics, education, and the mass media. The liberal perspective, at the other end of the continuum, sees schooling as a

- meaningful present;
- way to prepare for ever-expanding possibilities of the rapidly changing future, with its unknown challenges and successes;
- way to emphasize problem solving, critical thinking, and learning in cooperation with peers, for which individuals are judged on performance-based criteria; and
- way to value cultural diversity.

This perspective is held by the more liberal segment of academia and the political Left.

Glass (2000) points out that there have been certain fundamental contradictions, inherent in the ideology of public schooling from its beginning, that help explain public schools' mixed performance. Educators' sometimes-contradictory aims—preserving order and conserving dominant values versus fostering independence and transforming societal values toward more just values—have been entangled in the web of social and instructional practices of public schooling since its inception. Glass explains that public schools face the difficult and contradictory tasks of using their authority to foster the capacity among educated student-citizens to question that authority and to establish a framework of values and norms within an increasingly diverse society. These tasks represent tensions inherent in the dynamics of a pluralistic democratic culture that must balance demands of liberty, equality, and freedom without disintegration.

Cuban (as cited in Glass, 2000) suggests that problems faced by schools cannot be solved in a once-and-for-all manner because contradictions exist at levels of specific curricula and general purposes of schooling. Communities in the United States are plagued by a permanent set of dilemmas that persist as schools seek solutions in implementing the broad range of goals and mandates they have acquired because of decades of political debate and decision making.

In his article titled "Reading Patrick Shannon on Reading Instruction: Reflections on Politics and Education" (2000), Glass suggests that Patrick Shannon's ideas about reading instruction still resonate in current educational reform debates because these ideas address dilemmas involving fundamental values. These values, rather than being permanently fixed, must be readjusted continually to cope with changing circumstances and demands. Glass states, "The unrelenting force of institutions moving in time means that power and politics are determinative at any given moment, and what cannot be clarified or settled in principle gets lived in ambiguity and contradiction" (p. 287).

To understand what Glass means, one has only to look at three current issues: (1) the "reading wars," (2) epistemological and child development theories, and (3) research methodologies and inquiry paradigms. These issues also demonstrate how various political factions attempt to persuade one another (and the masses) to their mind-sets, and may have their own vested interests that do not correspond with the needs of classrooms or schools. These three issues directly pressure teachers, who increasingly receive mandates from various factions. Teachers also are pressured indirectly as they grapple with their own issues, trying to make informed teaching choices.

THE "READING WARS." Let us first examine the "reading wars," as the debate about reading methods and pedagogy was unfortunately dubbed by the mass media (e.g., Lemann, 1997; Rubin, 1997; Toch, 1997). This label caused even greater rifts in the literacy community than were already present prior to its use. The extreme perspectives on the groups involved in the reading wars are "phonics first and foremost" versus "meaning first and foremost." Of course, that terminology oversimplifies the issue and does not illustrate either position adequately. Both groups legitimately believe that children must gain understanding from what they read, value the place of literature in the classroom, and plan for and expect children to learn the alphabetic code of the English language. The beliefs of these groups diverge about the meaning of the word *reading*, the order of presentation, the methods of delivery, use of text composition, and the roles of context and prior experience in literacy acquisition. Less inflammatory terms often used to present these divergent views on reading instruction are *code-emphasis* and *meaning-emphasis* (e.g., Carnine, Silbert, & Kameenui, 1997; Chall, 1967, 1999). In her review of 50 years of research on this debate, Chall (1967) states that code-emphasis instruction promotes *mastering the alphabetic code* in initial reading instruction, whereas meaning-emphasis instruction believes that children learn to read best when *meaning is stressed* in initial reading instruction.

Advocates of code-emphasis instruction define reading as a psychological process with emphasis on reading words fluently and effortlessly so that readers respond to cues in the text to receive the author's intended message (e.g., Adams, 1990; Adams & Bruck, 1993; Grossen, 1998). The author's message is seen as fixed and non-negotiable, which means that a reader's personal experience and interpretation have little to do with the author's message; however, personal relevance and interpretation do receive attention later in the comprehension process (Adams & Bruck, 1993). A good reader can hear and manipulate phonemes (the smallest units of speech sounds). Advocates of code-emphasis instruction consider this skill, called "phonemic awareness" or "phonological awareness," a key influence in learning to read, and lack of this skill is called by some a "core deficit" (e.g, Foorman, Francis, Fletcher, & Lynn, 1996; Lovett, Steinbach, & Frijters, 2000; Lyon, 1996; Shaywitz et al., 1997; Stanovich, 1993/1994). However, advocates of meaning-emphasis instruction view this as possibly correlational, definitely not causal.

From the code-emphasis perspective, a good reader sounds out quickly and well, reading words even when there are no semantic context cues (Share & Stanovich, 1995; Stanovich, Cunningham, & Feeman, 1984). These authorities believe that children must learn how to decode the text in order to understand the author's intended meaning, and they must develop fluency and automaticity so that comprehension is not lost in a struggle to decode print (Chard, Simmons, & Kameenui, 1995). The most direct way to structure this process is through systematic, sequential phonics instruction that uses decodable text (Adams, 1990; Carnine et al., 1997; Chall, 1967, 1983; Ehri, 1991; Foorman, Francis, Fletcher, & Schatschneider, 1998; Foorman, Francis, Novy, & Liberman, 1991; Francis, Shaywitz, Stuebing, Shaywitz, & Fletcher, 1996). Beginning readers should hear stories, but their reading should come primarily from decodable texts that contain phonetically regular words and sounds they have learned previously, so they do not become confused (Adams, 1990; Foorman et al., 1998; Grossen, 1998). Most proponents of extreme code-emphasis instruction perceive reading as a solitary act, in which the reader passively receives information, and the teacher disseminates knowledge.

The prescribed order of literacy learning by code-emphasis instruction is relatively inflexible. Advocates of this perspective consider the following sequence to be the best way for children to learn to read: (a) learn the way sounds work in language first (phonemic awareness); (b) learn to identify each letter and connect it with its sound(s) through explicit and systematic phonics instruction (preferably in a set sequence, the exact order of which varies from expert to expert); (c) build and read both real words and nonwords from letters; (d) build and read sentences from words; (e) construct and read paragraphs from sentences; and (f) construct and read extended text from paragraphs. Individuals who believe in code-emphasis instruction do not negate the importance of comprehension. However, they believe there is an exact sequence of learning that begins with specific, isolated bits of information that are systematically and sequentially put together to form more and more complex pieces of language. (To read more about this method of literacy instruction, see Adams, 1990; Carnine et al., 1997; Chall, 1983; Ehri, 1991; Juel, 1988.)

Advocates of meaning-emphasis instruction define reading as making meaning of print (e.g., Clay, 1979, 1993; Goodman, 1976; 1986, 1993; Smith, 1971, 1975, 1985; Weaver, 1994). Reading is a transaction between the reader, the text, and the author (Rosenblatt, 1978/1994; Routman, 1994, 2000); therefore, the text has an intended meaning for the author *and* the reader—a negotiable reality. Children learn how to decode print more efficiently as they use a self-improving system of making meaning from print (Clay, 1979; Weaver, 1994). Children predict and confirm as they construct meaning (Ferreiro & Teberosky, 1979/1994; Manning, Manning, Long, & Wolfson, 1987). Proponents of meaning-emphasis instruction see reading as a social and cultural process in which the reader actively engages in constructing meaning (Bloome, 1993). The teacher facilitates learning.

The order of literacy learning espoused by proponents of meaning-emphasis instruction is more flexible than that prescribed by those who believe in code-emphasis instruction. Advocates of meaning-emphasis instruction believe the best way for children to learn to read is to have stories read to them from their earliest years; have children participate in lap reading (sharing books with a parent, guardian, friend, or other bonded person), classroom read-alouds (Trelease, 1979, 1995, 2001), shared book experiences (Holdaway, 1979), and interactive reading and writing (Fountas & Pinnell, 1996; McCarrier, Pinnell, & Fountas, 2000); or have children learn conventions of print through other rich connections with people and text (Clay, 1979, 1993; Routman, 1994, 2000; Weaver, 1994). From this perspective, phonics is an important part of reading but only one of three cueing systems: semantic (meaning), syntactic (grammar), and graphophonic (symbol-sound relationship) (Goodman, 1986; Goodman, Watson, & Burke, 1987). This instruction aims to help children understand from the beginning that print has meaning and to ask children if what they are decoding makes sense, sounds like language, and looks right. Teachers begin with connected text and instruct in ways that make sense for each individual learner. (To read more about this method of literacy instruction, see Clay, 1979, 1993; Fisher, 1991; Goodman & Burke, 1980; Goodman, Smith, et al., 1987; Goodman, Watson, et al., 1987; Routman, 1988, 2000; and Weaver, 1994.)

EPISTEMOLOGICAL AND CHILD DEVELOPMENT THEORIES. *Epistemology* is the branch of philosophy concerned with the study of knowledge. Theories are explanations or beliefs about how facts fit together to form meaning and organization. Epistemological theories, then, are structures that explain our beliefs about knowledge and learning. Child development theories explain our beliefs about children—what they are like, how they should be treated, how they learn and grow. With no dominant theory, or metatheory, of education, educators have traditionally drawn from psychology for their theories. Aldridge, Kuby, and Strevy (1992) discuss problems in applying psychological metatheories to education, using as examples Piaget's constructivist theory, which explains what develops naturally and spontaneously through a child's interaction with the environment but not what develops from direct instruction, and behaviorist theory, which describes ways in which learning takes place in contrived experimental conditions but not ways in which learning takes place in natural settings.

Thomas (1992) cites four questions people often ask as they seriously begin to investigate theories of development and learning, two of which have implications here: "(1) What difference does it make which theory you adopt?... (4) Why do scholars develop different theories rather than agree on an existing one?" (p. 4). In addressing the first implication, Thomas likens a theory of child development to a lens through which we view children and their growth. We could say the same of an epistemological theory as a way to view knowledge: A theory filters out some facts while attaching particular patterns to ones it lets in, coloring everything we see, hear, and understand.

In addressing the second implication, Thomas explains that one reason why scholars develop different theories is that they are not convinced that existing theories satisfactorily answer important questions. Scholars in different fields develop different mind-sets and are influenced by the types of problems they deal with in their daily work. For example, scholars in the field of science tend to think about problems in quantifiable ways, often looking at such factors as heredity and physical causes and behavioral solutions, whereas scholars in fields such as sociology and anthropology tend to think about problems relative to the contexts in which they are found, often looking at qualitative factors and environmental causes and solutions. These broad generalizations do not account for divergence in each field, but they point out how backgrounds and current situations can influence beliefs.

Vygotsky's (1934/1978) discussion of the four primary views of the relationship between learning and development also help to answer Thomas's questions: (1) Development precedes learning, (2) learning and development are the same, (3) learning and development interact and influence one another, and (4) learning precedes development. These views, based on psychological theories rather than educational ones, still influence educational beliefs and theories.

Other issues influence epistemological and child development theories. We see an array of beliefs ranging from radical behaviorism to radical constructivism, with everything in between, in the current debates about reading methods in literacy instruction. For example, people who favor code-emphasis instruction often support behaviorist theories and belief systems. Code-emphasis models (or "balanced" models that emphasize alphabetic code instruction) have many supporters in the field of special education. Influences on these supporters might be scientific backgrounds that have predisposed them to look at the world in quantifiable ways or a career in which they primarily work with students who have extreme difficulties with reading, writing, or speaking. These influences may cause them to perceive a higher percentage of people who struggle with literacy learning, and they may actively look for theories to support severely struggling learners.

Conversely, people who favor meaning-emphasis instruction (or "balanced" models that emphasize meaning instruction) often support constructivist theories and belief systems, especially social constructivist theories built primarily on Vygotsky's work. The meaning-emphasis model has many supporters in regular education, particularly in the field of early or emergent literacy. Influences on these supporters may be a sociocultural background, which may encourage them to look at the world in qualitative ways, or a career in which they primarily work with students in regular education, in which there is a wider range of literacy performance than in special education classes. Teachers in regular education classes generally have some students who learn easily, some who learn when they receive strong instruction that is appropriate for their learning, and some who struggle and need specific modifications and interventions to support their learning. These influences may cause these teachers to search for theories that support a wide range of learners, not just struggling ones.

In "Why Not Phonics *and* Whole Language?" Adams (1991) sees value in the goals of whole language, in which confidence and authority of teachers are restored; education is sensitive to strengths, needs, and interests of students; and compartmentalized instruction and learning of rote skills and facts are replaced with highly integrated, thoughtful, meaningful, and self-engendering engagement with ideas and information. As I read Adams, I began to think the beliefs of code-emphasis supporters and meaning-emphasis supporters might agree when she further notes that "These goals are of paramount importance to our nation's educational health and progress" (p. 52). Yet Adams calls these goals

> strictly independent from issues of the nature of the knowledge and processes involved in reading and learning to read. Only by disentangling these two sets of issues, can we give either the attention and commitment that it so urgently deserves. (p. 52)

So there is no agreement after all—supporters of the two theories are still miles apart in their beliefs. Perhaps Bruner (1986b) makes the wisest assumption about learning and development theories when he describes any learning model as appropriate or inappropriate for a particular set of stipulated conditions. He includes within those conditions the types of tasks being considered, the forms of intention being created in the learners, the learning specifics and generalities to be accomplished by learners, and "the semiotics of the learning situation itself" (p. 198), or what that learning situation means to the learners. Bruner states,

> You cannot improve the state of education without a model of the learner. Yet the model of the learner is not fixed but various. A choice of one reflects many political, practical, and cultural issues. Perhaps the best choice is not a choice of one, but an appreciation of the variety that is possible. The appreciation of that variety is what makes the practice of education something more than a scripted exercise in cultural rigidity. (p. 200)

I agree with Bruner—the key to education is situated within the variety of learners and ways of learning.

RESEARCH METHODOLOGIES AND INQUIRY PARADIGMS. Research methodologies are based on acceptance of particular epistemological theories and beliefs. In human and social sciences, inquiries work to understand social or human problems through *qualitative* studies, which build a "complex, holistic picture, formed with words, reporting detailed views of informants, and conducted in a natural setting," or *quantitative* studies, which test "a theory composed of variables, measured with numbers, and analyzed with statistical procedures, in order to determine whether the predictive generalizations of the theory hold true" (Creswell, 1994, pp. 1–2). Mixed methodology, which combines both these methods, is used sometimes as well. Quantitative and qualitative studies stand on opposite sides of a continuum, with mixed-method studies placed between the two.

The quantitative methodology also is called "traditional," "experimental," "positivist," or "empiricist" (Creswell, 1994). Smith (1983) credits early empiricists such as Comte, Mill, Durkheim, Newton, and Locke for establishing traditions of quantitative thinking. The qualitative methodology, which is sometimes called the "constructivist approach," "naturalistic inquiry" (Lincoln & Guba, 1985), "interpretative inquiry" (Smith, 1983), or "postpositivist" or "postmodern inquiry" (Quantz, 1992), began in the late 19th century as a countermovement to the positivist tradition. Smith credits writers such as Dilthey, Weber, and Kant for establishing traditions of qualitative thinking.

Attempting to differentiate the two research methodologies, Creswell (1994) bases a comparison of assumptions and questions of each paradigm on the works of Firestone, Guba and Lincoln, and McCracken (each as cited in Creswell). Creswell describes the quantitative researcher's view of reality as objective, singular, and separate from the researcher, whereas the qualitative researcher has multiple realities that are subjective and described from the point of view of participants in a study. Quantitative research is "context-free," searches for generalizations that lead to "prediction, explanation, and understanding" (Creswell, p. 5) and is deemed accurate and reliable through a process of validity and reliability. Qualitative research searches for patterns to promote an understanding of the data that leads to development of theories, and it is deemed accurate and reliable through a process of verification (Creswell, 1994). See Figure 1 for Creswell's quantitative and qualitative paradigm assumptions.

Systematic inquiry is guided by a set of concepts, procedures, and standards agreed on by a group of researchers. These patterns of inquiry are called "paradigms" (Kuhn, 1962). Some researchers (e.g., Soltis, 1992) describe three major inquiry paradigms in educational research:

- Positivist inquiry, or quantitative inquiry—often based on natural science methodology, in which quantitative experimental and statistical methods are used

- Interpretivist inquiry, or qualitative inquiry—often based on participant observation and analysis, in which researchers contend that the way people subjectively understand situations in which they are involved directly affects their actions (Erickson, 1986)

- Critical inquiry—often an investigation of the *hidden curriculum* or indirect instruction in habits and attitudes transmitted by the ways in which classrooms and schools are run (Apple, 1979)

Although positivist inquiry strives to be neutral, objective, and free from bias or value, interpretivists and critical theorists claim this is not possible or even desirable. Critics of positivist inquiry say it treats teaching, learning, and schooling as mechanical, technological processes rather than artful, creative human enterprises (Eisner, 1981; Schon, 1983). Critics of interpretivist inquiry assert it is too subjective, too relativistic, and not generalizable. Critics of critical inquiry, who usually are individuals of the quantitative persuasion, maintain it is too politically and ideologically motivated.

Taylor (1998), who cites Grossen's report on 30 years of research of the National Institute of Child Health and Human Development (NICHD) as problematic in many ways, agrees with Grossen that "in a true scientific paradigm, theories are tested by doing everything to try to prove the theory incorrect" (as cited in Taylor, 1998, p. 6). Taylor calls on schools and universities to respond to research by thoroughly analyzing the data and documentation on which decisions are

Figure 1
Creswell's Quantitative and Qualitative Paradigm Assumptions

Assumption	Question	Quantitative	Qualitative
Ontological Assumption	What is the nature of reality?	Reality is objective and singular, apart from the researcher.	Reality is subjective and multiple as seen by participants in a study.
Epistemological Assumption	What is the relationship of the researcher to that researched?	Researcher is independent from that being researched.	Researcher interacts with that being researched.
Axiological Assumption	What is the role of values?	Value-free and unbiased	Value-laden and biased
Rhetorical Assumption	What is the language of research?	Formal Based on set definitions Impersonal voice Use of accepted quantitative words	Informal Evolving decisions Personal voice Accepted qualitative words
Methodological Assumption	What is the process of research?	Deductive process Cause and effect Static design—categories isolated before study Context-free Generalizations leading to prediction, explanation, and understanding Accurate and reliable through validity and reliability	Inductive process Mutual simultaneous shaping of factors Emerging design—categories identified during researcher process Context-bound Patterns, theories developed for understanding Accurate and reliable through verification

Source: Based on Firestone (1987); Guba & Lincoln (1988); and McCracken (1988).

Creswell, J.W., Research design: Qualitative and quantitative approaches, p. 5, copyright © 1994 by Sage Publications, Inc. Reprinted by permission of Sage Publications, Inc.

based. Taylor notes that, no matter what our philosophy and whether or not we agree, in examining the facts we must ask,

> Is the research responsive to the social, cultural, and intellectual lives of children? How was the research conducted? What are the ethical issues? Were the scientific procedures rigorous? Were the tests and measurements relevant to the stated objectives of the studies? Were the hypotheses properly tested? Were the theories proven? What does the research really indicate? Correlation or causation? Are there alternative explanations for the results? What is the impact of the research on the lives of children and their families?
>
> And if, when this is done, we find that the theories we have tested are scientifically defective, filled with unsubstantiated assumptions and insupportable "evidence," and are essentially just "spin," then we must ask ourselves, what are the consequences for children of the widespread use of these studies in determining how they should be taught to read? (pp. 6–7)

Perhaps the most problematic issue regarding rigor of the research offered in NICHD reports concerning quantitative studies of phonemic awareness is that the studies that serve as the basis of these reports consistently cite one another, and four of the most prominently cited studies contain serious methodological flaws. (To read specifics of these criticisms, see Coles [1998b, 2000], Ohanian [1999], and Taylor [1998].)

Taylor (1998) also analyzes phonemic awareness research from a sociocultural perspective, building on the work of Michael Cole, Ann Haas Dyson, Emilia Ferreiro and Ana Teberosky, Jean Lave, Barbara Rogoff, Sylvia Scribner, Lev Vygotsky, and James Wertsch. Taylor's major criticisms of phonemic awareness research are (a) "the assumption of cultural and social uniformity" (p. 19) upon which the "experiments rest" (p. 19); (b) the absence of *children* in these studies that use only "labels, aggregates, and measures" (p. 20); (c) the separation of children's "performance on certain isolated cognitive tasks" from their "everyday worlds" (p. 21); (d) separation of written language forms from "meaningful interpretations of text" (p. 22); (e) the false assumption underlying the research that alleges "children's early cognitive functions work from abstract exercises to meaningful activity" (p. 23); (f) the fact that "tests given to children [in this research] provide measures of no value outside of the testing situations" (p. 24); (g) the unsubstantiated assumption of "a transfer of learning from isolated phonemic awareness exercises to reading texts" (p. 25); and (h) the fact that "direct application of [this] experimental research...to classroom situations changes relationships that exist between teachers and children" (p. 29).

Conversely, quantitative researchers have just as many criticisms of qualitative studies. The main criticisms are that qualitative research is not replicable, valid, reliable, scientific, or objective. For example, in California, politicians, the mass media, and a segment of the educational establishment frowned on the methodology of whole language, banned its use, and barred known whole-language advocates from speaking engagements in the state (e.g., McQuillan, 1998; Ohanian, 1999; Taylor, 1998). Texas, under the influence of reports by Foorman, (e.g., Foorman, et al., 1998), Lyon, and the NICHD studies (both as cited in Coles, 2000), also rejected the use of anything but scientific methodology to promote the Texas Reading Initiative (Coles, 2000). The trend has been escalated through media (e.g., Manzo, 1997, 1998; Markley, as cited in Taylor, 1998) and government entities that provide monetary grants to U.S. educators (e.g., Reading Excellence Act, 1999). Presently, there is a general prohibition against any research other than robust "reliable, replicable research" (Coles, 1998a, p. 7) in governmental grant funding, especially research that is connected with the NICHD. Lyon claims, "Indeed, the education of our children is too important to be determined by anything but the strongest of objective scientific evidence. Our children deserve nothing less" (1998a, p. 5). This growing bias against qualitative studies has frustrated researchers who have built on the qualitative investigations of the past half-century. This frustration is apparent in a 1998 letter to the editor of *Education Week*, in which Gerald S. Coles criticizes the NICHD; Duane Alexander, director of NICHD; and G. Reid Lyon, chief of NICHD's child development and behavior branch. Coles specifically condemns

> NICHD's funding of reading research dedicated to an unremitting partiality toward one interpretation of..."effective" reading instruction.... Dr. Alexander has never voiced an objection to Mr. Lyon's active encouragement of federal and state legislation that would narrowly—and undemocratically—define "reliable, replicable research" along lines that accord with the purported "findings" from NICHD reading studies. All

other approaches are dismissed as "unscientific".... Similarly, Dr. Alexander has never himself raised a question about the legislative efforts that would enshrine the NICHD studies as the "gold standard" of reading research and diminish the validity of journal peer review as a standard of research quality. (Coles, 1998a, p. 7)

Pedagogy and Pragmatics

Pedagogy, the art or science of teaching, and *pragmatics*, the practicalities of real situations, do not always align in the classroom. Compared to what teachers are taught in preservice education courses, what is required of them when they enter real-life classrooms may leave them feeling ill prepared. High-caliber universities and colleges of teacher education in the United States receive accreditation from the National Council for Accreditation of Teacher Education (NCATE). This accreditation ensures that preservice and inservice teachers are taught in accordance with NCATE standards, which require that candidates meet standards that are grouped into five major areas:

Development, learning, and motivation; curriculum; instruction; assessment; and professionalism. These closely follow the ten "model standards" for teacher licensure from the Interstate New Teacher Assessment and Support Consortium (INTASC), a project of the Council of Chief State School Officers. The INTASC models were made part of the NCATE "unit" accreditation standards in 1995. These *Program Standards* elaborate on those from INTASC for development, learning, and motivation; add detail on curriculum for the subject content of elementary teaching; and make collaboration with families a separate part of professionalism from collaboration with colleagues and the community. The intent is to align NCATE program standards with the work of INTASC and trends in teacher licensure practices, and also to build on the moves toward the performance-based accreditation system that NCATE is developing. (NCATE, 2000, p. 3)

The content of the standards illustrates the high-level expectations that teacher candidates must meet by graduation. In order to have positive effects on student learning, teacher candidates should know and be able to do these things, which are listed in the following categories:

Development, Learning, and Motivation—Candidates know, understand, and use the major concepts, principles, theories, and research related to development of children and young adolescents to construct

24

learning opportunities that support individual students' development, acquisition of knowledge, and motivation.

Curriculum...Candidates know, understand, and use the central concepts, tools of inquiry, and structures of content for students across the K–6 grades and can create meaningful learning experiences that develop students' competence in subject matter and skills for various developmental levels [including] English language arts...Science...Mathematics... Social studies...The arts...Health education...Physical education...[and] Connections across the curriculum...[so that they] know, understand, and use the connections among concepts, procedures, and applications from content areas to motivate elementary students, build understanding, and encourage the application of knowledge, skills, and ideas to real world issues.

Instruction...Candidates plan and implement instruction based on knowledge of students, learning theory, subject matter, curricular goals, and community; [includes] Adaptation to diverse students...Development of critical thinking, problem solving, performance skills...Active engagement in learning...[and] Communication to foster collaboration.

Assessment for instruction—Candidates know, understand, and use formal and informal assessment strategies to plan, evaluate and strengthen instruction that will promote continuous intellectual, social, emotional, and physical development of each elementary student.

Professionalism—[includes] Practices and behaviors of developing career teachers...Reflection and evaluation...Collaboration with families...[and] Collaboration with colleagues and community. (NCATE, 2000, pp. 6–7)

These standards of expertise set forth by NCATE depict instruction that is complex and not easily attained. Teacher candidates work hard as they complete course work, gain clinical experiences, and engage in after-hours reflection and planning. Candidates who are taught in these far-reaching ways anticipate their first classrooms with enthusiasm and a desire to make a difference in the lives of children.

In increasingly fewer situations, however, are these well-prepared novice teachers ushered into teaching situations by supportive administration, faculty, and students' parents. In fact, first-year teachers report lack of support as one of the most crucial of their problems (Farkas, Foley, Duffett, Foleno, & Johnson, 2001; Stewart, 2000). For example, Farkas and colleagues report that 70% of teachers whom they surveyed felt left out of the decision-making process in schools, and a majority of the surveyed teachers expressed a desire for support from administrators and parents alike. Many times, what awaits these excellent teachers is a less-than-perfect opportunity to implement what they have learned. As societal problems and demands on schools and teachers increase, more and more novice teachers find themselves overburdened by multiple pressures in the classroom. For example, teachers may encounter overcrowded classrooms, students who are behind in their learning, harried administrators who are pressured to have students achieve higher levels of test performance, parents who have less time to give to their children but demand more of schools, overabundance of paperwork, and curricula that are increasingly crowded with mandates. Add the multiple layers of the teacher's newness—trying to teach new content, plan for a new situation, manage a new classroom, learn procedures and policies of a new school, and get to know new students, students' parents, faculty members, and members of administration. Then consider the fact that some administrators and many fellow teachers advise novice teachers to forget what they learned in school and just make sure children are ready for the high-stakes testing, the results of which will make or break these new graduates as teachers. It is not surprising that novice teachers, who transition from university programs into the often-chaotic real-world classrooms, are overwhelmed by the problems they are expected to handle on their own.

STANDARDS.   Some educators adamantly oppose standards because they believe standards result in curricula that are insensitive to specific needs and contexts of students and teachers. These educators disapprove of the cookie-cutter sameness that the standards seem to assign every classroom. Many teachers are professionals who have personal standards that far exceed the minimum standards often prescribed in standards documents. Educators who oppose standards believe that if minimal standards are set, minimal progress will be made, and minimal may become the norm. One of the most vocal adversaries is Ohanian, whose book *One Size Fits Few: The Folly of Educational Standards* (1999) warns of the dangers of educational standards. Ohanian wants to tell

> Standardistos who rely on skills charts and standardized test scores for their notion of children..."People, those aren't children, those are numbers." Members of the media have a singular inability to look beyond charts and see real children. (p. 1)

Ohanian asserts that schools should have teachers and curricula that are flexible enough to serve the needs of *each* student. She advises readers to note the increasing importance of teachers' curricula choices during this time of society's devaluation of children.

Zemelman et al. (1998) voice similar concerns, as they are deeply troubled by the "heartless, authoritarian way" (p. 19) in which the U.S. standards movement talks to and about children. Zemelman and colleagues state that this tough, no-nonsense tone comes across through demands, consequences, and warnings to children—with disregard for making school safe and comfortable, let alone fun. These authors provide examples of schools that have achieved high standards in other ways, such as setting high expectations that balance teacher-designed activities with predictable spaces and time for students so that students have opportunities to achieve their own successes and have them recognized as such.

On the other hand, there are educators who herald the standards movement as worthwhile and necessary. Advocates of standards believe that it is imperative to set ground expectations to ensure that every child achieves *at least* that level of educational accomplishment. They also believe that standards guide the instruction of individuals who may be uncertified, teaching out of their field of expertise, or whose training is incomplete. Advocates of standards stress that elements of a high-quality education are built into the standards.

One of the most vocal supporters of standards for teachers is Darling-Hammond (1997), who believes that standards ensure that all children will have competent and qualified teachers. Darling-Hammond notes, "Perhaps the single greatest source of inequity in education is this disparity in the availability and distribution of well-qualified teachers" (p. 273). McMillen, Bobbitt, and Lynch (as cited in Darling-Hammond, 1997) also support this stance by noting, "The common belief that anyone can teach turns out to harm most intensely those students who most need good teaching" (p. 273). Standards are an important step in the process of creating a learner-centered vision, which is the vision Darling-Hammond believes we can use to improve U.S. education.

CONSENSUS.   Specific educational groups within the United States strive to reach consensus on how literacy should be taught to young children. For example, the National Council of Teachers of English

(NCTE) developed the Standards Consensus Series (1997) in recognition of a set of core beliefs about English language arts revealed by "innumerable standards-related documents and ideas generated by teachers" (p. v). Four notable consensus documents that were published in the late 1990s also affirm some areas of agreement in the field of literacy, especially early literacy.

In 1996, the International Reading Association (IRA) and NCTE copublished *Standards for the English Language Arts*, which is a core document outlining national standards in language arts. In 1998, IRA and the National Association for the Education of Young Children (NAEYC) created a joint position statement on developmentally appropriate literacy instruction for young children. The U.S. Department of Education and the U.S. Department of Health and Human Services requested that the National Academy of Sciences create a committee, which first met in 1996, to investigate what is known about preventing reading problems. That request produced *Preventing Reading Difficulties in Young Children* (Snow et al., 1998). The goals of Snow and colleagues were to investigate and understand the diverse database of studies concerning reading problems; translate their research findings into guidance and advice for educators, parents, and others; and make this guidance available to the general public. The fourth consensus document, *Reading & Writing Grade by Grade: Primary Literacy Standards for Kindergarten Through Third Grade* (New Standards Primary Literacy Committee, 1999), goes beyond general statements of what students should be able to accomplish and provides specific examples of desired learning performances. *Reading & Writing Grade by Grade* sets high expectations, demanding much of students, teachers, and students' parents, although it claims to "set out realistic expectations for children who are taught well. They are demanding because nothing less will prepare children for their futures" (pp. 8–9).

As standards documents become more common, they may further increase pressure on classroom teachers who may be asked to correspond instructional practices to multiple standards and to detail inclusion of these standards in their lesson plans.

PROFESSIONAL READINGS.   Teachers and others who engage in reading within the field of literacy or within other content areas must investigate the validity of professional reading sources. For example, Grossen's report titled *30 Years of Research: What We Now Know About How Children Learn to Read* (1998) sounds quite impressive until we remember that this report is based on research studies only within the NICHD network, which disregards other studies because of their supposed lack of scientific rigor. Grossen's report declares that the best solution for reading problems is appropriate and early direct instruction, and the report goes on to outline a system for this type of instruction in the classroom. All information in her text is delivered as scientifically proven fact based on evidence in the NICHD studies, but readers face a dilemma when they recall that researchers outside the NICHD found these studies to be significantly flawed.

Focusing on an emerging consensus for reforming U.S. schools, Zemelman et al. (1998) take on a different perspective in the second edition of *Best Practice: New Standards for Teaching and Learning in America's Schools*. The authors summarize research in six main subject fields: reading, writing, mathematics, science, social studies, and performing arts (visual art, music, dance, and theater). Zemelman and colleagues present summaries of research in each subject field, describe at least one exemplary program within the subject field, and present real-life scenarios from several classrooms. Each chapter concludes with a chart of teaching recommendations within a subject field. The authors openly acknowledge their biases and beliefs, which makes this text anything but impartial; however, many of their ideas are sound, allowing for broad curricular frameworks that accommodate the specific needs of schools, teachers, and students. The negative aspect for readers, however, is that Zemelman et al. do not represent other perspectives, which leaves readers to question whether the perspective is believable.

Best Practices in Literacy Instruction (Gambrell et al., 1999) is a practical text that also serves as a research base for people who are interested in learning about exemplary literacy practices, teaching and learning strategies, and special issues in education. As Strickland writes in the foreword, the book provides a rich knowledge base for improving literacy and "the scholars contributing...are representative of many of those whose work has contributed to that knowledge" (p. xx). The editors aim to amass "in one volume recent insights from the research that have direct implications for classroom practice...to help beginning and experienced classroom teachers become more effective literacy teachers" (p. 1). Gambrell et al. address both the *what* and the *how* of literacy instruction and pay careful attention to influences such as student-teacher interaction, the context of classrooms, methods of instruction, the social context, and learners' motivation. This book exemplifies how teachers and researchers are learning to fit instruction to the students rather than students to the instruction. Yet readers may themselves question the validity of the perspective because other perspectives of literacy instruction are not represented in the book.

MULTICULTURAL ISSUES.　How do multicultural issues affect *what* and in *what ways* we will teach? How will our choices impact realities of our classrooms—the learning, the individuals, and the group as a whole? Giroux and Simon (as cited in Ladson-Billings, 1994) note,

> Pedagogy refers to a deliberate attempt to influence how and what knowledge and identities are produced within and among particular sets of social relations. It can be understood as a practice through which people are incited to acquire a particular "moral character." As both a political and practical activity, it attempts to influence the occurrence and qualities of experiences. When one practices pedagogy, one acts with the intent of creating experiences that will organize and disorganize a variety of understandings of our natural and social world in particular ways.... Pedagogy is a concept which draws attention to the processes through which knowledge is produced. (p. 14)

Ladson-Billings agrees with Giroux and Simon's view of pedagogy. Her book *The Dreamkeepers: Successful Teachers of African American Children* (1994) investigates why a certain kind of teaching not only helped students succeed academically, but also supported and encouraged the students to use prior knowledge to understand and improve their world.

Ladson-Billings (1994) differentiates *excellent teaching* from *excellent teachers*, focusing more broadly on shared teaching ideology and behavior than on individual styles and personalities. Much of the reform debates center on *what* we should teach, "But it is *the way we teach* that profoundly affects the way that students perceive the content of that curriculum" (p. 13). Ladson-Billings discusses the importance of culturally relevant teaching, which "helps students work collectively toward a common goal of academic and cultural excellence" (p. 58). She notes that "Culturally relevant teaching honors the students' sense of humanity and dignity. Their complete personhood is never doubted" (p. 76). Building a classroom community is an integral part of culturally relevant teaching, in which individuals who are acknowledged as worthy of being part of a loving, supportive group have their self-worth and self-concept promoted in a very basic way. Key components of culturally relevant teaching are the teachers' attitudes toward students and students' cultures, teachers' expectations of students, and teachers' behaviors toward students. There is no set prescription for successful culturally relevant teaching, but the result "fosters the kinds of social interactions in the classroom that support the individual in the group context" (Ladson-Billings, 1994, p. 76).

Ladson-Billings and other researchers (e.g., Delpit, 1994; Paley, 1979/1990) note the importance of "seeing color." Delpit (1994) says that teachers—particularly white teachers—learning to teach diverse children—particularly African American children—often struggle with the issue of color. The prevalent attitude of teachers seems to be that to acknowledge students' color would be to insult students. Delpit reports that one of her colleagues uses Paley's *White Teacher* (1979/1990) to help teaching students

> understand that to say you don't see color is to say you don't see children.... Students were then able to understand that people could be proud of their color and their differences and that the teacher could help this process. (p. 131)

Delpit mentions other behaviors and attitudes that Paley exemplifies: Teachers should observe children, look within themselves and their own lack of knowledge about other cultures as sources of problems in the classroom, realize that implications about intelligence of children of other cultures are often lost on teachers because of differing backgrounds, and learn from adults of the same cultures as their students, especially the students' parents. Although these issues are discussed, explored, and even experienced in field placements during preservice education, it is not until teachers enter the reality of the classroom that they are forced to come to terms with these issues daily.

Our beliefs shape our teaching. We must examine our beliefs closely and realize how the *way* we teach affects the *students* we teach. In her earlier writings, Delpit (1988, 1990) argues that it is our responsibility as teachers to convey to our students the rules and conventions of the culture of power. By the culture of power, Delpit means the culture of people who know how the system works and how to work the system—people who use grammatically correct standard English and who understand the codes of school and society. In their book titled *Teaching/Learning Anti-Racism: A Developmental Approach* (1997), Derman-Sparks and Phillips discuss the growth their university students experienced as they moved from a racist consciousness to an anti-racist consciousness. The authors explain that their approach to "Anti-racism education is not an end in itself but rather the beginning of a new approach to thinking, feeling, and acting" (p. 3). Because of tension in the discourse between teachers who have choice in the matter and students who are born into situations—without choice—teachers must gain those new ways of "thinking, feeling, and acting."

Brophy and Good (as cited in Knapp, Shields, & Turnbull, 1995) assert that children from low-income backgrounds need instruction with more review, more drill and practice, and more low-level questions. They believe that emphasis should be on "mastery" of the material that is taught, even if that means that less material is covered across the school year. Brophy and Good believe children from low-income backgrounds need more "structuring from their teachers, more redundancy and smaller steps with higher success rates" (as cited in Knapp et al., p. 183). Their statements suggest that they view these children as having learning deficits that can be overcome by drill and practice through direct-instruction models. Knapp et al. (1995) disagree with this type of rigid direct instruction with an emphasis on learning deficits, which has been the conventional wisdom of many practitioners for many years and bolstered by research. Knapp (1995) bases his book on a large-scale, systematic attempt to look at both skills-oriented and meaning-oriented instruction in a range of high-poverty elementary school classrooms. Findings from Knapp and colleagues' study reveal that teachers who emphasized meaning constructed and maintained learning environments that were rich, orderly, and varied. The teachers in these high-poverty classrooms responded "actively and constructively to the students' diverse cultural, linguistic, and socioeconomic backgrounds" (Knapp et al., p. 184). They report that when teaching mathematics, reading, and writing, the teachers "posed cognitively demanding tasks from the earliest stages of learning," taught "discrete skills within contexts of their use," and "connected academic learning to the children's experience base" (p. 184). Knapp et al. state that this instruction produced "superior learning of 'advanced' skills and comparable or better learning of 'basic' skills by *both* high and low achievers" (p. 184). However, Knapp et al. conclude that the teachers were most likely to attempt and sustain this type of instruction when the right combination of conditions and supports were in place at school, district, and state levels.

ALLINGTON'S "CONFUSIONS." In *The Schools We Have. The Schools We Need* (1998), Allington discusses other practical pressures that exist within the classroom; he calls the pressures "confusions." Arguing that we can help virtually all students achieve types of literacy historically expected from only a few, Allington speaks of heightened expectations in areas of literacy development. U.S. schools now educate more students to higher levels than at any time, although this fact is seldom acknowledged by the mass media. Historically, schools were expected to advance literacy of only their top students. Now, schools are increasingly challenged to develop advanced literacy in almost all students. Allington stresses that confusions about teaching and learning literacy must be resolved before all children can achieve.

Although Allington (1998) points out seven confusions, he also offers solutions for teachers.

1. Confusing children's lack of experiences with books, stories, or other print with a lack of ability.

Solution: Give children rich experiences with reading and print.

2. Lowering expectations for students who have limited print experiences and giving them restricted learning opportunities based on tests that ostensibly measure reading abilities and intellectual capacities.

Solution: Set high expectations and model good teaching practices for *all* children.

3. Spending time, money, and energy sorting children rather than supporting them.

Solution: Provide high-quality classroom instruction—*support* children.

4. Questioning whether curriculum or instruction is more important to literacy learning.

Solution: Recognize teachers as the key to learning, expand instructional time, personalize instruction, and intensify the intervention (i.e., *increase* the amount of reading and writing for less successful or less experienced children).

5. Comparing the effects of real reading and writing (less than 10% of time during the school day in many classrooms) with other time-consuming classroom activities, such as workbook exercises and test preparation—*books* versus *blanks*.

Solution: Provide both *access* and *time* for real writing and real reading.

6. *Assigning* student work and mistaking that with *teaching*.

Solution: Give all students good models, explanations, and demonstrations of how reading is accomplished. Provide *many* demonstrations of how to go about thinking through strategies while reading and writing. Make these elements central to instruction.

7. Mistaking *remembering* for *understanding*.

Solution: Rather than interrogate students about facts, converse with them to get them to summarize, analyze, synthesize, and discuss their understandings about their reading.

To Allington's confusions, I add other practical pressures that affect the art of teaching—pedagogy—and the practicalities of real teaching situations—pragmatics. Some of the most obvious pressures are overcrowding of classrooms, increasing diversity of the population, busing, inclusion, and time constraints. The solution? The coming together of concerned citizens and educators in local spaces to ponder these complex issues and collaborate to find equally complex and contextually relevant solutions for *those* students in *those* schools in *those* places.

Programs and Professionalism

Mandated curricula or prescribed programs that have been made "teacher-proof" do not treat teachers as knowledgeable professionals who are able to make informed decisions to support learning in their classrooms. Teacher-proof programs or curricula allow no flexibility in delivery. Regardless of how knowledgeable a teacher is—or how inept—the *material*, rather than the teacher, provides the instruction. This material is designed and scripted to tell the teacher exactly what to say; what activities to do; and when, in what order, and how long to say and do them. The material is delivered in exactly the same manner for all students. Every student is expected to "master" every skill and skill lesson, usually in a set order, regardless of his or her individual level of accomplishment or prior knowledge. These programs are "teacher-proof" in that teachers cannot mess it up, so to speak. As previously noted, Ohanian (1999) describes these programs as being at the heart of the "Standardisto" argument, which she believes endorses the belief, "Choose the right technique/text/program and any teacher can deliver it" (p. 49). Speaking of the goals of the Standardistos, she further notes that "The goal is clearly stated: Get rid of teacher variability. Put out a manual that tells the undifferentiated work force exactly what to do to their undifferentiated students" (p. 50). These teacher-proof programs are a scary thought. Especially during this time when so much attention is placed on struggling readers, teachers are bombarded with mandatory programs for their classroom instruction that claim to be the way to "fix" this problem. For example, in my state, it is law that one of five explicit, direct-instruction programs must be provided for students evidencing characteristics of dyslexia. If schools are to receive grant funding from the state, they must choose one of the five programs, or design a program they can *prove* is equally effective with students who have dyslexia. All five programs are supposed to be research based; any self-designed program must be as well. The state pressures schools to "train" teachers to use one of these programs. Unfortunately, some districts within the state send a principal and at least one teacher to receive "training" just so they meet the law's requirements. Many schools feel it is too difficult to fight the system and they need the grant money; therefore, schools give in and take the training. Some teachers who receive this training implement it indiscriminately, commenting that it "won't hurt the others." As Allington's (1998) confusions make clear, anything that takes time away from real reading and real writing hurts students.

Teachers must make their own curricular decisions. Burnaford (1996a) proposes the idea that curriculum is something that is *lived*: Teachers go beyond curriculum guides as they make instructional decisions by watching and listening to their students. Qualified and expert teachers carefully observe children, noting when students need to move on or when time is needed for assistance. These teachers choose activities and strategies based on needs and abilities of the children they are teaching at that time. Teaching should not be deprofessionalized through teacher-proof curricula that tell teachers what to say, when to say it, and how much time is spent saying it. When we consider the troubled state of many of our classrooms, do we really want any less than the best-prepared teachers in charge of the learning? Many studies have revealed that the teacher is the most important element in the effectiveness of classrooms (e.g., Berliner & Biddle, 1995; Darling-Hammond, 1997; Ladson-Billings, 1994).

We must celebrate teachers because of their role in creating the future, but we often fail to do that. Of the teacher shortage in the United States, Ogle (2001) writes, "At the same time that we are putting underprepared teachers in schools, our society is demanding more from teachers" (p. 8). She laments short-term solutions to the shortage of well-prepared teachers—which often make use of teacher-proof materials to support student learning—because children deserve highly prepared, well-qualified teachers. Ogle implores the decision makers to make sure that such shortcuts do not replace excellent professional development. Citing a table used by Berliner and Biddle, Ogle states that there is a "clear positive correlation between states that have the highest percentages of certified teachers and student achievement. Better teachers produce higher levels of learning" (p. 8).

Processes and Products

As pressures increase for teachers to spend more and more time preparing for high-stakes testing, literacy processes and products often are put on the back burner. Students who engage in *processes* of literacy have the deepest learning. Learning is active; therefore, readers learn best through reading, and writers learn best through writing. Smith (1999) compares learning to read to learning to ride a bicycle. For example, just as someone supports us as we are learning to ride a bicycle, readers need support when they are learning to read. It is this social nature of teaching and learning that makes learning meaningful. We must make constant decisions about what will help our students learn best at any given moment. Smith encourages teachers to be responsive to the condition of each learner as an individual; we must address those conditions on the spot, not leave them to some outside expert.

Routman provides a definition of process orientation in *Invitations: Changing as Teachers and Learners K–12* (1994), in which teachers notice and value what students and teachers do during the process of writing, reading, speaking, and listening. Although products are still valued, process orientation emphasizes *how* students reach their goals because learning takes place within the process. Process orientation celebrates students' approximations that show evidence of thinking and learning, trusts students to learn, and gives students' recognition as they learn. Routman notes that process orientation

> applies to us teachers in transition, too. We need to value ourselves in the learning process even if we are not "there" yet. Implicit in process orientation is lots of risk taking, which acknowledges that learning happens gradually over time. (p. 17)

Interconnectedness is also an important aspect of the literacy process (e.g., Strickland, 1998b; Weaver, 1994, 1996, 1998a, 1998b)— especially connections between reading and writing (e.g., Nelson & Calfee, 1998). Because we construct meaning as we read and write, we are both readers and writers at once. Our identities as readers and writers are established in the context of our social relationships with other writers and readers (Nelson, 1998). Such social construction is at the heart of my teacher research.

Conversely—whether we agree or not—we teachers and our students are judged on the *products* of literacy. For example, people are judged on the conventions of writing just as much as they are judged on the content of writing. Often, readers devalue content of writing because they cannot get past poor spelling or grammatical incorrectness. Readers frequently make these judgments based on the appearance of handwriting alone (Graves, 1994; Shaughnessy, 1977).

Attending to conventions in the writing product, however, does not mean we must give up our work on the processes of literacy. For example, Graves (1994) advocates teaching handwriting "within the act of composing itself" (p. 254). Regarding the process of spelling, Giacobbe (as cited in Graves, 1994) advises teachers not to tell their students not to worry about spelling but to say, "When you write, try your best. Spelling words as best you can is helping your readers"

(p. 255). Graves (1983) encourages teachers and children first to write about what we know, say it the way we want to say it, and do it as quickly as we can. Then, by revisiting and reflecting on our writing, we have the opportunity to make our writing say exactly what we want it to say—to ensure that final products are high-quality, edited pieces of which we can be proud.

We also need to encourage students to build on oral language so that they actively engage in and support all literacy processes. Braunger and Lewis (1998) call today's literacy "a higher stakes literacy" (p. 1). Learning to read is so important that entire elementary schools are judged as successful or not based on students' reading proficiency (Boyer, as cited in Braunger & Lewis, 1998). We need to model the processes of writing, thinking, reading, and speaking so that our students can learn how to engage in these processes. As we go about the difficult work of fitting curricula to students, it is important to balance processes and products so that students and teachers attend to both.

A scene from Calkins's *Lessons From a Child: On the Teaching and Learning of Writing* (1983) captures the essence of this issue. In this scene, a visitor in Calkins's class overhears a student's (Susie's) writing revisions and says to Calkins, "I guess I got here just in time" (p. 4). Thinking of the changes in Susie's writing over the previous 2 years, Calkins remembers,

> Over the course of third and fourth grade, Susie and her classmates had developed as writers, gaining experience in the craft of writing. Our visitor hadn't seen the changing interactions between Susie, her teachers and her classmates, or the accompanying changes in her writing strategies.... Now many of them were relentless revisers. They'd learned to wrestle for the words to convey memories, images and information. They'd written personal narratives, content area reports, letters, stories and poems. Our visitor had seen the product but he'd missed out on the process. He'd missed the story of Susie's growth in writing, and of how writing was taught and learned in her classrooms. "I guess we see it differently," I said to him. "I'd say you got here just too late." (pp. 4–5)

Prerequisites and Praxis

In addition to the Interstate New Teacher Assessment and Support Consortium (INTASC) standards, colleges and universities of education must meet their own preservice prerequisites with core principles in various areas of education set forth by INTASC. This consortium is made up of the Council of Chief State School Officers (superintendents), state education agencies, institutions of higher education, and national education organizations. In 1992, this academy developed the following 10 core principles for elementary education. I have included interpretations that summarize these principles, which are included in brackets immediately following the principles.

"Principle #1: The teacher understands the central concepts, tools of inquiry, and structures of the discipline(s) he or she teaches and can create learning experiences that make these aspects of subject matter meaningful for students" (p. 14) [content knowledge].

"Principle #2: The teacher understands how children [students of all ages] learn and develop, and can provide learning opportunities that support their intellectual, social, and personal development" (p. 16) [development of learners].

"Principle #3: The teacher understands how students differ in their approaches to learning and creates instructional opportunities that are adapted to diverse learners" (p. 18) [diversity of learners].

"Principle #4: The teacher understands and uses a variety of instructional strategies to encourage students' development of critical thinking, problem solving, and performance skills" (p. 20) [strategies for teaching].

"Principle #5: The teacher uses an understanding of individual and group motivation and behavior to create a learning environment that encourages positive social interaction, active engagement in learning, and self-motivation" (p. 22) [motivational aspects of teaching].

"Principle #6: The teacher uses knowledge of effective verbal, nonverbal, and media communication techniques to foster active inquiry, collaboration, and supportive interaction in the classroom" (p. 25) [communicative aspects of teaching].

"Principle #7: The teacher plans instruction based on his or her knowledge of subject matter, students, the community, and curriculum goals" (p. 27) [instructional planning].

"Principle #8: The teacher understands and uses formal and informal assessment strategies to evaluate and ensure the continuous intellectual, social, and physical development of the learner" (p. 29) [evaluation].

"Principle #9: The teacher is a reflective practitioner who continually evaluates the effects of his or her choices and actions on others (students, students' parents, and other professionals in the learning community) and who actively seeks out opportunities to grow professionally" (p. 31) [reflection].

"Principle #10: The teacher fosters relationships with colleagues, parents, and agencies in the larger community to support students' learning and well-being" (p. 33) [community connections].

Questions about what to do with standards once they are in place are raised within the INTASC document *Next Steps: Moving Towards Performance-Based Licensing in Teaching* (1995) in a section titled "Reshaping Teacher Licensing and Preparation" (p. 6). Of special concern is the question, "How do we create a coherent system for ensuring that teachers can teach in the ways that new standards for students require?" (p. 7). This section goes on to provide suggestions such as modeling teaching after other professions that require rigorous licensing examinations and requiring that teachers graduate from professionally accredited institutions and complete approved internships. Performance-based assessments replace course-counting strategies for licensing. There are many ways in which the INTASC principles and standards will be evaluated, including assessment of learning portfolios, assessment of institutions by NCATE, and review of specific individuals through a series of examinations, including entry and exit examinations that are being developed. The most prominent of these examinations are the *Professional Assessments for Beginning Teachers: Principles of Learning and Teaching* (Educational Testing Service, 2001), which are part of The Praxis Series. *Praxis I: Academic Skills Assessments* measures writing, reading, and mathematical skills of teaching students during their early educational careers. *Praxis II: Subject Assessments* measures students' knowledge of subjects in which they are seeking certification; students generally take this examination toward the end of their education programs. *Praxis III: Classroom Performance Assessments* evaluates all aspects of novice teachers' classroom performance; students usually take this examination in the first year of teaching.

Two of Shulman's seminal articles help explain the emphasis on praxis—or reflection on practice—in the United States, as well as the emphasis on helping teachers understand the relationship of their practice to theoretical and ethical concerns of teaching. "Those Who Understand: Knowledge Growth in Teaching" (Shulman, 1986) compares what teachers were expected to know, understand, and do in the 19th century to the same expectations of teachers in the 1980s. Shulman specifically compares attention to content during the 1870s when pedagogy was basically ignored to the absence of attention to content in the 1980s. Shulman's comparison introduces a discussion of the "Missing Paradigm" in which he asks important questions that suggest interconnecting knowledge and pedagogy:

> The sharp distinction between knowledge and pedagogy does not represent a tradition dating back centuries, but rather, a more recent development.... How does the teacher prepare to teach something never previously learned? How does learning *for* teaching occur?... How do teachers take a piece of text and transform their understanding of it into instruction that their students can comprehend? (1986, pp. 7–8)

Shulman further suggests three forms of teacher knowledge— prepositional knowledge, case knowledge, and strategic knowledge— which are the very pillars on which the INTASC core principles are built.

Shulman's 1987 article, "Knowledge and Teaching: Foundations of the New Reform" discusses teaching reform built on the idea that "comprehension and reasoning...transformation and reflection" (p. 13) are the cornerstones of teaching. Shulman examines the sources of the knowledge base of teaching, terms in which those sources can be conceptualized, the processes of pedagogical reasoning and action, and implications for teaching policy and educational reform. The idea of praxis as reflection on practice is built on Shulman's model of pedagogical reasoning and action, which includes comprehension, transformation, instruction, evaluation, reflection, and new comprehensions. What distinguishes a teacher from others is

> the capacity of a teacher to transform the content knowledge he or she possesses into forms that are pedagogically powerful and yet adaptive to

the variations in ability and background presented by the students.... We must achieve standards without standardization. We must be careful that the knowledge-base approach does not produce an overly technical image of teaching, a scientific enterprise that has lost its soul. The serious problems in medicine and other health professions arise when doctors treat the disease rather than the person, or when the professional or personal needs of the practitioner are permitted to take precedence over the responsibilities to those being served. (pp. 15, 20)

Lather (1986) defines praxis as "the dialectical tension, the interactive, reciprocal shaping of theory and practice which I see at the center of an emancipatory social science" (p. 258). Her research is directed at building a more just society through critiquing the status quo. Namenwirth (as cited in Lather, 1986) writes, "Scientists firmly believe that as long as they are not *conscious* of any bias or political agenda, they are neutral and objective, when in fact they are only unconscious" (p. 257). Lather disputes the idea of neutral and objective research, citing research support (i.e., Bernstein; Fay; Habermas; Hesse, each as cited in Lather) that research paradigms reflect personal beliefs, although she contends that research programs that disclose their value base often are discounted as overly subjective and unscientific. Therefore, Lather urges theory building that is grounded in studies respectful of people's everyday experiences and in which social science looks at the intersection of choice and constraint and focuses on questions of power. According to Lather, research from the emancipatory perspective goes beyond Lewin's concept of action-research because it allows the researcher to become "the changer and the changed" (Williamson, as cited in Lather, 1986, p. 263). Action-research is explained by Tripp (1993) as traditional research that "consists of initial observation of current practice, analysis of the observational data, planning changed practice, implementation, observation of the new practice...etc." (p. 148).

Critical inquiry responds to the experiences, desires, and needs of the people being studied in an attempt to inspire and guide these people in cultural transformation. At the core of this process is a "reciprocal relationship in which every teacher is always a student and every pupil a teacher" (Gramsci quoted in Fermia, 1975, as cited in Lather, 1986, p. 268). Teachers who engage in praxis at this intense level gain deeper understandings of their specific situations, as well as of teaching practice in general.

Issues to Consider

Many educational professionals discredit the polarization of literacy issues in the United States. For example, Strickland (1998a) deplores seeing "complex issues reduced to quick, two-sided arguments" (p. 12), while Routman (1996) notes that such "polarization forces people to take sides and ultimately shuts down the conversation, as each side spends all its time defending its position" (p. 10). Teachers typically are not the people who polarize literacy issues because they desperately want to reach each individual in their classrooms. Teachers, from positions inside the reality of classrooms, understand that these complex issues will not be resolved easily. Allington and Walmsley's book *No Quick Fix: Rethinking Literacy Programs in America's Elementary Schools* (1995) discusses how U.S. education demands different kinds of literacy and teaching skills, such as thoughtful literacy (Brown, 1991) and new literacy (Willinsky, 1990). Allington and Walmsley call for this change:

> Thus, a first order of change in elementary schools must be in the kind of work that both teachers and children do. To create thoughtful readers and writers, we must focus on topics worth knowing and evaluate understanding, not remembering. To create thoughtful readers, children must spend large parts of the school day engaged in reading and writing. Thoughtful schools focus children's attention on understanding and communicating information and ideas to each other.... We must accept that all children can become literate before we design schools to achieve that end. Schools are, primarily, collections of classrooms staffed by teachers. It is the teachers who are the key to rethinking our elementary schools. (p. 11)

This chapter has presented a number of important educational issues. It ends by listing some possibilities for consideration.

Possibilities to Celebrate

Celebrating the Unique Contributions of the Students and the Teacher

Greene (1973) comments, "There are no final answers, nor are there directives to govern every teaching situation. If he is to be effective, the teacher cannot function automatically or according to a set of predetermined rules. Teaching is purposeful action" (p. 69). Teachers, key people in the classroom, determine by their purposeful actions the possibilities therein—possibilities for themselves and for each child in their care.

Reciprocity means that we learn from one another. Children and adults learn from each other. Children learn from their peers. Although this is obvious, many adults have seemingly given it little thought (Bussis, Chittenden, & Amarel, 1976). Isaacs (1948) writes, "It is not the mere presence of other children but active participation with them doing real things together, an active interchange of feeling and experience, which educates the child" (p. 226). I celebrate the possibilities brought about by the people in the classroom—specifically the students—during my teacher-research study. The community created by the students and me illustrates this active interchange of feeling and experience that Isaacs describes.

Celebrating Discourse as a Possibility

In his 1989 article "What Is Literacy?" Gee discusses a *discourse* as a count term (meaning "many discourses"),

> a socially accepted association among ways of using language, of thinking, and of acting that can be used to identify oneself as a member of a socially meaningful group or "social network." Think of a discourse as an "identity kit" which comes complete with the appropriate costume and instructions on how to act and talk so as to take on a particular role that others will recognize. (p. 18)

This use of discourse is important because of its implications on gaining insights into discourses of the different paradigms and political groups mentioned in this chapter. As we have seen, discourses in that regard are ideological and involve values and points of view. It seems equally important, however, to think about discourses as they are evident in Chapters 3 through 6 of this book, which present specific data from my study. Discourses are

> intimately related to the distribution of social power and hierarchical structure in society. Control over certain discourses can lead to the acquisition of social goods.... The critical question is: how does one come by the discourses that he or she controls? (Gee, 1989, pp. 19, 20)

In the remainder of the text, readers should observe for instances in which the second-grade students *acquired, learned,* and *practiced* various discourses.

CHAPTER 2

Research in the Classroom: Foundation and Methodology

Foundation of My Perspective as Teacher Researcher

Teachers' beliefs about teaching and learning are influenced by how they learn from their experiences, as well as how they perceive teaching (Duckworth, 1987; Fosnot, 1989). These beliefs are reflected in *what* they teach and *how* they teach it (Clark & Peterson, 1986; Deford, 1985; Duffy & Anderson, 1984; Fang, 1996; Harste & Burke, 1977).

The social constructivist foundation underlying this text is based on the works of Vygotsky, Dewey, Bruner, and others. I have also drawn from more recent works that consider children's multiple constructions of reality and expressions of that reality through their many "languages," or modes of expression (e.g., Edwards, Gandini, & Forman, 1979/1994), that contribute to understandings about learning communities (e.g., Dyson, 1989, 1993; Fraser & Skolnick, 1994; Peterson, 1992), and that investigate children's writing in real-life classrooms (e.g., Calkins, 1983, 1986; Dyson, 1986, 1987; Graves, 1983, 1994). As a participant, an observer, and a teacher, I was also influenced by work about the systematic observation of children and the methods of recording that observation (e.g., Clay, 1979, 1993), and by work about the importance of looking closely and carefully at children as they work and learn, or "kidwatching" (Goodman, 1985).

My experiences with literacy instruction in first-, second-, and third-grade classes, combined with my own scholarly studies, have encouraged me to express my theoretical beliefs and philosophy.

Luijpen (1969) helps me feel less intimidated about doing so, noting that "Authentic philosophy is an attempt to give a personal answer to personal questions" (p. 19). Luijpen also notes that philosophy is authentic only when a person philosophizes for himself or herself, raising questions, searching for answers, and personally trying to "clear away the obstacles to insight" (p. 20). The following sections describe my philosophies as a teacher-researcher.

A Philosophy of Teaching and Learning

Knowing that my beliefs affect my classroom and the lives of each student, I have scrutinized them carefully over the years. I believe that learning is a process of knowing, that teachers must provide classroom settings that suggest ideas to students, allow students to explore those ideas, and instill confidence in students that enables such exploration (Duckworth, 1987). This exploration of constructivist perspectives has expanded my own beliefs through ideas gleaned from other researchers who value the construction of personal knowledge and the assimilation of new experiences through prior knowledge (c.f., Duckworth, 1987; Fosnot, 1989; Kamii, 1979, 1989; Piaget, 1955).

When I heard Sinclair's (1994) explanation of the similarities and differences between Piaget's and Vygotsky's beliefs on collaboration, argumentation, and coherent reasoning, I struggled to understand how their theories are complementary. (Sinclair was a guest speaker at the school where I did my doctoral studies.) However, I understood Sinclair's assertions that Piaget viewed knowledge as being objectified through discussion, arguments, and collaborative dialogues among equals and that Vygotsky viewed knowledge as coming from interaction between novice and expert, with emphasis on instruction. Sinclair's illustration of these theories raised questions then and continues to push me to investigate Piaget's and Vygotsky's ideas through deep, ongoing reading and reflection.

ACTIVE LEARNING.   As a teacher, I believe that learning is something students do rather than something that is done to them. We must empower students to think for themselves, remain open to new experiences, and become lifelong learners who participate in self-directed growth (Fosnot, 1989; Piaget, 1955). Vygotsky (1934/1997) says,

The curve of development does not coincide with the curve of school instruction; by and large, instruction precedes development.... What the child can do in cooperation today he can do alone tomorrow. Therefore the only good kind of instruction is that which marches ahead of development and leads it; it must be aimed not so much at the ripe as at the ripening functions. (pp. 185, 188)

For me, Vygotsky's words take even more meaning in light of Calkins's (1983) comments: "Teaching—in the richest sense of the word—interacts with development and changes it. Teaching can be the cutting edge for learning" (p. 60). Stressing the importance of interactions between students and between students and their teachers, Calkins reminds readers that "Instruction does not necessarily come from a teacher" (p. 60). The classroom should be an active, alive place in which children work and talk together about what they are learning.

In his introduction to *The School and Society* and *The Child and the Curriculum* (Dewey, 1900, 1902/1990), Jackson suggests that if we view humans as "being inherently active and engaged" (p. xxv), the educational challenge lies in putting that view into practice without relinquishing the educational outcomes valued by society as a whole. I also believe that students who are interested in learning and who move and talk and think together about their learning learn more than students who sit passively waiting for their teachers to tell them what is important and what they should think. I also value the attainment of educational outcomes that society generally considers important in developing informed, knowledgeable citizens who will continue to be lifelong learners. Content should not be sacrificed for active learning. This is not an either-or dichotomy. Children should be given opportunities to learn rich, exciting, and important content through meaningful, relevant, and connected experiences. My experience tells me that Jackson is right—this is quite a challenge.

Various dimensions of the teacher's role in early childhood classrooms, as explained by Edwards et al. (1979/1994), sum up ideals toward which to work: "The teacher's role centers on provoking occasions of discovery through a kind of alert, inspired facilitation and stimulation of children's dialogue, co-action, and co-construction of knowledge" (p. 154). Edwards and colleagues assert that intellectual discovery is essentially a social process during which teachers can help even very young children learn to listen to other people, consider ideas and goals, and communicate successfully.

CLASSROOM COMMUNITIES AS LEARNING COMMUNITIES. We should be open to the unexpected and value and accept students for who they are, although we should also give students the tools to be full participants in U.S. society. I believe in fostering autonomy (Kamii, 1989; Piaget, 1955), which allows students to empower themselves, and I believe in building a supportive community within the classroom and school. In all subject areas, I encourage students to *understand* rather than simply *memorize* facts. I emphasize pride of product as well, stressing cooperation and collaboration while de-emphasizing in-class competition. We must experience and express delight in students and their efforts and encourage students to do the same for their peers

As I read and reflect on the particular classroom context of my study, in which not even one student consistently used standard English, I begin to understand perspectives of educators such as Delpit (1988), who argues that it is our responsibility to make explicit to all students the rules and conventions of the culture of power, and McLaren (1989), who says we must keep students' needs and problems foremost in our practice in an effort not to marginalize them. I find that the longer I teach young children—especially students whose backgrounds transmit cultures they need to survive in their own communities but do not necessarily make them successful within the culture of school— the more I come to believe that we, as teachers, must fit our model of schooling to the needs of the children we teach.

Delpit (1988) asserts that "schools must provide these children the content that other families from a different cultural orientation provide at home" (p. 286). This does not suggest separating children by their backgrounds; rather it suggests providing appropriate strategies for all children in each classroom. I think we must balance our classrooms to empower students as both learners and citizens; that is, we must accept our students just as they are, support them, and affirm them as important individuals who have worthwhile ideas and values. At the same time, we also must take responsibility for teaching students the codes of school and of the prevailing culture of the United States. The "codes of school" are unwritten customs or rules. However, unless these customs are made explicit to those students of different cultures, those students may make social or academic blunders. For example, these students may not turn in typewritten assignments on clean white paper, or they may come to school wearing unwashed clothes. Effective teachers have a variety of strategies to use with their students and are not afraid to be *experts* within their classrooms. Effective teachers view themselves and their students as experts who collaborate to create a community of learners. Mutual respect and caring acceptance—with the teacher's and the students' willingness to push for the best in both process and product—are catalysts that convert *classroom* communities into *learning* communities, in which growth occurs and relationships extend beyond school.

Peterson (1992) articulates practices that help teachers move toward promoting classroom community. He encourages teachers to help students "grow in complicated and critical ways" (p. 6). I believe "people construct meaning by bringing meaning to and taking meaning from their experiences," and I believe that "knowledge is personal—people search for meaning, structure, order" (Peterson, 1992, p. 6). I recognize, with Peterson, that skills are best learned while students are engaged with meaningful curricula that are connected to their lives and through which they are encouraged to take a critical stance, expressing and further developing their learning. I agree with Peterson that approximations and collaborations are essential as students and teachers construct learning communities together. I support his assertion that "intuition, feeling, and conceptual knowledge are valued ways of knowing...social, emotional, and cognitive interests are important" (p. 7). In the schooling that Peterson and I value, there is an important and meaningful *present* in which students demonstrate discipline and accountability as they become empowered and responsible for themselves and the group. According to Peterson, students' work is meaningful, collaborative, relevant, connected, and competent, based on their demonstrations of solving problems, working with others, expressing meaning, and providing perceptive critiques.

WAYS OF HELPING STUDENTS.   The students I have taught who were not as successful as might be desired despite our best efforts, moved me to learn as much as I could about ways to help them at the time. I *have* found teaching ideas that have been successful, largely because of what I have learned about children in four ways. I first learned about children from years of close and careful kidwatching, as described by Goodman (1985), in my classrooms and in other teachers' classrooms. The second way I learned how to help children was through many years of careful study of classroom-based research about children's literacy learning (e.g., Calkins, 1983, 1986; Clay, 1979, 1993, 1998; Graves, 1983, 1994; Heath, 1982, 1983; Holdaway, 1979; Rosenblatt, 1978/1994). The third way I learned how to help children occurred as I advanced my expertise in coming to know theory and methodology from multiple perspectives through various graduate courses. The final way I learned about helping children came from my participation in workshops, seminars, and conferences over the years.

Believing that it is important for teachers to remain avid learners who stay at the cutting edge of their field, I continue to observe children carefully, read current books and journals in the field, and attend and participate in conference sessions at every opportunity. Shulman (1986, 1987) considers it important to have knowledgeable teachers who grow in their understanding in three dimensions: (1) subject-matter content knowledge (what to teach), (2) pedagogical knowledge (how to teach), and (3) curricular knowledge (including, among other things, an understanding of the breadth of curriculum students are studying, as well as alternative curriculum materials available to meet the needs of learners at varying stages). Beattie (1995) adds a fourth dimension, personal practical knowledge, that pertains to teachers' knowledge gained through experiences with students' needs, interests, strengths, learning styles, etc. Teachers' personal practical knowledge is informed by their theoretical knowledge in their content fields and child development, social and learning theory, and other areas (Elbaz, 1983).

In his seminal article on knowledge and teaching, Shulman (1987) defines *comprehension and reasoning, transformation,* and *reflection* as crucial aspects of teaching. At the time of his article, most effective teaching studies looked primarily at teachers' management of classrooms. Shulman, however, advanced these studies by adding the management of *ideas* to the concept of effective teachers, stressing that ideas must not only be comprehended, but they must be "transformed in some manner if they are to be taught" (p. 16). Shulman also discusses the importance of the following for teachers: preparation for instruction; representation of ideas through new metaphors, analogies, and the like; selection of teaching methods and models; adaptation of these representations to the students being taught; and tailoring of these adaptations to the specific children involved. I believe that these important attributes are significant in helping us become and remain expert at what we do. As a teacher, I am obligated to increase my knowledge in all the areas that Shulman describes.

Ultimately, my ways of helping children become successful learners lead to one principle: I have learned to fit curriculum to the needs of each learner rather than to mold every learner into the same curriculum. When I received special permission to incorporate different ways of exploring learning with my students, I broke with traditional instruction of my school district. Thanks to supportive administrators who were willing to allow my students and me to be inventive in our approaches to literacy learning, my beliefs were strengthened and new avenues of successful learning were opened for my students.

A Philosophy About Students

Generally, many students in my study would be referred to as "at risk" by various educational authorities, although I prefer not to use that term. (Later in this chapter, I provide an in-depth description of the demographics of the students in my study.) Unfortunately, over the years, I have seen an increasing number of students whose circumstances make it more difficult for them to succeed in the world of school. In many schools, classes made up of these students are the norm. For me, the keys to working successfully with students—no matter who they are or what their backgrounds—are as follows:

- Know and love them as individuals;

- Look for the good in them;

- Accept them as they are, while challenging and encouraging them to higher levels of thinking, performance, and behavior;

- Instruct them to use tools that will lead to success in school and society;

- Allow them choices; and

- Appreciate their approximations toward their goals.

CONSTRUCTIVE ERRORS. Ferreiro and Teberosky (1979/1994) stress the importance of allowing children to work through periods of constructive error. "Constructive errors" refer to the systematic errors that differ from correct responses; however, rather than impeding progress in language processing, these errors subsequently permit learners to develop closer and closer approximations toward conventional language and ultimately to gain fully conventional language. Allowing learners to go through periods of constructive error is a long-term task that necessitates observant, knowledgeable teachers who understand how to support this learning process. Because of their Piagetian stance, Ferreiro and Teberosky view these systematic types of errors as ways to allow children to arrive at solutions; however, they caution readers to differentiate constructive errors from nonconstructive errors. They write, "Progression in knowledge is only attained through 'cognitive conflict'" (p. 18), but advise that not every activity is intellectual activity, and not every conflict is cognitive conflict. Ferreiro and Teberosky urge teachers to watch for crucial moments when they can help students to move forward in their new reconstructions.

My value of *approximations*, or constructive errors, was the element that most changed the tone of my classroom. Peterson and Eeds (1990) discuss approximation as achievement of competence over time, in which children are encouraged to share their thinking in settings that look at the direction of their responses to literature as much as the specific content of their responses. The students and I were genuinely enthusiastic and excited for each person who accomplished some small feat in his or her journey toward a more complete competence. Mayeroff (1972) reminds us how encouraging it is for a person "to realize that his growth evokes admiration, a spontaneous delight or joy, in the one who cares for him" (p. 44). He says that admiration affirms to the person that he or she is not alone: "It is as if I said to him, 'Look at yourself now, see what you did, see what you can do'" (p. 44). Mayeroff suggests that we must understand other people from within their worlds—seeing with their eyes—so we get a sense of who they are striving to become and what they need to grow. He states that we must also work to comprehend and respond to our own needs so we can use this understanding of ourselves to strengthen our understanding of others. Similarly, Fosnot (1989) observes that the teacher's ability to probe the learner's understanding, or skill in the art of "getting inside the student's head" (pp. 2, 3) is central to good teaching. This teacher research permits me to enter students' worlds from an *insider's* viewpoint (e.g., Spradley, 1980) in my effort to understand my students and my practice.

ACCEPTANCE AND ENCOURAGEMENT.   The success of each child also depends on his or her feelings of success and pride in what he or she legitimately accomplishes. By building a classroom community, teachers have an outstanding opportunity to encourage feelings of individual and group success. We must de-emphasize competition within the classroom and encourage cooperation and collaboration, although competition between classes can increase effort and collaboration within the classroom. When we accept each student as he or she is, we unlock opportunities for success within the classroom. This willing acceptance helps to build a risk-free learning environment in which students can flourish.

In his preface to the second edition of *Motivation and Personality*, Maslow (1970) writes that sweeping social and educational changes would take place quickly if we could teach our students to give up their demands for perfectionism—in people, society, parents, teachers, or friends. Imagine what we might accomplish if we could give up our demands for perfection from our students and if they could give up their demands for perfection from us.

A Philosophy About Literacy Learning

As an enthusiastic believer in the process approach to literacy learning, I support integration of semantic, syntactic, and graphophonic cueing systems (e.g., Goodman, Watson, & Burke, 1987; Weaver, 1994, 1998a, 1998b). I encourage students to use those systems simultaneously as they process print, by asking themselves, "Does it make sense? Does it look right? Does it sound right?" (e.g., Clay 1979, 1993, 1998; Dorn, French, & Jones, 1998; Strickland, 1998b). I support the use of self-correcting strategies to unlock meaning in all content areas, especially in reading and writing. I see reading, writing, spelling, listening, and oral language as interconnected components of a whole, and I communicate this interconnectedness to students as essential if they are to be proficient, effective users of language.

SCAFFOLDING. Reading is making meaning from print, and once a child has a good processing system in place, he or she is well on the way to self-improving behaviors every time he or she reads (Clay, 1979). I have explored many teaching methods and models, and I have come to agree with Clay, who cautions teachers against matching teaching methods to strengths of groups of children. She tells us,

> Such matching attempts are simplistic, for English is a complex linguistic system. The way to use a child's strengths and improve his weakness is not to work on one or the other but to design the tasks so that he practises [*sic*] the weakness with the aid of his strong ability. (p. 13)

One way I accomplish this is through scaffolding, or supporting, classroom experiences. Bruner's (1978) use of the term *scaffolding* describes what mothers do to make children's language learning more manageable: The mother's support includes helping the child focus his or her attention to pertinent aspects of the task and modeling her expectations of the child. Bruner notes that mothers extend or widen the range of contexts and serve as "communicative ratchets" (p. 254) to keep children from sliding backward once they have made a forward step. I believe teachers must be the communicative ratchets within schools, helping children build and maintain literacy expertise. For example, after pointing out positive aspects that students have accomplished, I propel this learning by suggesting a particular aspect for them to consider in their next effort.

Wood, Bruner, and Ross (1976) describe scaffolding as a support system that helps children achieve success on tasks that would be too difficult for them to achieve on their own. Dorn et al. (1998) build on the ideas of Bruner (1967, 1986a), Vygotsky (1934/1978), Rogoff (1990), and others in their support of building literacy development through an apprenticeship model in which students acquire knowledge and skills under the support and guidance of more knowledgeable people. I encourage students to talk about their lives and their work, because I agree with Piaget's (1955) perspective that talk between peers strengthens and objectifies knowledge. I value Vygotsky's (1934/1978) view of language as a social process in which students are supported in their zone of proximal development, which is "the distance between the actual developmental level as determined by individual problem solving and the level of potential development as determined through problem solving under adult guidance or in collaboration with more capable peers" (1934/1978, p. 86). Culture determines talk; thus, talk in school is important to help all children grow in their use of language (Heath, 1982, 1983). Having used these teaching approaches in my classrooms, I know their effectiveness. Teachers provide assistance as needed and remove it when it is no longer needed through a system of "adjustable and self-destructing scaffolds" (Dorn et al., 1998, p. 17). It takes knowledgeable teachers who are aware of the students with whom they work to accomplish such scaffolding. Knowing *which child* needs specifically *what assistance* for exactly *how long* are important aspects of teachers' work.

CONCEPTUAL FRAMEWORKS FOR LITERACY LEARNING.   I agree with other researchers (e.g., Calkins, 1986; Clay, 1979; Goodman, Watson, et al., 1987; Graves, 1983; Manning, Manning, & Long, 1989) that holistic literacy processes are the most beneficial way to help students construct meaning from print. Strickland's (1998b) "whole-to-part-to-whole conceptual framework" (p. 43) of literacy learning (in which children first work with whole selections of text, then have skill instruction in appropriate segments, and finally use those skills in speaking with or reading or writing meaningful, connected text) seems to be the most effective way of teaching students literacy skills. Wagstaff (1999) builds a whole-part-whole instructional model: Teachers and students establish a literacy context; students accomplish skill and strategy work; and students revisit the literacy context in order to practice the skills and strategies through shared, guided, and independent writing. All phases are interactive, and the model is supported by assessment that is connected to all phases.

I build on Strickland's and Wagstaff's conceptual frameworks of literacy instruction by envisioning the classroom as a sphere (see Figure 2) in which the *literacy context* of *authentic literacy events* and *whole, connected*, and *meaningful text* surrounds the students and me. Embedded within that literacy context is *ongoing assessment* that connects *authentic literacy* to the *parts of written language*, or the *skills and strategies* that learners need to know and use. By formally and informally assessing students' needs, I am able to plan meaningful skills and strategies at the cutting edge of the students' development, which enables them to work in their zone of proximal development.

Figure 2
Model of Literacy Instruction

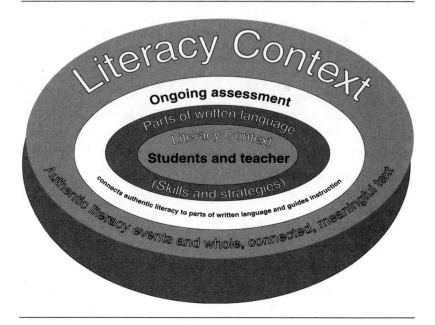

In other words, this ongoing assessment *guides my instruction* as I deliberately take these skills and strategies back to the authentic context, so children have multiple opportunities to use them in real reading, real writing, and real speaking interactions.

LEARNING CHOICES.   I agree with Dewey (1900, 1902/1990) that school must be unified and organized so all of its factors are connected as an organic whole rather than a composite of isolated parts. Cambourne (1988) notes that the following conditions of learning are requisites for success with students' learning literacy: immersion, demonstration, expectations, responsibility, use, approximations, response, and engagement. My goal in designing a literacy learning environment is to provide children consistently with Cambourne's conditions of learning, although I would add *reflective attention*, which goes a step beyond engagement. As Dewey (1900, 1902/1990) puts it,

True, reflective attention...always involves judging, reasoning, deliberation; it means that the child has a *question of his own* and is actively engaged in seeking and selecting relevant material with which to answer it.... The problem is one's own; hence also the impetus, the stimulus to attention, is one's own; hence also the training secured is one's own—it is discipline...that is, a *habit* of considering problems. (pp. 148–149)

It is this habit of personal "reflective attention" that I strive to encourage in every learner, including myself.

I value a language arts program for children similar to that of which Dyson (1993) speaks, which displays dialogic curricular activities in which there is "space for child choice as well as for adult plans and a willingness to consider changing adult plans at a child's suggestion" (p. 35). In discussing the importance of choice in negotiation of curriculum, Routman (1994) reminds us that if we do enough modeling, students are better able to develop their own questions and projects, and teachers who have a philosophy and solid theory of learning are better able to develop meaningful plans. Weaver (1994) also mentions choice in such curricular negotiations, noting that teachers set the parameters in which student and teacher choices are made. I believe that teachers have a responsibility in the negotiation of curricula and that a collaborative process is best to determine curricula (e.g., Dewey, 1938/1997; Short et al., 1996). I especially like the way Short et al. (1996) express that idea: "Curriculum is most powerful when teachers, with their experiences, interests, and knowledge (including state and district curriculum mandates), and students, with their experiences, interests, and knowledge, come together" (p. 4). Chapters 3 through 6, which document my teacher-research study, explore in depth the importance of choice.

A LITERACY ENVIRONMENT. The more I think and read about the social aspects of the classroom, the more I understand their significance for students' literacy growth. The timeliness of Dewey's comments about the classroom environment in *The School and Society* and *The Child and the Curriculum* (1900, 1902/1990) continues to impress me each time I reread it. Dewey describes a busy environment in which children are interested and fully engaged in their learning activities, and "there is a certain disorder [as] in any busy workshop" (p. 17). This is an environment in which a deep and wide form of discipline comes from working cooperatively and responsibly in constructive activities. Dewey portrays the school as a "miniature community, an embryonic society" (p. 18), in which discipline grows out of the spirit of social cooperation and community life. Here, "a spirit of free communication, of interchange of ideas, suggestions, results, both successes and failures of previous experiences, becomes the dominating note" (Dewey, p. 16). I am encouraged by seeing Dewey's insights reflected in my classroom, as children genuinely want to know and work together for extended periods of time to find out. Dewey's theories remain relevant and are applicable to my beliefs about the literacy environment and the larger environment of school.

Dyson's (1989) comments about "the very human desires to create and enact relationships with others and to organize and store information about a jointly shared world" (p. 3) ring true for me because I became even more convinced that part of the reason my students in this study seemed eager to produce and share written pieces about class experiences had to do with their jointly constructed community. Setting in place circumstances to foster the development of a classroom learning community was not an easy task, but it is important. Peterson (1992) states, "Bringing students together as a group and nurturing tolerance for their ways and beliefs while celebrating their differences challenges the talents of the most experienced teachers" (p. 13). It is essential that we teachers do just that. Other researchers (e.g., Fisher, 1991; Fraser & Skolnick, 1994) also endorse the importance of a community of learners as a support for children's literacy learning. We also must establish a sense of connection between the home and school, which Shields (1995) claims is "fundamental to our conception of 'meaning' in teaching and learning" (p. 44).

Knowing their importance, I worked toward establishing predictable time and predictable structure in our literacy environment, especially in the area of writing with children (e.g., Atwell, 1990; Calkins, 1983). My goal in designing the classroom's literacy learning environment was to provide children with many opportunities to love reading and writing. I immersed the classroom in many forms of print; I included core literature to encourage reflection and rereading, as well as a constant supply of new literature to ensure interest, excitement, and surprise. I tried to involve children with books, reading to them often and having them read to me at every opportunity. I believe that allowing children to connect with books by becoming authors themselves unlocks a new perspective for many students who have never thought of writing as a way for people to share their thoughts, so I had them write regularly in many genres and for as many purposes as possible. For example, I had them write thank-you letters after touring the lunchroom, create picture books of shared experiences, and design book advertisements to convince friends to read a book that they enjoyed.

LISTENING TO CHILDREN.   Possibly, the most important idea I have learned from working with children is to listen to them—*really* listen. Graves devotes a section of his book *A Fresh Look at Writing* (1994) to teachers' learning from students, and he strongly advises us to "practice listening to children" (p. 16). This idea is not new, nor is it unique to Graves, but it is perhaps the most enlightening single action teachers can take in the process of coming to understand students and as they support students' learning. When we actively listen to children, we allow children to inform our understandings about what the children know. For example, I commented on one child's book advertisement and said, "I like the way you're writing that book advertisement. How did you know how to spell those hard words?" The student then told me, "Well, I wrote the words the way they sounded and tried to see if they looked right." My comment and question and the student's subsequent explanation prompted me to move this student forward in the learning process. When we comment on something positive and ask the child to tell us how he or she went about the learning process, it allows us a window into that child's thinking. This window offers us the opportunity to confirm to children that what they are doing is correct and to *listen* to children teach us about their learning.

I am not the only teacher or researcher to have discovered the power of actively listening to children. In addition to Graves, other authorities note that they talk less themselves and are listening more to their students as readers and writers who are becoming critical talkers, listeners, and thinkers (Fraser & Skolnick, 1994). Peterson (1992) values thoughtful listening and responding to meaningful collaborations between inquirers. In the *Spying Heart: More Thoughts on Reading and Writing Books for Children* (1988), Paterson reminds readers that children do not necessarily say what we want to hear at the time when we want to hear it, but for teachers who listen patiently and who perceptively attend to what children say, the words of children can be revealing and can transform learning and relationships.

The students and I experienced an unsettled beginning as they tried to understand what I expected of them, and I attempted to learn what they needed from me. At the beginning of the school year, we had no common cause, no common experiences as a community. We had far to go academically, socially, and emotionally. Many children, by shouting at will across the classroom and disrupting the class, often put their needs before those of others. Arguments and conflicts abounded. For many students, assignments seemed to be mandates, and there appeared to be little investment in learning. Isolated instances of compatibility and even moments of joy occurred as we shared a story, which let me know what our classroom *could* be like. Feeling overwhelmed as our year began, I wanted to find a way to transform our classroom to what it could be. I had to set up circumstances to shape us into a unified group.

People who are not involved in everyday classroom life have a difficult time understanding that in our current educational environment, in which the students often have many risk factors, teachers often cannot attend to academics until they first attend to the children. I believed my class would not change the poor academic situation until each child took responsibility for altering the classroom conditions. I determined on the first day of class to change our direction, and I set up circumstances to move us from looking at what was wrong to looking at what was right. My experience as an early childhood teacher tells me that successful literacy instruction is not so much about which method teachers use to enable children to read, write, and talk, but more about the connections teachers help children build— connections to other students, connections to their teachers, connections to parents and other adults, and connections to literature and the world of print.

My teaching style supports my beliefs about teaching, as I try to be open and caring with my students in a child-centered and process-oriented classroom. I help students meet high academic and behavioral expectations by supporting them with acceptance and encouragement and providing classroom modifications as necessary to ensure their success. It is my hope that educators will heed the words of Greene (1994) and "come together in local spaces and struggle to create humane communities, playful communities, at once beautiful and just" (p. 459).

Methodology

As stated, the everyday classroom provides many opportunities for teachers and students to form classroom communities. In these communities, teachers and students launch investigations in their quest for knowledge, reflecting as individuals and as a group about what works and what does not in their classroom community. My particular study follows a year in the life of one classroom, and it reflects the culmination of my career of teaching young learners.

I always have been captivated by the many ways young children pursue reading and writing as they come to know the written forms of language. Over the last 5 years of my elementary school teaching career, as I actively conducted research in my own classrooms, my teaching has changed from being centered on what *I* do to focusing also on what the *children* do. The eager, active learners have infused the classroom with freshness and anticipation in their quest for knowing about their world. Their enthusiasm has been contagious and has helped me maintain my own eagerness for teaching and learning. Anderson et al. (1994) report that teachers who conduct practitioner research often remark on this kind of excitement. Although there have been daily crises and mishaps inherent to any group situation, the positives far outweigh the negatives. My students and I have become a caring community—interested in one another, our work, and our lives. The following sections describe the specific methodology of my study, which includes the purposes of the study, why I chose practitioner research, a description of the participants, my role as researcher, data collection, and data analysis.

Purposes of the Study

More qualitative research is needed to explain the complexities inherent within a self-contained elementary school classroom, particularly regarding literacy learning. This study examines those complexities in one such classroom to accomplish six purposes:

1. To describe and interpret the social organization, actions, interactions, and attitudes within the classroom centered around its literacy activities and instruction.

2. To describe how and why a teacher facilitates students' learning.

3. To add to the current body of knowledge about the ways in which children gain meaning in reading, writing, speaking, spelling, and critical thinking through language literacy experiences within a supportive learning environment.

4. To modify conditions to facilitate the teaching-learning process and to encourage positive attitudes toward learning and self-direction in gaining meaning.

5. To improve my own teaching practice (an idea that I found supported in the research of Anderson et al., 1994; Bissex & Bullock, 1987; Burnaford, 1996a; Cochran-Smith & Lytle, 1995; McNiff, Lomax, & Whitehead, 1996; Oja & Smulyan, 1989; Patterson, 1996; Patterson, Stansell, & Lee, 1990; Tafel & Fischer, 1996).

6. To add to the body of knowledge concerning the ways in which practitioner research can enhance the classroom practice of teacher-researchers.

My study began with this focus, although as is the case with qualitative research, this focus took some twists and turns as the study proceeded, not always leading where I had expected it to go. What began as a study looking at my own practice and the learning of my students ultimately helped me isolate exemplary practice for the students in my classroom.

The Practitioner Research Method

I chose practitioner research as the appropriate method to answer my questions because it allowed me to take on the *emic*, or insider, perspective (Anderson et al., 1994; Bogdan & Biklen, 1982, 1998; Cochran-Smith & Lytle, 1993; Lincoln & Guba, 1985), adding breadth and strength to my understanding of language literacy and classroom community in a classroom of young children. I did not feel that any other methodology would have allowed me to gain the same level of insight in the context of this particular study.

Practitioner research has become a well-established methodology during the past 25 years, but there is no one specified set of practices or methodology that is respected by all authorities. I prefer to think of practitioner research from Britton's (1987) point of view—a discovery process in which I am allowed to take seriously the ordinary life that my students and I experienced at school.

One of the strengths of qualitative work is that the researcher enters the study without preconceived notions of what the research findings will be. As Fetterman (1989) notes, however, the ethnographer enters a study with an open mind, not an empty head. I entered this study prepared to document and describe the literacy events, activities, actions, and interactions of my class in various settings over the school year. Because I was concerned with both multiple meanings and perspectives, I designed this study to rest on theoretical underpinnings of symbolic interactionism, which has three premises, according to Blumer (1969): (1) People act toward things according to the meanings they have assigned to those things; (2) those meanings come from social interactions with other people; and (3) those meanings are dealt with and modified through a person's interpretations when dealing with those things.

The Participants and the Setting

Similar to Pollard (1985), I found the selection of site and participants to be more a matter of pragmatism than a matter of careful consideration of the advantages and disadvantages of a particular situation. Having immediate access to my own classroom, as well as being subject to time restrictions and job requirements that did not permit observation of other classrooms, I elected to study my own second-grade classroom. I had immediate access to the site and the students.

I also chose to study my students because I have come to understand that practitioner research brings multiple benefits to students and their teacher. This intensive study of my own classroom allowed me to look in-depth at individuals—their ways of working, their strengths, and their difficulties—to better support their learning and to challenge them in appropriate and meaningful ways.

WHO WE WERE. This study took place in a rural school—approximately 50 miles from the nearest large urban area—in a southern state during the 1997–1998 school year.

Demographics of the school's student body were as follows: 75% were European American and 25% were African Americans; 50% were male and 50% were female; 66% were bused to and from school; 64% received Title I reading services, math services, or both (Title I is a federally funded program in the United States to improve students' skills in reading, math, or both); 61% received free or reduced lunches; 54% lived with either one parent or neither parent; and 15% had special needs (e.g., students who had speech or hearing impairments, mental retardation, learning disabilities, or physical handicaps). An added risk factor was that 34% of the students were transient.

The demographics of my second-grade class closely paralleled the overall school statistics. Nineteen students were in the class, and I, a middle-aged white female, was their teacher. The children ranged in age from 7 to 9 years old. There were 6 African American children— 3 males and 3 females—and 13 European American children— 6 males and 7 females. The children came from primarily working-class homes. These students' risk factors were heightened because of the minimal education obtained by most of their parents, the lower socioeconomic status of many of their families, and the below-grade-level reading performance of many of the students. In *Preventing Reading Difficulties in Young Children* (1998), Snow et al. discuss implications of such risk factors as being detrimental to language and literacy progress. Snow and colleagues note that these risk factors include group risk factors (e.g., attendance in low-achieving schools and residence in low-income families and neighborhoods), as well as individual risk factors (e.g., parental history of reading difficulties, a poor home literacy environment, and little or no verbal interactions prior to schooling). Snow et al. caution that although many children who begin their schooling with weak language and literacy skills— possibly because of these risk factors—do become successful readers, most do not.

In this study, the economic status of families seemed to correlate to parental levels of education; that is, the families with less education had poorer economic statuses than the more educated families had. Parental education levels also may have affected the priority that these families gave their children's education. From the students' enrollment forms and from the 35 parents who cited their educational status, I was able to determine the following about the students' parents: 20 graduated from high school; 10 were high school dropouts (some as early as eighth grade); 3 had 2 years of college education; 1 earned a general equivalency diploma (GED); and 1 had a college degree.

Home situations of the students varied: 11 children lived with both biological parents, whereas the remaining 8 students lived with either a biological parent, a biological parent and a stepparent, or a biological parent and two grandparents. Most of the students had adult supervision after school at home, at the school's extended-day program, or at a day-care facility. One third of these second graders had attended more than one school since kindergarten, and of this one third, some had attended two, three, or four schools since kindergarten. One student required intensive counseling and visited the school counselor at least twice weekly because of previous traumatic experiences. The County Department of Human Resources removed and returned the student to her mother's care numerous times, which kept the student in constant turmoil.

Several children in the class had been diagnosed with special needs. One student was placed in the class for students with mental retardation but was mainstreamed into my second-grade class for brief periods during the day. One boy who had been diagnosed as having attention-deficit hyperactivity disorder (ADHD) took Ritalin at home and twice daily at school. Overall, 12 students received Title I reading services, and 10 received Title I math services.

WHERE WE BEGAN.   At the beginning of the year, reading scores from the Qualitative Reading Inventory (QRI) (Leslie & Caldwell, 1990), a commercially prepared measure of reading proficiencies, placed almost three fourths of my students at levels below the conventional second-grade level of reading. Eight students were below primer level. Of the remaining students, one was at primer level, four were at first-grade level, two were at second-grade level, one was at third-grade level, and two were at fourth-grade level. (The student placed in the class for students with mental retardation was unable to take this test and was not considered in these figures.)

We did have three advantages. First, we were fortunate to have a principal who supported the active learning and informal structure in our classroom. Second, we had a caring woman, experienced in working with school children, who was assigned as the Title I instructional assistant for our class. Third, we had an enthusiastic and dedicated classroom volunteer—a young college sophomore who came twice weekly from mid-September until mid-March to work with students while she was trying to decide whether she wanted to continue her studies in either teaching or nursing. (At present, she has accepted her first teaching assignment and credits her experiences in our classroom for her career choice.) It is important to note that all of these advantages involved *people*.

My Role as Researcher

The following quote from Pollard (1985) seems appropriate as I reflect on my role as researcher:

> I find it hard to comment in detail on how "the type of person I am" affected the research, although I am sure it did; indeed, it was my deliberate intention to use my "self" as a tool in the research process. (p. 231)

As I assumed the dual role of teacher-researcher, I also became the research instrument, attempting to produce a wide spectrum that contained the details of everyday classroom life and generating a thick description of the thoughts, actions, and interactions of everyone within the classroom. The year-long study began with an exploratory phase in which my students and I began to construct a caring and trusting relationship, building a sense of community while engaging in literacy learning. I gained permission to conduct the study from the students, the students' parents, the Title I instructional assistant, the classroom volunteer, the school principal, the school district superintendent, my doctoral dissertation committee, and the Institutional Review Board that oversaw the study.

I found that I constantly made modifications to this study, modifying the context of my research, as well as the students' learning. This would be regarded as a weakness in some methodologies, particularly quantitative studies that consider modifications during a study to confound the variables, thus weakening the study; nevertheless, this modification surfaced as a strength in this practitioner research. Practitioner research gave me the opportunities to document situations, reflect about ways to respond to these situations, actively modify instruction or conditions as needed, and carefully study changes I made in order to determine what the best action could have been. My students and I gained knowledge and experience as we reflected together about these changes. The logistics of assuming two roles at once simply necessitated finding appropriate ways of collecting data, which served two purposes: facilitating children's learning and documenting rigorous research practices.

Data Collection

This research study employed the following methods of data collection: participant observation; formal and informal interviewing; student and teacher journaling; photography, audiotaping, and videotaping; and collection of artifacts (student-produced books, stories, and group projects). All of these data-collection methods followed the procedures of four qualitative researchers (i.e., Bogdan & Biklen, 1982, 1998; Seidman, 1991; Spradley, 1980). These systematic methods of data collection were used in conjunction with other naturalistic methodologies (i.e., collecting field notes, triangulating data sources, verifying interpretations of data with participants), as I attempted to capture the essence of our classroom and produce data on instruction, following suggestions by Patterson et al. (1990) and Shipman (1985). Using observational research methods to understand this classroom, I was aware of the impact of my "human judgments and perceptual abilities" (Genishi, 1982, p. 564) as I looked, listened, noticed, and recorded data. This awareness brought a carefulness and attention to detail to my observation. For example, many times I referred to videotapes, audiotapes, or photographs to confirm my observations.

All of these methods, although they are available to researchers from other paradigms, took a more prominent role in my data collection as a teacher-researcher. For example, student journals were a wonderful way to combine an educational assignment with a form of data collection. Photocopying students' journal entries, reflecting about them in my field notes and in discussions with the students, and periodically returning to the entries throughout the year, enabled me to give a comprehensive picture of the students' growth.

Use of reflection in the students' journals and in oral discussions sparked divergent points of view. Hubbard's (1996) method of questioning students—"What went right? What went wrong? What happened here? What could we have done differently? What would we continue to do in the same way?" (p. 116)—could have come straight from the pages of my field notes. These types of questions enabled growth in the students' questioning, as well as my own. Discussion based on Hubbard's method of questioning was a constant in my process of data collection.

Photography emerged as another tool that fit especially well in the data collection of a working teacher who is also a researcher. Walker and Wiedel (1985) call photographs a complex kind of data, which are "in many ways the visual equivalent of the ethnographic field-note...with a surface validity and undeniability always denied the second-hand account" (p. 214). They also state that the issue of selectivity, which is inherent with the use of photographs, is reduced in importance as it is juxtaposed against the documentary power of photographs and their relation to memory. Photographs were an invaluable tool of data collection because they initiated reflection and an invaluable teaching aid because they triggered collective memories when students were writing about group experiences.

Observing the classroom through these means allowed me to step out of the role of teacher and into the role of researcher, or outside observer. The *familiar was made strange*, as described by Erickson (1973) and Pierce (1990), by the use of audiotapes and videotapes. In other words, I was able to notice patterns of body language and behavior that were not observable from my insider position as classroom teacher.

Data Analysis

As the researcher, I used three of Lincoln and Guba's (1985) techniques for gaining credibility in a naturalistic study: (1) prolonged engagement, which enabled me to learn the context and reduce distortions in data and which provided me with time to build trust and rapport with the participants; (2) persistent observation, which enabled me to identify and assess the salient factors and to explore them in detail; and (3) triangulation of data, which may be accomplished by using different sources, methods, or investigators. In this study, I used different sources to triangulate the data. I also found it helpful to use *member checks*, which Lincoln and Guba define as continuous formal and informal testing of data, interpretations, and conclusions with participants from whom the data were originally collected (e.g., the students, the Title I instructional assistant, and the classroom volunteer). Lincoln and Guba differentiate member checks from triangulation by noting that triangulation is carried out with respect to data and member checks are carried out with respect to constructions. I have included both to gain credibility for this study. For example, see Appendix A for the time frame for this study, which documents the rigors of teacher research.

I also used Spradley's (1980) ethnographic research cycle to collect and analyze data. I started the cycle with broad ethnographic questions, collected ethnographic data, made an ethnographic record of the data set (through interviews; field notes; audiotapes, videotapes, and photography; and classroom artifacts), and analyzed the data, which in turn, generated more questions and continued the cycle. The constant comparative method (Glaser & Strauss, 1967) enabled me to collect and analyze data simultaneously. Each day, I jotted down field notes; each night, I fleshed out the field notes by reading and rereading them. At least 3 nights per week and on weekends, I transcribed audiotapes and videotapes, reflecting on patterns and hidden meanings and noting my comments and insights. I used inductive analysis of my actions and those of the students, as well as the interactions between the students and those between the students and me, with some triangulation furnished by interviews I had with the classroom volunteer and the Title I instructional assistant. I used member checks throughout the study.

Multiple collection procedures allowed triangulation of observations; field notes; interviews; photographs, audiotapes, and videotapes; and classroom artifacts. I triangulated my field notes and videotapes with secondary data (i.e., interviews with the Title I instructional assistant, the classroom volunteer, and the students to gain their perspectives) to generate a description of the social organization within the class. I had other researchers, such as a fellow doctoral student and another teacher-researcher, view videotapes in an attempt to obtain interrater reliability. I am confident that using both triangulation and interrater reliability made the study less subjective.

As I collected data, I actively looked for recurring themes that emerged from the data. On finding these, I devised coding categories and marked my notes with colored dots to indicate codes. I translated these codes into symbols on the word-processor versions of data for ease of replication. Following this coding, I looked for ways to group or bracket the data. From this process, which was ongoing throughout the study (as is prescribed in the constant comparative method of analysis), I was able to focus my data collection to particular times that emerged early in the year as being salient. Those times that appeared to be influential to both literacy and community included writing workshop; reading workshop; after-lunch storytime; Elsewhere Expeditions (purposeful journeys outside the classroom); various conversations that took place at the lunch table, as we walked to and from various school activities, and en route to and from field trips; and experiences that occurred during our two field trips. Chapters 3 through 6 document these meaningful experiences.

I conducted analyses at least biweekly, with more extensive efforts monthly. I kept all the physical artifacts in folders, which I first grouped by date and topic but later grouped by students' names. The exception to that were some artifacts that were so outstanding as group examples of literacy efforts that I kept them together in manila envelopes coded with event names and dates. Five times during the year—October, January, March, May, and June—I sorted, categorized, and continued to code the physical data. At each of these intervals, I had more data, and the categories shifted. The largest shift came in June, when I was finally able to distinguish two major splits in the data. These splits came from reciprocal directions of the teacher's roles and the students' roles and the ways in which each influenced the other, the community, and literacy.

As I struggled to analyze my data, I found truth in assertions by Bogdan and Biklen (1982, 1998), Pierce (1990), and Spradley (1980): Nothing is too insignificant to be noted by qualitative researchers, and we must alternate between the perspectives of *insider* and *outsider*, sometimes having both viewpoints at the same time. As Bogdan and Biklen affirm, "Data are both the evidence and the clues" (1982, p. 73). Conclusions from the data are discussed in Chapter 7.

CHAPTER 3

My Role as "Architect"

[Architects] design much more than the façade...of a building. They develop its basic concept—its inner space, its feeling, its look. The contemporary architect must be a very versatile person...a dreamer and a doer at the same time. (Feldman, 1970, p. 335)

Teachers are architects who design much more than the appearance of their classrooms. They establish its underlying composition—its character, its temperament, its intentions, its goals. Teachers, too, must be versatile—part artist, part architect, part poet, part philosopher, part supportive advocate, part demanding task master—dreamers and doers at once. Teachers create spaces that allow students to thrive.

Teachers must have a vision that attends to the overall concept of the classroom. This vision accounts for both the external and internal structure of the classroom and requires that the teacher pay attention to not only basic classroom needs, but also the needs and desires of the students within the classroom. Teachers must envision spaces that foster human interactions. Just as no two buildings are ever identical, no two classroom designs are exactly the same either. Wise teachers provide a flexible outer structure that allows them to redesign the inner structure as students learn and grow.

Setting the Foundation: Establishing Access and Routines

Teachers prepare the foundation of the classroom structure before the beginning of the school year, although their work continues throughout the year as needed. Architects design buildings to serve the needs of the people who will live and work there; teachers create frameworks to serve and support their students. Believing that a supportive environment provides the best structure for learning, I worked from the beginning to provide a consistent and predictable classroom structure and expectations to facilitate active and ongoing learning—students knew what to expect and could plan for their work.

Planning the Classroom Environment

As the classroom's architect, one of my responsibilities was to create a physical environment that supported all aspects of literacy learning, particularly reading and writing. I organized my classroom so children could locate and access needed materials easily. For example, some of the first work areas I created were for the students' use for reading, writing, and art. I stored writing supplies such as pencils, pens, markers, paper, stapler, and tape in or near the writing work area so students who needed these supplies did not disturb others who were working elsewhere. Duplicate supplies were kept in both the writing and art work areas so students did not argue over supplies or have to wait to use supplies.

Books of many genres and various formats covered virtually every area in the classroom to encourage students' exploration of books. For example, I kept most books on old greeting-card racks, which allowed the students to view book covers easily. I used prominent places such as the chalk tray, windowsills, and work-area tables to *feature* certain books. Laundry baskets provided me with an easy way to separate library books from my own books. I put textbooks on low bookshelves, which left the books within the students' reach.

I designated specific areas throughout the room for use by large groups of students, small groups of students, and individuals. I decided on the location of these areas by the students' level of noise and the activities in which the students were involved. For example, I placed quiet reading areas away from the more active art areas. I also arranged desks to facilitate student interaction and to leave pathways for students, knowing from experience that our arrangements and pathways would shift as our unique patterns of work emerged.

I decorated the classroom's bulletin boards with brightly colored fabrics and borders, although I left them clear of anything else in anticipation of the student work I would soon be able to display. By displaying the students' work on bulletin boards, walls, and windows, I let the students know their work was important. Indeed, I wanted everyone who walked into our classroom to realize that these creations were made by children who were readers, writers, thinkers, and doers. Our classroom—even though it was often messy and cluttered with projects under construction—portrayed a literacy and learning community that valued learning, accomplished difficult work, and enjoyed reading and writing. This community allowed the students and me to make connections to each other, authentic purposes, and integrated curriculum.

Fostering Family-School Connections

On the first day of school, I spoke briefly with the few parents and grandparents who came to ease their children into this strange new environment. I invited all of them to return to the classroom to help us if they were interested in returning and available. The few parents who came back to the classroom helped the children feel valued: They read to the children, listened to the children read, and acted as scribes for the children who had difficulty writing on their own. Visits from students' family members eventually became less frequent, but the access to the classroom was still there. By opening our class and asking for families' assistance, I removed a barrier to home-school partnerships—the lack of understanding about what students experience in school.

I also promoted access to the classroom by being available to parents; that is, I gave parents my home phone number and asked them to call me when they had questions, concerns, or suggestions. This availability also helped me learn about students from the people who knew them best. Delpit (1994) suggests that listening and talking to parents helps teachers understand students who have cultures different than their own. My willingness to communicate with students' parents promoted a strong home-school connection in which parents felt welcomed into the classroom and nonthreatened. Parents became my allies as they helped me to get to know their children; this knowledge improved student-teacher learning interactions.

Photography also provided students' families with access into our classroom. The children and I took pictures to document our experiences. The students eventually used these pictures to create stories

73

and books for their family members and friends to read. This glimpse into school life helped families—especially those who could not visit the classroom—understand the structure and significance of our work and learning.

Managing the Environment

Managing the classroom environment is a crucial element in helping teachers and students maintain a productive learning environment. Part of my management included guiding the students by establishing routines. Believing that we all take more ownership of and interest in devices that we help design, I invited the students to plan these routines with me. For example, we discussed how to use the three work areas in the classroom. We decided how to arrange books on the bookshelves in the reading work area, how to use writing supplies in the writing work area, and how to use art materials in the art work area. We talked about the best times to go to a work area, how many students were allowed in one area at a time, and how long students could stay in one area. Once we established procedures for these work areas, I expected the students to follow these procedures consistently; this took time and practice.

Also key in managing the classroom was a daily schedule. The students quickly learned our daily schedule, which included but was not restricted to the following:

- A language arts block (i.e., journaling, class meeting, and reading and writing workshop)
- A math block
- An integrated content area block (i.e., social studies, science, health, and language arts)
- Daily read-alouds
- Drop Everything And Read (DEAR) time

Our daily schedule enabled the students to learn my expectations of the class structure. For example, when it was time for group lessons, the students learned to sit together either on the rug, beanbags, or pillows without distracting those around them, and they knew they were supposed to listen when others spoke and take turns when speaking.

When working on independent assignments, the students discovered that they were free to work wherever they chose, speak in soft voices, and ask for and give assistance as needed. When I wanted to see what they could accomplish without assistance, the children learned to sit at their desks and work completely independently. Through student interviews, I discovered that the students worked independently without complaint because they knew they had many other opportunities to work in different ways.

Like McCollum (1995), I found that alternating instructional patterns and creating distinctly different learning environments worked toward the success of our classroom and helped the students reach specific academic goals. McCollum notes that successful management of the learning environment—students engaged in academic tasks, few classroom disruptions, and smooth transitions between instructional segments—is readily apparent to an observer. For example, on observing my second-grade class, the school's principal commented:

> When I come into your classroom, you all are always busy—the children are working and talking about what they are doing, you are busy with children. Everyone knows what they can and can't do. The children always come up to me as soon as I come in the door to pull me over to where they're working. They want to show me what they're doing and tell me all about it. I can tell there's real learning going on in here. (R. Roberts, personal communication, May 29, 1998)

McCollum (1995) further reports that teachers who successfully used whatever combination of right moves to fit their personal teaching styles succeeded in making their classrooms "highly productive learning environments where students not only completed assigned tasks but also clearly enjoyed being and learning...children felt successful, were respectful of one another, and willingly approached the tasks of the school day" (p. 17). The data from my study suggest that such a combination existed in our classroom. The following sections set forth this "combination of right moves."

MOVEMENT AND PURPOSE.   My encouragement of movement and purpose, which connected physical and social aspects of our environment, influenced the success of my classroom. All the students were active members of a working community: They worked on self-designed projects, as well as assigned lessons. Freedom of movement in and out of the classroom helped them remain engaged in their learning. This aspect of the classroom design promoted flexibility and social interaction, although I also used it to acknowledge the importance of their work. Students needed ample time and space to accomplish their work, which required them all to come together as working partners who moved freely within the class—using supplies, finding space, and talking to one another about work. By incorporating movement into students' work, I affirmed that their active involvement was important and necessary.

Dewey (1900, 1902/1990) speaks of the importance of purposeful work in his discussion of thinking, in which he defines purposeful work as a mentally projected plan that a person devises as a solution to a problem that has arisen. This mentally projected plan begins as the person reflects about the best way to solve the problem, then decides on necessary steps to solve the problem and determines the order in which to accomplish these steps. Dewey notes, "This concrete logic of action long precedes the logic of pure speculation or abstract investigation, and through the mental habits that it forms is the best of preparations for the latter" (p. 135).

The students took more interest in careful observation when they were in the midst of what they thought was an important experience; therefore, the students left that experience with deeper knowledge than they might have if they had not thought it was important. Students were willing to work at follow-up projects, such as books, letters, charts, and graphs, for extended periods of time. They became willing to read or write in-depth about their experiences and eventually *expected* to read and write in connection with every experience. Students told me that after each experience, they had thought about and planned for ways to read and write. This became apparent in a year-end interview I had with one student, Jimmy:

> Stewart: Do you plan out before you come to school what you're going to write about that day?
>
> Jimmy: I do it...in the nighttime.
>
> Stewart: When you're in the bed?
>
> Jimmy: Um hum.
>
> Stewart: What do you do?

Jimmy:	Stay up real late.
Stewart:	Are you lying there thinking about what you're going to write about the next day?
Jimmy:	Um hum. I just let it grow and it grow and it grow....

Other researchers have documented witnessing this similar phenomena in students (e.g., Calkins, 1986; Dyson, 1989; Graves, 1983).

HIGH EXPECTATIONS.   High expectations emerged as an important part of the success of the classroom community and the children's language literacy. The students realized that I expected them to be considerate of and respectful to everyone in the class and put forth their best efforts in their work. From the beginning of the school year, I tried to communicate to the students to be on time for class, have the necessary working supplies, and complete assignments in a timely manner. I also implored the students to make the products of their assignments as "perfect" as they could be because "If it goes public, it's perfect!" (Manning, 1991, p. 5). Even though I allowed the children to turn in first drafts of their writing, I expected that the students would have reviewed the drafts several times since they had been written. Emphasizing both the conventions and content of writing, I expected students to reread their drafts to find places where they could use stronger words, circle possible misspellings, and add needed punctuation while looking for places where their writing needed to be reworded for a better flow of ideas.

The students' efforts to meet the high expectations within our class elevated not only the level of student achievement, but also the students' levels of effort and commitment. Both the students and I helped and encouraged each other to do his or her best. If one student had difficulty, another student was there to encourage him or her to keep trying or to ask for help when he or she needed it. And someone—whether it be another student or me—was always there to give that help. In his year-end interview, Jimmy and I discussed how this help affected other students:

Stewart:	Do we help each other?
Jimmy:	Yeah. Um, in writing workshop, we can have partners, or we have to work by ourselves at our seats.

Stewart:	So what are some ways that we help each other?
Jimmy:	Well, um, when we do group stories we, you know, um, have ideas....
Stewart:	So we're helping each other with ideas? Do we help each other with other stuff?
Jimmy:	Yes, ma'am. Helping with writing workshop, reading, telling...I mean, sounding out words for 'em... telling like that....
Stewart:	What about reading and writing and telling stories? Is there anything you can tell me about that?
Jimmy:	Um, Jeff, Matthew, and I like to do reading and writing together.... Like, I'll be writing it, Jeff will be telling pictures, and Matthew, he'll tell us what to write. Then we all talk about it and decide if we want to change it. When we read, um, sometimes Jeff don't know any words, so I help him with 'em, and all of a sudden he pops up and knows some words.

RELEVANT STRATEGIES.   I tried to engage children so that they worked in cooperation with me—or other adults or students—at higher levels than they would have been able to negotiate by themselves. Strategies that I modeled and taught in this classroom were consistent with my underlying philosophy and emerged as a theme under my influence as architect. The students and I valued both the processes and products of our literacy efforts. We all realized and talked about the importance of the predictable routines of our daily reading and writing workshops, such as those described by Calkins (1983, 1986) and Graves (1983, 1994).

During our reading and writing workshops, I found many opportunities to model strategies for literacy development that supported the students' thinking and learning. Sometimes, I modeled thinking, reading, or writing in front of the students; I often stopped to share my thought processes as I worked through some difficulty that I thought might help their processing. Although we did not always follow every step of the writing process (Calkins, 1986; Graves, 1983), we did it often enough that the students were thoroughly familiar with every step and realized that the steps were not linear but recursive. A description of these steps in the writing process is given later in this chapter in the section titled "Writing as a Literacy Framework." Over time, the students began to feel comfortable with and successful in carrying out the entire writing process.

I often explained strategies by using students' pieces of work, although at other times, I explained strategies in a more didactic way. In general, however, I taught the students to use strategies to make their reading and writing stronger by stressing metacognition—thinking about their thinking. I wanted the students to be aware of which strategies they chose and why. We spent a great deal of time discussing those choices and the reasons behind them. For example, when I listened to the tape of Jimmy's year-end interview, I found myself suggesting relevant strategies even as I questioned him:

Stewart: We've finished talking about retellings, and I want to know what good readers do.

Jimmy: [thinks a minute] Well, um, at first they'll get a book, and they'll read what it's dedicated to...and if they didn't know a word, they'd go, "I didn't know *production*—pr-o-duc-tion." That would give me a clue at the end of *shun*, so I'd have to figure it out. *Shun*. [We had discussed in earlier lessons the fact that *t-i-o-n* is pronounced *shun*.]

Stewart: All right, so you're using the sounds of the words. What else are you using?

Jimmy: [His face lights up, and he replies with a huge grin.] I can also use my friends!

Stewart: [laughing] How do you use your friends?

Jimmy: They help me with the words. [The preceding comment demonstrates an aspect of the bonds of this learning community in that the children considered their friends to be important literacy resources.]

Stewart: OK. What if you're reading all by yourself?

Jimmy: Um, let's see.... I'd probably just happen to do it one way and not tell anyone..."pro-duction."

Stewart: OK. OK, so you'd use the sounds?

Jimmy: [cocking his head to the side] No, I'd use syllables.

Stewart: Oh, syllables. Good for you! Good for you. Well, do you pay attention to meaning?

Jimmy: Meaning? What's that mean?

Stewart: Well, do you pay attention to what the sentence is trying to tell you?

[The conversation/interview jumps from reading to writing in the following section because we worked on both simultaneously in the classroom. Jimmy thought of himself as both reader and author; therefore, he considered his own writing to be important, real reading.]

Jimmy: Yep, see, after I write about...10 sentences one at a time, I'll just go over there and read them [*sic*] 10 sentences all together, and if I have 'em right, I don't do anything. I write 10 more sentences. If I have anything wrong in 'em, I have to fix it.

Stewart: [I jump in before he has time to finish. As I listen to the tape, I notice we constantly talk over each other.] So you kind of write your stories a section..

Jimmy: ...or I don't fix it; I just circle it. I circle right there....

Stewart: [nodding] And then you go back? And fix it later?

Jimmy: Yeah, 'cause...so I'll remember where it is.

Stewart: Oh, well, that's a smart idea.... If you were reading, though, and you tried to sound out your words and you didn't have anybody to ask, what are some other things you could do?

Jimmy: Well, you could just go, like, you'd see what it sounds like...p-r-o-d-...

Stewart: [I jump in.] Well, that's using your...

Jimmy: u-t-i-o-n.

Stewart:	Yeah. That's using your sounds. You almost spelled the word *production*. Whew, you were really close!
Jimmy:	[looks intrigued] What'd I spell?
Stewart:	P-r-o-d-u-c-t-i-o-n.
Jimmy:	What did *I* spell, though?
Stewart:	[I can't exactly remember how he spelled it without rewinding the tape, which I do not want to do at this point.] I don't know.... You might not have spelled it exactly right. I think you left out one letter, but I'm not sure.
Jimmy:	Yeah, *c*.
Stewart:	Um, OK.

Jimmy's preoccupation with what *he* spelled demonstrated his determination and persistence to make his work as correct as he could make it, whether in reading, writing, spelling, or any other aspect of his literacy performance. This type of effort and attention to detail is typical of students who view themselves as having important, real work to accomplish. As Jimmy and I continued our conversation, I began using a "teachable moment" as I introduced a new idea:

Stewart:	One of the things I hope you would remember is that you could use your pictures for clues. Do you ever do that?
Jimmy:	Sometimes, but I'll...
Stewart:	But you don't have to do that very much, do you, Jimmy?
Jimmy:	It'd give me an idea.
Stewart:	Yeah, if you did that, you'd have to go back...
Jimmy:	...and read it again...
Stewart:	Read it again, so it'd make sense, wouldn't you? [Even in this setting I find myself scaffolding a child's learning.]

Jimmy: Yeah.

Stewart: That's what I was talking about "sense" a while ago.

Although I thought I had ended this interview successfully, Jimmy was not ready to stop talking. He wanted to tell me what he knew and how he knew it, knowing I was always interested in the "whys" behind every response:

Jimmy: But you can find out how that word is...like, you could just look down at the pictures, you know, um...about *My Home* [naming a book just across from him on the windowsill]. You could just look down at the picture and see what it is, like, you wouldn't know how to spell *lion*, but you could just look down there, and there's *lion* down there. And you'd say "lion."

Stewart: [nodding] That's true.

Jimmy: Li-on.

Stewart: All right [in my mind, moving on to the next question].

Jimmy: You want to know how I thought about that?

This excerpt is definitely not an example of good interviewing in the sense of being a method of data for my teacher research. I originally had intended to ask an open-ended question, wait for Jimmy's complete response, follow up on his response, then move to the next open-ended question on my list. But at the time of the interview, my teaching instincts unconsciously took over. I will always choose to do what is right for my students over what is expedient for me, even though I realize that this is one reason some people dismiss teacher research as invalid. Rather than view my actions as a weakness in my research techniques, I choose to view it as a strength in my teaching techniques.

I also realized that I "jumped" into Jimmy's answers without fully giving him time to respond. This was a conversational pattern that the students and I had established across the year; we often finished others' sentences in this way. We did not consider this to be rude, rather we were involved in one another's thoughts to the extent that we were anxious to convey our understanding of just what the other person was trying to say. This "shorthand" conversational style evolved as we developed into a learning community.

RESPONSIBLE CHOICE. Responsible choice seemed to enhance the sense of ownership experienced by the students. I purposely arranged a wide range of choices into the instructional design, so that the students could experience making choices, reflect on which of those choices were good ones, and take increasing responsibility for consequences of those choices. From my data analysis, I realized that many instances supported the fact that when students were given some aspect of choice—whether in the assignments themselves, in the order of assignments, or some other aspect of the assignment—they invested themselves more completely in that assignment. Having a choice in genre, length, topic, or format appeared to give students a deeper interest in completing their writing piece. When children had choices in their environment (e.g., seating, light, temperature) or social interactions, an exciting variety of situations emerged that supported both literacy and community. Choices seemed to help children feel ownership of literacy tasks. By sharing products of literacy events, students learned to take part in discussions about them and to make insightful comments about shared pieces of writing and the authors of those pieces. That ownership—particularly of written pieces—seemed to encourage children to listen to one another, comment on ways in which the pieces were strong, and sometimes, suggest ways in which pieces could be improved. Specific examples of ways in which they accomplished these discussions are included in Chapters 4, 5, and 6.

Record-keeping sheets that I used during writing workshops illustrated the importance of choice and ownership. I prepared these sheets by listing students' names down the left side of the page, with specific categories to be filled in by me across the top of the sheet. I used separate record-keeping sheets for students' reading workshops and writing workshops (see Stewart, in press, for examples of these forms). These categories listed the title or topic of each student's daily writing or reading workshop, as well as the genre and format that each student used. I also asked the following questions and recorded the students' answers on the sheet:

- Did you complete your piece?
- Will you continue to read and write about this topic?
- Did you use your time well?

I used record-keeping sheets for both writing and reading workshops for several reasons. These sheets were a practical tool for managing the logistics of the workshops; they let me know who was working on which project at any given time, and they documented students' growth across time. Record-keeping sheets also provided more formal structure and seriousness to reading and writing because they allowed students to make choices about topic, genre, and format and served as a record of these choices. Students were permitted to revise their plans, but I asked that they have me mark their changes on this sheet also. When the time came for sharing at the end of each workshop, I referred to this sheet to determine whether students actually had written or read what they initially recorded. This choice and responsibility produced more effort in the students' selections in the first place and eliminated much of the wavering from topic to topic that many children had experienced very early in the year.

The students, the Title I instructional assistant, the classroom volunteer, and I were aware of and commented on the influence of choice within our classroom. The following excerpt from my year-end interview with the instructional assistant, Mrs. Collins, exemplifies the importance of choice:

Stewart: What do you see as the most important part of our classroom?

Mrs. Collins: Choice...you know, all the kinds of choices the kids could make. I think that made the biggest difference.

Stewart: In what ways?

Mrs. Collins: Well, you know, you let them choose where they would work lots of times and who they would work with. They could choose what to write about and which books to read—that was really important as far as I could tell. When they came back to me they usually brought books they had chosen.

They liked that. And I liked that too. You know, they didn't have to keep reading the same old stories like they did in some classes. They could find books they were interested in. I thought that was one reason they liked to read so much, because they had a choice in it. Yeah, I think choice was a really big thing in here!

Building the Edifice: Creating Experiences and Memories

After setting the foundation for the classroom, teachers build on it in ways that personally have an impact on each class member, which allows the students to engage in common experiences and create joint memories. As architect, it was my job to create experiences on this foundation. Throughout our year together, the students referred to our shared experiences by saying, "Do you remember when...?" or "That's like the time we...." These common references allowed us to reflect on our past experiences with one another; we nodded in recognition when someone mentioned a favorite book or poem, and we smiled at the memory of something funny. Experiences and memories bonded us just as a family is bonded by memories of their experiences together. This family feeling—this sense of community—is what helped us to be understanding when students took risks in their learning or exposed their feelings to the rest of us, to be patient and supportive when problems arose, to celebrate one another's successes, and to plan together for meaningful group efforts.

Photography as Documentation of "Good Things"

Photography emerged from the data set as one of the most important factors of my influence as architect. It focused our classroom on positives and promoted the importance of valuing the strengths of each class member. For example, I introduced photography on the morning of the first day of second-grade year: I took pictures of each child as he or she created an *All About Me* book (see Figure 3 for a student's example) and placed the picture at the end of each child's book. An *All About Me* book is a "step" book—which is a book composed of

Figure 3
Example of *All About Me* Book

All About Me

by Jamiel Crowder

This is some thing I am Proud of.

These are my favorite things to do.

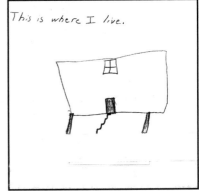

This is where I live.

This is my family.

Me

This what I looked like on August 19, 1997.

six increasingly longer pages that are stapled at the top—on which children wrote and drew illustrations about themselves, their families, and whatever else they chose to write about. (Specifics on creating these books can be found in Stewart, in press.) We included an instant photograph of each child at the end of his or her book to show how each child looked on the first day of school. I then invited the students to become the "photographers." I told them to tell me when they saw "good things" happening in our classroom, and I would let them take a picture of it. The students and I talked about what some of those good things might be and why it was important to look for them:

Stewart: What do you think I mean by taking pictures of "good things"?

Adam: Would it be somethin' like somebody workin' real hard?

Stewart: Yes. Great answer! How might someone be working hard? [Looking at the students]

Frances: Well, they could be writing a story.

Stewart: Yes, that would be important work. What else?

Jessica: They could be reading.

Stewart: Yes. Would it have to be just people who were working by themselves?

Jimmy: Could it be two people working together?

Stewart: Yes, if those two people were really working hard and not playing around, then that would be a very good thing.

Even from the first day, it was important to think aloud with the children and to scaffold their understanding and not assume that they interpreted ideas as adults would. Therefore, I took a great deal of time conversing with them that morning about the work they would be doing in class. This helped set the stage for a respectful, risk-free learning environment. The following discussion revealed a typical pattern in our classroom, as I asked a question, allowed waiting time for response, then asked the same question again and elicited responses from the children by nodding or smiling at those who looked eager to speak:

Stewart: Now I want you to think about how important it is that we have "smart" people as photographers. It's not easy to be that kind of a photographer. Take some time to think about why this might be hard. [I wait several minutes, allowing the students to think silently.] Why would this be hard?

James: Well, you might be working yourself and not notice other people.

Stewart: That's right, but do you know what? Then somebody might catch *you* on film doing something good!

James: Well, you could just stop every once in a while and take a quick look around, I guess.

Stewart: Yes, that's just what you should do. Every once in a while, take a quick rest and see if somebody's doing something good. I think you'll be surprised at all the people who are working hard.

That morning, I also guided the students to think of many situations that would be good for learning, but I also wanted them to consider the importance of the person who found the good things.

Stewart: You have to know what good things are.... Why do we need to have photos of the good things in our room?

Matthew: We could put 'em on the bulletin board so people could see 'em.

Stewart: Why is that important?

Matthew: So people will know we work hard?

Stewart: Yes, that's so important. You know your mothers or fathers or aunts and uncles have important work, don't you? They go to jobs every day because that's their work. Well, you come to school every day because that's your work. Your work is to learn as much as you can and to help the rest of us in our classroom learning as much as we can.

Jimmy: What about makin' a book and writin' about what we do?

Matthew: Yeah. We could do that!

Stewart: Of course. That's a great idea! We could do that. What else?

This type of discussion was an important tool to have the students think about the purposes and procedures of classroom activities. It was important to have the students start this type of thinking on the first day of school, which immediately set the tone of our classroom. By holding serious conversations with them in a group setting, I was able to build a shared sense of respect for hard work and to scaffold their understandings of the processes of working together in a learning community.

Tangible evidence of our hard work amassed as we used our photographs to create bulletin boards and class books. Everywhere we looked, we saw validation of good things happening in our classroom. We labeled pictures with photographers' names, so not only were the students in the photo recognized for good work, but photographers were respected for finding it.

Of all the types of photography I used with my class, instant photography emerged as the most crucial, because it enabled students to immediately connect with events and feel ownership of their photographs. These photographs were true documentation of authentic events, providing concrete reminders as we reflected on our successes together. As a class, we consciously tried to find something good about every class member; thus, we affirmed our diversity in powerful and obvious ways. Shields (1995) confirms, "In classrooms where teachers proactively engineer constructive responses to student differences, students may have a better chance of success in both basic and higher-order skills" (p. 44). Photography played an important role by consciously calling our attention to worthwhile contributions of each member of the class, regardless of differences in race, gender, socioeconomic status, or achievement level. This tool was effective in helping us focus early on these good things about each student. We always found something to celebrate in our photographs.

Reading as a Supportive Structure

On that all-important first day of school, I also began reading aloud to the students. I continued to read aloud many times a day, every day. Read-alouds emerged from the data as one of the most important scaffolds that I provided for the students. Just as important, I modeled not only processes of reading, but also enjoyment of reading. Two distinct and powerful ways to explore sources of language are (1) to introduce students to new literacy experiences every day through either new poems, songs, or stories and (2) to provide literacy events connected to the world of experience—the world outside of books (Holdaway, 1979). The children and I used both of these sources every day in our classroom.

Huck, Hepler, Hickman, and Kiefer (1997) affirm that literature brings enrichment as well as proven education value to the lives of children. For example, Huck et al. note that literature provides enjoyment, builds critical thinking, develops imagination, provides escape, and shapes insights into human behavior. In addition to these intrinsic aesthetic values, Huck and colleagues specifically cite educational values of using literature, particularly in helping children learn reading and writing. Trelease's (1979) research on the effectiveness of read-alouds confirms the importance of literature in children's lives, especially with regard to helping children become readers themselves. Reading aloud builds a lifelong love of reading; supports and extends oral and written language; and improves vocabulary, spelling, and writing; however, Trelease proposes that "story does not exist to teach reading skills. Story is the vehicle we use to make sense out of the world..." (p. 57).

Shared reading became central to our classroom structure as we came together to read and learn more about the processes of reading and writing. Like Fisher (1991), I wanted my students to become more confident in their abilities as language users and learners. Expecting all the students to listen, share, and learn, I worked to keep the sessions interesting, relaxed, noncompetitive, and focused on meaning. From these shared experiences, we moved to reading-workshop sessions, in which I worked with smaller groups of children while others read independently, with partners, or in small groups. The primary activity that occurred during reading workshop was reading—real reading—because it is the active engagement in reading real texts that moves children forward in their reading (Allington, 2001; McQuillan, 1998).

Between meeting with groups of children, I held conferences with individuals. In these conferences, students told me what they were reading, answered my questions, and talked about problems they were having and about possible projects. When children read aloud to other students or to me, or when they read by themselves, they used many strong reading strategies. This favorite time was often buzzing with quiet sounds of children softly reading aloud to themselves or others. Children were not pressured to read in front of others, but many supports were in place to enable them to succeed in reading. For example, children read by themselves, but there were many times when they read with me or with others who listened carefully, who whisper read along with them to support them, who echo read with them, or who helped them with words when the struggle was too great for them. Vygotsky (1934/1997) writes that "what a child can do in cooperation today, he can do alone tomorrow" (p. 188). Dorn et al. (1998) talk about apprenticeship in literacy and the importance of using this model with children. Bruner (1978) speaks of scaffolding children's learning and reminds readers how this helps children attain higher levels and "ratchets" them to keep them from slipping back. Heath (1983) reminds us that the ways of schooling must be accessible for children regardless of their cultures and language experiences. All of these authorities stress the power of supporting children in their learning processes. I found this to be particularly true in the process of learning to read. Indeed, the children in my class were aware of the supports available to them. Comments from year-end interviews reveal this helpfulness: "It really helps that you let us read with somebody else," and "I like it that it's OK to have help to figure out my words."

Writing as a Literacy Framework

Another tool that contributed to the structure and interactions within our classroom was making writing an expected component of daily class life. From the first day of school, I asked the children to write about the experiences, interests, and things that were important to them. They quickly came to expect to write about everything! As is evident in examples provided in Chapters 5, 6, and 7, the children wrote about stories we read, adventures we had, and times that they spent with their families. The students wrote about science experiments by taking notes about the experiment itself and then explaining the experiment's results. They also wrote in math to solve problems and explain how they used different problem-solving methods and why they chose those methods. They often came together to write in groups, especially when using photographs to help them remember specific experiences (see Figure 4).

I encouraged children to write in many formats such as whole-group and small-group stories based on their interests, Big Books, "bare" books, bi-fold books, step books, flip books, journals, and content area logs (see specifics in Stewart, in press). Students also created flip books and step books when they needed quick ways to write down something or specific formats for their writing (see Figure 5 for an example of one student's first-draft flip book). To create a flip book, students folded one piece of paper lengthwise, then cut the top layer in four equal-sized sections, or flaps. They drew illustrations on each flap and wrote on the layer below or vice versa. This is a versatile format because it can be used in any content area for a variety of purposes.

Figure 4
Children Using Photographs to Help Them
Write in Groups

Figure 5
Example of a Student's First-Draft Flip Book

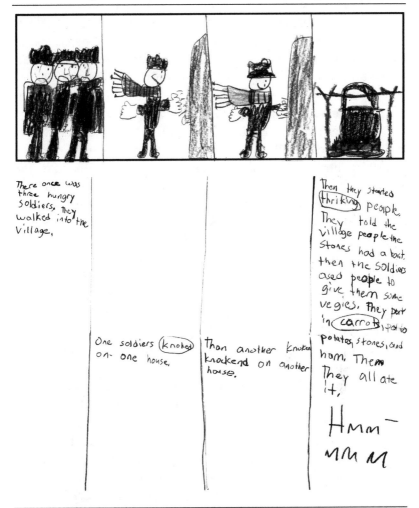

The students liked using the format of step books because it allowed them to record steps in a science experiment or math problem; recall the timeline of a story's events; or summarize a story's characters, setting, problem, and solution. As previously noted, I encouraged with first-draft formats that it was most important to write out ideas, but even in these first drafts, I found evidence of attempts at revision such as circled words and crossed-out corrections. Students also used writing as a tool to engage others in reading and writing. When students wanted to convince others in the class to read a particular favorite book or poem, they created book advertisements to share with each other. If a student had a large writing project, he or she gathered friends to help with the project. No matter what form of writing students chose, it seemed that my underlying expectation for them to continually engage in writing helped embed that process in the daily structure of our curriculum and sustain its importance in our work.

Teaching children the processes of writing helps them build a cohesive framework for literacy learning that supports them as thinkers, readers, writers, and speakers. The writing process is based on the work of Graves (1983, 1994), Calkins (1986), and others who have written extensively in this area. The process, which can be thought of as made up of recursive stages, includes the following stages: Prewriting, drafting, revising, proofreading/editing, and publishing. It is important to remember, however, that within the classroom, this process is not neat and linear but flexible, recursive, and spiraling.

Graves (1994) refers to the *prewriting* stage as a place of beginning, of choosing a topic, and of actively thinking and planning for writing. This stage involves both unconscious and conscious rehearsal or preparation for writing. It especially helps young writers who are learning to compose. Brainstorming as a group is often a good way to help children become familiar with this process. Writers often will return to this stage again and again as they expand their written projects.

During the *drafting* stage, writers jot down preliminary ideas, then conduct research that is required to complete the draft. In this stage, ideas are more important than the conventions of writing. Writers choose their subjects, compose (in their minds or on paper) what they want to say, read what they have said, and make necessary changes or move on to select what they will say next. Graves (1994) notes that the common composing pattern is "select, compose, read; select, compose, read" (p. 80). Different writers attend to these steps differently, but each writer uses all these steps in some way to complete the process of putting ideas on paper.

At the *revising* stage, writers will improve their drafts, work to make sure the story makes sense, and work on the flow of ideas, wording, and the order of sentences. Writers continue to compose during this stage, as they choose to read a portion of their working draft, decide how they can improve it, think of ideas for improving their piece, then reread the piece to judge the effectiveness of their revisions. "Re-vision," literally means to "re-see." Graves (1994) encourages teachers to set up conditions that invite writers to revise. Allowing time to write, preferably daily, helps writers stay connected to their work. When teachers disrupt writers' involvement with writing for even a day, students must reorient themselves to their thinking and what they wanted their writing to say. Graves suggests that teachers interview students about "chunks" of writing that they feel best about (approximately four pieces at a time). This enables teachers to tell students elements that delight or interest them in the students' work and enables students to point out in their own writing what specific parts they like, do not like, or wish could have turned out better.

Writers in process-oriented classrooms learn that when they are satisfied that the content of their piece is right, they move to the *proofreading/editing* stage, in which they look for errors in grammar and other mechanics of writing and make necessary changes. When writers are sure that their drafts are as good as they can make them, they have peer conferences and teacher conferences for final proofing. However, children who are writing every day and who are writing for many purposes cannot be expected to revise, proofread, or edit every piece of writing. These children are writing first drafts constantly, then selecting pieces that they believe are important enough to publish. In these selected pieces, the revision of ideas is more important than the revision of mechanics. It is important, though, that students learn the conventions of standard English and that they progress toward including those conventions in their writing.

The last stage of the writing process is *publishing*, or presenting the writing in a final format. Again, this final stage is not required for every piece of writing that a child does. When students have selected pieces for publishing, several options are available. For example, in my class, I typed stories for students (or had parents, older students, or other volunteers do that for the students), or some students typed the stories by themselves if they were experienced at using a computer. Other students wrote stories in book formats, as posters, or on chart paper or other special paper used specifically for display in the classroom or hallway. At other times, I wrote the students' final drafts, and they included photographs or illustrations to accompany their piece. In whatever format the children chose, they took care to ensure that the final draft was neat, conventionally correct, and appealing to other readers. Final drafts were products of which the children could be proud. Sharing the students' work publicly also emerged from the data set as essential to learning, because sharing validated students' hard work and enabled them to experience the pleasure of authorship.

Even though Graves (1994) presents these various stages of deliberation and action in the writing process, he cautions teachers against taking children through a set sequence of choosing, rehearsing, composing, and rewriting. Graves states that teachers must be aware of the writer's *voice* in the whole process and must allow that voice to convey the child's potential. Good writers move back and forth between stages as often as necessary until they are satisfied with their finished piece. One of the biggest challenges in teaching writing—or any subject—is looking for the potential of the students and setting appropriate expectations for them as learners. Teacher can best challenge students by setting high expectations that are based on knowledge of the students as learners and of the subject matter involved. We teachers obtain that knowledge by studying our classrooms, looking closely and carefully at our students and ourselves, as both teachers and learners together.

Oral Language as a Support for Written Language

Oral language was a pivotal aspect of the design of the classroom because, as with most young children, the oral abilities of the students greatly surpassed their reading and writing abilities. Even students who were successful with print were more successful with oral language, and oral language was particularly crucial for struggling readers. Therefore, I used oral language to build a way into written language. I purposefully included discussion in every lesson. Arranging desks and work spaces to accomodate talk, I deliberately made working conversations a part of our classroom environment. At times, I also explicitly instructed students to talk with their partners or groups about their work and ideas. I planned for and pointed out ways in which we turned our ideas into spoken words and our spoken words into written words. I talked to the children about print as our words written down. I found that capturing their own words, their oral language, onto paper was an effective "way in" to print that many times surpassed every other attempt to connect spoken and written language—especially with struggling readers. Chapter 5 provides an in-depth discussion of how oral language opened literacy learning for some students.

Sharing as a Deliberate Process

Many aspects of sharing have been and will be mentioned in discussions throughout this book, because sharing was a key element that emerged from the data analysis. This sharing enabled the many connections that the children and I made. We shared from the first day of school and continued to do so throughout the year in many ways. Our sharing of books, stories, poems, experiences, adventures, emotions, reactions, troubles, and triumphs was evident within every data source of my study. This element was key in our class becoming a bonded family of colearners. That sharing, which was planned for and consciously included in the space of each day, was often difficult because our instructional time was so crowded with essentials we needed and wanted to accomplish. That is, we did not want to cut short reading and writing workshops, math and science explorations, or daily read-alouds. But sharing allowed us to *know* one another, to build on what each person contributed and learned, and to bridge our differences by celebrating small and large successes alike. Although the real importance of sharing unfolded across our time together, it was the deliberate inclusion of it in the design of the learning community that made it possible for us to acknowledge and understand one another and our accomplishments. Teachers who intentionally make time for intensive sharing and discussion of children's work will find, as I did, that the benefits far outweigh the time constraints involved.

Elsewhere Expeditions as Learning Experiences and Collective Memories

While planning for the second-grade class at the beginning of the year, I intentionally designed time and space outside the classroom for the students. Specifically, the students and I took Elsewhere Expeditions around the school's grounds. See Appendix B for a timeline of our Elsewhere Expeditions (and related activities) that reveals the increasing complexity of *purpose* in our journeys.

During the first day of school, I explained to the students what Elsewhere Expeditions were and how we would form a routine around them. I tried to make Elsewhere Expeditions into special shared times that were rich with learning opportunities, interesting, and without stress. I wanted these to serve as one cornerstone of our literacy lives together. An excerpt of my conversation before taking the children to physical education follows:

> We're going on an adventure today. In fact, we'll be taking these adventures almost every day on our way to physical education class.... We're going to have a special name for our adventures—"Elsewhere Expeditions." That just means we're going somewhere else else—somewhere that's not in our classroom—so that's the "elsewhere" part, and we're going on a small trip that has an important purpose. [I looked around at them.] When you take a trip, or you can call it a "journey"—to find out more about something, you can call it an "expedition." So that's why we're going to call our purposeful trips "Elsewhere Expeditions."
>
> Today on our way to physical education, we're going the long way around, so we can be scientists. We're going to learn to *observe* the way scientists observe. That means we're going to look very carefully at everything we see. Then when we come back to class, we're going to write our *notes* about what we saw. We'll do this every day and see what important discoveries we can make.

The students shortened "Elsewhere Expedition" to "EE" when writing, although they continued to call them "Elsewhere Expeditions" when discussing them. The students and I usually took 5 to 15 minutes to walk around the school just before physical education. We were particularly interested in science—plants and animals—and social studies—community helpers, transportation, and types of houses. We became interested in observing changes over time in environments such as the growth of an ant bed, new plant growth, the construction of a bird nest, and community helpers at work.

The students and I used snack time (after physical education) to record our observations: I sat at the computer typing the students' observations as they dictated them to me, and the students used quarter sheets of photocopy paper to illustrate what they saw. Because not everyone was able to have his or her name credited to typed notes, the illustrations helped to give each child a more complete sense of ownership of the observations. We concluded the Elsewhere Expedition by pasting the notes and illustrations (with artists' names on them) on large sheets of construction paper, dating the observations, and displaying them in the hallway so others could recognize our hard work.

We found that neighboring classes were eager to read about our Elsewhere Expeditions each day, making suggestions to us about where we should go and wondering what we would see. Mrs. Mettinger, a third-grade teacher who taught across the hall from us, came into our room each day to compliment us on what we had done or, as she did a few times, to question why we had not mentioned something that she had noticed that day. One day, Mrs. Mettinger stepped into our classroom and commented,

> Boys and girls, my class and I enjoy reading your notes every day. You are getting to be good scientists and good observers. We stop by and read what your notes say each day on our way back to our room. But today, I think we were better observers than you were.... You didn't write about the bird nest that is being built under the awning right outside our back door. I know you had to pass right under it to go on your Elsewhere Expedition! You're going to have to be very careful observers to see more than we do!

This camaraderie, gentle teasing, and friendly competition between our classes bonded our classes in a way that differed from interactions between any of the other classes. That early event of her commenting on our notes spurred our class members to be more careful observers. The children began to make statements showing their increased seriousness: "We have to look better. We're really good scientists. Mrs. Mettinger will be surprised when she reads our notes today!" The students also began to express a feeling of friendly competition with Mrs. Mettinger's class, even though they really seemed to like her and her students. The students would tell me, "Let's try to trick Mrs. Mettinger! Let's see if we can see more than she does today." Mrs. Mettinger's interest and involvement in our Elsewhere Expeditions gave an added seriousness to the students' purpose and seemed to create a group connection within my class as we worked together to be even more careful observers.

Indeed, our daily Elsewhere Expeditions paid off bountiful dividends in literacy and community building throughout the year. Elsewhere Expeditions seemed to invest our group with a common experience and a collective "memory," such as Dyson (1989) describes. These excursions became predictable routines, which were made exciting by numerous small unanticipated pleasures, such as a butterfly hovering over a particular child or the rumbling of a freight train on the train tracks along the edges of our school grounds.

To make our Elsewhere Expeditions even more productive, I wanted the students to learn to take notes by themselves, thereby shifting the responsibility from me to them. I found it easy to teach them to take notes by showing them the video titled *Mr. Know-It-Owl's Video School: All About Animals* (Wright & Naderi, 1986). This video—designed to introduce young children to mammals, fish, amphibians, reptiles, and birds—uses video clips of animals in their natural habitats, catchy tunes, and flash words to enhance learning. Over a 2-week period, I showed students one 10-minute clip every other day to help them learn the characteristics of animal groups mandated for study in second grade. The clips that I showed were ideal for the students to use to practice taking notes within a time frame; students were able to grasp the concept of taking notes as they copied words that flashed on the screen and learned to associate tunes with particular animal groups. For those children who could not write fast enough to keep up with the flash words, I wrote those words on the chalkboard. The students opened their spiral notebooks, which they used as their science logs, and transcribed words from the video onto the left page and made drawings of the animals on the right page (see Figure 6 for an example of a student's notes on mammals).

This video activity combined with practicing taking notes allowed the students to move rapidly to taking notes during Elsewhere Expeditions. Once the students began taking their own notes, I observed even more seriousness in our Elsewhere Expeditions. The students intently tried to capture their observations on paper and referred to their notes for in-class writing or discussion. Taking notes in their science logs helped them to gather information through their senses and realize that observation was a basis for thinking. The students created a "living textbook of their knowledge" (Thompson, 1990, p. 39).

One Elsewhere Expedition that took place shortly after the children began taking notes stands out as an example of a collective memory. I noticed that comments about Elsewhere Expeditions turned up in class more frequently. On one Elsewhere Expedition, we met a

Figure 6
Example of a Student's Notes on Mammals

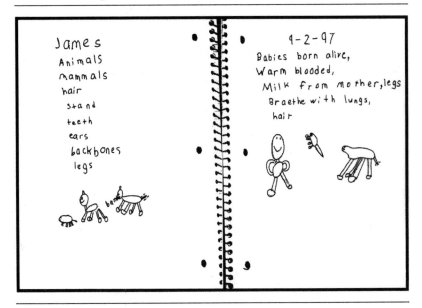

district maintenance worker who was inspecting our school's buses. I asked "Mr. Randy" if we could interview him, and he was very gracious about letting the children ask him questions and took time to explain how he used his tools and instruments. During that afternoon's snack time, as I typed observations, the students used their own notes to help me get the details right. They also referred to their notes to make their illustrations even more accurate, portraying Mr. Randy working on the buses and using specific tools he had mentioned. (See Figure 7 for some examples of these illustrations.)

As the illustrations and notes confirm, the episode with Mr. Randy provided all of us with a wonderful group memory and seemed to work toward bonding us as a learning community. Peterson (1992) notes that in a learning community, "Each encounter leaves behind a residue of meaning that contributes to the shared history, thereby enriching the meaning-making potential of the group" (p. 132). Experiences like the ones we had with Mr. Randy forged strong links through collective memory and shared history.

Figure 7
Students' Illustrations of Mr. Randy
From Elsewhere Expedition

Conclusion

In this chapter, "best practice" refers to the ways in which a teacher works within constraints of his or her environment to design appropriate learning contexts for his or her students. The practice is best for these *particular students* in this *particular setting* during this *particular year*. This chapter connects the generic concept of best practice to the specific everyday world of this classroom by examining ways in which my initial construction of time, space, and activity influenced what *these* second graders were able to accomplish during our year together. The design of our classroom was not static but grew and developed as students' needs and goals changed.

Knowledgeable teachers stand firm in their convictions that multiple classroom designs are needed in the service of providing the best teaching possible—teaching that is most appropriate for each individual in each specific situation. Teachers who are architects of their own classrooms make that happen.

CHAPTER 4

cMy cRole as "cArtist"

As teachers we are called upon to be artists. We must remember that artistry does not come from the quantity of red, green, and yellow paint...but from the organizing vision that shapes the use of these materials. It comes from a sense of priority and design. If our teaching is to be an art, we must remember that it is not the number of good ideas that turns our work into an art, but the selection, balance and design of those ideas. Instead of piling good teaching ideas into the classroom, we need to draw from all we know, feel, and believe in order to create something beautiful. To teach well, we do not need more techniques, activities, and strategies. We need a *sense of what is essential* [italics added]. (Calkins, 1986, p. 9)

A teacher does not oversee learning activities and strategies; a teacher "selects, balances, and designs" a powerful combination of ideas based on what is right for each student. As with any masterpiece, the whole is greater than the sum of its parts. Only through the students does the teacher know "what is essential."

Teachers should concentrate on finding their own vision according to what is essential is in their classrooms. This chapter focuses on interactions between two students and me, their teacher, to illustrate how I set into place my organizing vision in the second-grade classroom. For my classroom, it was critical to have the students recognize self-success and the success of their peers. I consciously observed the students for examples of things they could do well and pointed out those strengths to students, using them as a support on which to build future successes. The teacher as artist carefully studies elements of students' work in progress. What areas need more attention? What works well? What can be learned by comparing the vibrant colors of competence with the subdued shades of struggle?

Establishing a Productive Entry Point for Instruction

One critical element of helping each child prepare for the year's instruction is determining how far along each student is in his or her learning so that instruction may be aimed "not so much at the ripe as at the ripening functions" (Vygotsky, 1934/1997, p. 188). Teachers should support students in their zone of proximal development (Vygotsky, 1934/1978). It was very important for me to know right away where each student was as a reader; thus, I would be able to design reading plans to *best* serve each student's specific needs. I used Leslie and Caldwell's (1990) Qualitative Reading Inventory (QRI) with each student at the beginning of the year to assess where each student was as a reader.

A well-developed sense of timing on the teacher's part is also essential to finding entry points into instruction. During the period in which I assessed students using the QRI, I was very conscious of the need to time those assessments so that I would secure the students' best performances. For instance, in the case of one particular student, Judy, my concern appears in my early field notes about her:

August 25, 1997 entry (7th day of school)
I saved Judy until last because I sense from her performance in various class situations that she is a struggling reader. I want to give her as much time as possible to become comfortable with our classroom setting in general and with me in particular....

Judy's performance on the primer word list indicates that she is having great difficulty recognizing words in isolation and has little automaticity or skill with decoding, putting her at what the instrument developers term the "frustration" level for this task. I can see almost no pattern on which to build.... The only strengths I see are that she appears to look at words from left to right and sometimes seems to indicate an awareness that words are composed of sounds which can be "stretched," though the sounds she stretches do not often correspond with the letters in the printed words.

September 5, 1997 entry (16th day of school)
I began last week with the easiest list from the QRI (primer level) because I want Judy to succeed, but even that was too hard. Many times struggling readers have difficulty with isolated words and read more easily from connected text, so I am going to continue the assessment by administering the narrative assessment passage at this lowest level. I

have waited a little longer than a week to give her more time to "settle in" to the routines of school. Maybe she will remember more of what she learned last year in first grade....

Judy reads haltingly and with great difficulty at a rate of 7.9 words per minute on the QRI primer passage—an extremely slow rate.... At this point in time, Judy cannot even read back to me what she herself has just written. We seem to struggle at every turn when it comes to any aspect of language literacy learning, though I can tell by talking with her and by listening to her that this is a child who understands many things. She seems able to learn. I am searching for a way to tap that potential so that she can successfully enter the world of print. (Stewart, 1997)

It is important for people who have never used or seen this type of assessment to understand the amount of effort—on the part of the teacher as well as the student—that goes into this type of assessment. Readers who are not familiar with qualitative assessments, such as the QRI described here, may be interested in visiting a school to see a teacher administer this type of instrument with students.

Facilitating Success

It is essential for teachers to choose the most appropriate technique to facilitate students' displays of competence. I found that one of the best strategies for calling attention to students' strengths was retelling. We retold in many ways in our classroom—both spoken and written—and retold in quick, more general ways (e.g., using flip books and step books) and in lengthier, more detailed ways (e.g., using picture books, plays, multiple-page stories, and "television" scripts). We retold selections from various literary genres, and we retold from our own life experiences in and out of school. Following the retelling procedures of Brown and Cambourne (1993), I had the students listen to a literature selection more than once while reading with the class or reading independently, and then produce a retelling of that selection. This following scene, which took place earlier in the school year, documents this technique as I explain it to the students:

Stewart: Boys and girls...I want you to do what we call a "retelling" of a story we all know. That just means you are going to take someone else's story and tell everything you can remember about it.

Jessica: Is it kind of like the *Goldilocks* book you read to us that said "retold by" that lady? [She refers to *Goldilocks and the Three Bears* (Brett, 1992).]

Stewart: Yes, Jan Brett's *Goldilocks and the Three Bears* is a retelling of a story we all know. Can you get it from the shelf, please, Jessica? [Jessica gets the book and hands it to me, and I ask her to read what the front cover says.]

Jessica: *Goldilocks and the Three Bears*, retold by Jan Brett.

Stewart: That's exactly right. Even authors who have their books published by big companies sometimes do retellings of their favorite stories. We have lots of retellings in here. When you're looking for books to read, keep your eyes open for retellings. They're always special because everyone who does a retelling changes a few things about the story. Sometimes they mean to change it, and sometimes they do it by accident. But that's something we almost always notice about retellings...how are they like the original stories, and how are they different? We're going to do a special retelling this morning. How many of you remember lots of things about *The Wolf's Chicken Stew* [Kasza, 1995]? [Hands go up around the room.] Well, today during writing workshop...I want each of you to go off in the corner by yourself and tell everything you can remember about that story into the tape player. You can't take your book. In fact, the only thing you can take is yourself and your good brain. See how that desk is turned with its back to the class? [There is a chorus of yes'es.] That's so you won't be distracted by what's going on in here. You have to be really smart to do this. You have to be able to *concentrate*. Do you know what that means?

Adam: Is that kind of like that game Concentration?

Stewart: Yes. Can you explain that to us, Adam?

Adam: It's a game where you try to match a card that you turn over with another one just like it somewhere else

on the table. You have to think about what you're doing or you won't remember where the other one was.
I'm real good at it. I beat my sister all the time!

Stewart: You're right on target, Adam. Concentration is when
you really think about what you're doing. This morning, I want you to think about that story of *The Wolf's
Chicken Stew* and tell *everything* you can remember
about the story. You can't ask anyone anything about
it. You have to depend on your own brain to remember. Later in the year we will try to write our
retellings, but this first time we're just going to make
a tape of them. I'll listen to them tonight. I can't wait
to hear what you can remember. Try really hard. I
want your best thinking. Can you do that? [There is
a chorus of yes'es.]

This was not an easy task for the children, especially so early in
the year, but they seemed to understand that I wanted them to retell
as many of the story's details and ideas as they could. I had read *The
Wolf's Chicken Stew* to the class three times in the days before the
retelling; I also used this story because it is included in the basal literature collection mandated for use in all second-grade classrooms in
my school district. After the retellings, the students and I discussed the
story several times, laughing at our mental pictures of various scenes.
Using their ingredients of the story, the students had made their own
versions of chicken stew. True to my word, I listened to all the students' tapes and transcribed and typed retellings that I thought were
outstanding for future in-class sharing.

Finding a Way In for Each Student: Judy's Retelling

Intuitive "knowing," which is a critical aspect of the artistry of
teaching, or understanding what is essential, develops through close
and careful observation of students and their learning and through
thoughtful reflection of that observation. Because of Judy's poor performance on her QRI, as well as her other poor academic performance, I was not expecting the high-quality retelling she gave. I was
overwhelmed with Judy's potential, as evidenced through her strong

use of oral language in her first taped retelling. Right away, I knew this was Judy's *way in* to literacy learning.

Heath's (1982, 1983) work, which talks about children like Judy who have a rich oral heritage but struggle in school, sprang to mind as I listened to Judy's rich retelling. I remember laughing aloud with delight at Judy's rendition of the last line of the story. I was not only proud of her choice of words and the animation in her voice, but also excited to recognize that oral language was the way to reach this child. Here was a medium in which she could excel.

Judy became more fluent and relaxed as she recounted elements from the story. She used dramatic pauses and employed words used in the original story. To truly appreciate Judy's achievement, see Figure 8, which shows her retelling of *The Wolf's Chicken Stew* (Kasza, 1995). In the original story, Kasza uses the phrases, "scrumptious pancakes," "scrumptious doughnuts," and "scrumptious cake" to describe the food. Although Judy used a different word, *delicious*, it was clear that she understood the word *scrumptious*. Kasza also employs the use of the following refrain in the original story: "Eat well, my pretty chicken. Get nice and fat for my stew" (p. 127). As the reader can see from Judy's retelling, she understood the basic sense of the refrain, and although her adaptations were not exact, the rhythm and texture were definitely there. The concluding line of the original story is "Ah, shucks. Tomorrow I'll bring the little critters a hundred scrumptious cookies" (p. 132). Judy's final line lost nothing in the translation.

Selecting Student Work to Use as Teaching Pieces

One of the strongest designs in my classrooms has been choosing and showcasing excellent student work—especially from students whose work in other classes often had been unacknowledged because of their learning struggles. Selecting and presenting good examples of student work is a good way—though not the only way—to interpret teaching and learning because it extends the ideas of other students. The student and the student's product exemplify success in the classroom. For example, after asking Judy for permission to use her successful retelling with the class, I used it to teach the class. First, we listened to the audiotape of Judy's retelling; then, I used an overhead transparency of Judy's retelling to point out good things Judy

Figure 8
Judy's Retelling of *The Wolf's Chicken Stew* (Kasza, 1995)

1   One day a fox was in the…<u>he think of dinner a</u>…after another and

2   another…He thought a delicious dinner. It was ch-…<u>chicken stew</u>. He…he

3   was…<u>he looked for a chicken</u>. He spotted one! But just as he was fixing to get

4   his prey, he thought a…<u>of another one</u>. He cooked a delicious cake. "Eat well,

5   my pretty chicken. Get nice and fat for my chicken stew."

6   The next day he brung delicious looking doughnuts. "Eat well, my good

7   chicken. Be fat and smooth for my chicken…<u>chicken stew</u>."

8   Then the next day he brung pan…<u>delicious pancakes</u>. "Eat well, my…

9   pretty young chicken. Be nice and good for my chicken soup…<u>chicken stew</u>."

10 The day was today. He was ready for his…his food. He creeped to the

11 door and opened the door. What a prey he was. By…By…By seeing the

12 chicken, it was as small as it was. The chicken opened up the door. She was at

13 it…him…"<u>It wasn't the</u>…the Santa Claus that brung that goody stuff. It

14 was Mr. Wolf! He brung that delicious…<u>delicious cake and delicious doughnuts</u>

15 and delicious pancakes. Come here, childrens. Aaah…This is the one who

16 brung the delicious cake, delicious doughnuts, delicious pancakes."

17 They all ga-…<u>jumped</u> around him and gave him a big kiss on the cheek.

18 He was…"<u>Oh, Shoot!</u> I'm gonna make them buzzards a dozen of cookies!"

19 The end!

20 I ready.

(Excerpt from Transcription of Audio Tape #14, September 22, 1997)

did. I used markers to highlight each important aspect that I wanted the students to notice:

Stewart: Boys and girls, look at these words I'm marking in blue—*thought, looked* and *spotted, thought* and *cooked, brung* [*sic*].... This lets us know that Judy is paying attention to the different things that happened in the story. Did all these things happen right now or at some time in the past—which means some time before now?

[Some students tentatively say, "In the past?"]

Stewart: That's right. Those things happened in the past, and Judy was smart in her retelling to let us know that by *the choice of words she used.* She paid attention to when things happened and used good word choices to let us know that. All those words she used are verbs that show action and all this action is in the past. We'll be looking for words that show past tense a lot this year, and Judy's retelling is the first time we are talking about it.... Judy even came very close to using some of the words from the story when she used "brung" and "creeped." The story had *brought* and *crept,* and even though her words are a little different, they show us that she was really paying attention to the words in the story and that she knows that the action happened before now—in the past. Now I want you to look at these words I'm marking in green— *prey* on line 4 and *prey* again on line 11. She is so smart that she used a word exactly from the story. Can anyone remember what the word *prey* means? [Jessica and other students raise their hands.] Jessica?

Jessica: Well, a prey is something that's being hunted. I think it's usually an animal.

Stewart: That's exactly right. All of you read Judy's retelling on line 4 and on line 11 and decide which time she used it to mean something that is being hunted. [The students raise their hands. Several children are saying, "I know. I know."] Mark?

Mark:	Well, I think she used it right on line 4 when she said he was fixing to get his prey.
Stewart:	Who was he "fixing" to get?
Mark:	The chicken...but then he changed his mind.
Stewart:	That's right. On line 4, Judy knew just the right use of the word *prey*. The chicken was the prey that was being hunted by the wolf. [I make eye contact with Judy, then I look at the other children.] I'm so proud that you really are paying attention to the words in the story. Do you know something else great that Judy did? She paid attention to the details of the story and to the order in which they happened. Judy, you knew exactly which foods the wolf cooked for the chicken— let's mark them with red—a delicious cake, delicious looking doughnuts, and delicious pancakes. Those are the correct details in the story. Then you mentioned those same details again on lines 14 and 15 and again on line 16.... You accidentally flipped the order—pancakes really came first and the cake came last—but you knew which foods he cooked, and you knew that they came one after the other. That is really good thinking. Maybe when you do a retelling again, you can put a picture in your mind of the order things happen so that it will be easier to do a retelling.

I continued to "teach" how important it was for the students to use thinking in their retellings. For example, I pointed out how Judy paused during her retelling to think of just the right words and how she revised what she wrote to make it sound better. I kept emphasizing that Judy's retelling let us see how smart it was to do certain things in a retelling. (At this point in the year, I looked for every opportunity to teach using the students' authentic work as examples.) The following excerpt shows how I helped the children begin to think about self-correction strategies not as mistakes, but as problem-solving opportunities to show how smart they were. This is the constructive error of which Ferreiro and Teberosky (1979/1994) speak:

Stewart:	It is a really good thing that Judy was thinking so much during her retelling. She did what smart story-tellers do...she stopped when she needed to give her-self time to think of just the right words. Sometimes she even went back and changed what she started to say to make it better. For example, what good thing did Judy do on line 9?
Frances:	She started to say "chicken soup," but then she re-membered that it was really "chicken stew." So she just changed the words to make 'em right. You can do that.
Stewart:	Perfect, Frances. That's exactly what she did. Class, is that a mistake?
Class:	No.
Stewart:	You are so smart, boys and girls. I can't even trip you up! I wonder if you can spot the good thing Judy did on line 17. Who can find it?

[Jimmy raises his hand.]

Jimmy:	I know! I know! She started to say that they gave him a kiss—but then she went back and made it better. She said, "They jumped around him and gave him a big kiss on the cheek."
Stewart:	Jimmy, you are super smart to spot that. Judy, you were really smart to go back and fix that sentence when you were telling it. Look how much more in-formation you are giving your listeners when you added all those good words. All those strong words help us get a much better picture in our minds of what was happening than if you had just said, "They all gave him a kiss."

Do you remember what I've been telling you every day—smart readers and writers and storytellers and thinkers all know how to go back when they make a mistake or leave something out and make it better...and that that's not a mistake? That's a really smart thing to do. Well, Judy's retelling lets us see just how smart that is. Judy, I'm so proud of you. You were a very smart reteller!

To bring this minilesson to a close, before the children went off to write, I said,

> Wow, class, we have a star storyteller in here. Judy, thank you for letting us share your retelling and learn so much from what you did. Boys and girls, you were wonderful detectives in finding good things in Judy's retelling. I knew I had the smartest class in second grade, but I just didn't know how really *smart* you were! Now that I know, I can't wait to see what you'll do in writing workshop this morning. I hope that some of you will think about doing a retelling of another story that you really like. Be sure to get started right away so we'll have time to share some of them.

These comments were my way of affirming Judy as being a good storyteller. I also sent the children to write with an expectation of more successful writings and retellings.

Engaging in Reflective Practice

Teachers must make use of reflective practice to evaluate the balance of their teaching strategies and efforts in the classroom. It was essential for me to balance my views as teacher and researcher, so I stepped back from the immediacy of the students' work to assess what it meant to my overall teaching practice. Therefore, I was compelled to step back from the episode with Judy to reflect on the greater meaning of that event—what it meant to my classroom. Two entries from my teaching journal capture this reflective process:

First Entry

> How did this one early episode change the potential for Judy within this classroom? What did she learn? What did I learn? What did the other children learn? Again, I am reminded of Heath's (1982, 1983) work. I continue to think of the rich oral tradition of Heath's Trackton children and the ways in which their strengths were devalued and lost in their larger schooling experiences. I am determined at this moment to build on Judy's strengths—to share with Judy and the class her wonderful gift for story.

Second Entry

I keep thinking about Judy's retelling of *The Wolf's Chicken Stew* (Kasza, 1995). At the time, I knew it was important, but just not how important. By playing back and discussing specifics of Judy's tape with the whole group, I set a precedent in our class for looking for all the good things that we could specifically find in each person's work.... I remember noticing a beaming Judy who seemed to begin to see herself as a teller of tales. Over subsequent weeks, I have noticed other children coming to Judy for advice and encouragement as they are retelling other stories...

During the past month, I have noticed that Judy's status has changed from being one who cannot do to one who can. I have also noticed that when she shares her own original written stories, she "reads" from her mind rather than from her paper. This gives me a new appreciation for Judy's talents and an avenue from which to teach. I now encourage her to go back and add details from her mind and to search for ways to get those words out of her head and onto her paper. I often notice her pairing up with stronger writers who can help her make this transition from thoughts to written words. I am watching as she becomes able to read her own stories, as well as stories written in large and small groups or with partners. I am watching her begin to act as an author with worthwhile stories to share and to act as a reader who is capable of connecting with authors' ideas.

Looking back to Judy's retelling, I realized that it had three powerful implications on the structure of our classroom. First, I became aware of Judy's competence in one particular area of language—oral language—which gave me a foundation on which to support her learning. Second, because Judy began to see herself as being able to use language successfully, she appeared to have more confidence when attempting class work. Third, as Judy's classmates and her parents began to see her as capable in certain areas of literacy, she also saw herself as more capable in these areas. Furthermore, Judy's successful retelling had an important implication for other students' learning because it served as a teaching model of one successful way to do a retelling.

By year's end, even though Judy was not the strongest reader or writer, she could recognize her strong points, which allowed her to move forward in her learning. For example, Judy was developing a "self-correcting system" of processing in reading, which Clay (1979) sees as being essential to making meaning of print. She established specific strategies for reading, spelling, and writing that unlocked language literacy *for her*. Judy built on her area of competence to become more proficient in other areas of literacy. By celebrating and supporting Judy's strengths, the students accepted Judy as a contributing member of our classroom community, which further unlocked Judy's potential for connecting her own rich experiences to the larger experience of school. Judy's retelling was important not only because of *her demonstration* of strength in oral language, but also because of *my recognition* of that strength. Both these factors must be present for the effective selection of teaching pieces. Reflective practice recognizes both.

Encouraging Multiple Modes of Representation: Adam's Retelling

Teachers who design flexible classrooms let students show their learning in many ways; teachers who encourage multiple modes of representation create possibilities for various visions and re-visions. Just as I needed many strategies to accomplish teaching, so the students needed many ways to represent their learning. Adam's story illustrates how I supported a flexible design.

Adam's parents and I were frustrated with his poor academic performance, which was evident in his low grades. As student and teacher, Adam and I were often in adversarial positions. Looking back, I really do not know which one of us was more stubborn that first semester. Although Adam's verbal responses indicated to me that he seemed perfectly capable of doing his written assignments, he rarely did; I was determined that Adam would do his assignments. Adam seemed determined not to pick up a pencil and write. I often became so caught up in the power struggle to make Adam do his work that I was not successful in looking for or finding his strengths. However, Adam and I genuinely liked each other. He frequently chose to sit across from me at lunch and was never intentionally disrespectful to me; I could never stay mad at him long because of his infectious grin.

Adam specifically disliked the physical act of writing. As I struggled to understand why Adam tried so hard to get out of his work, I constantly looked for different ways in which I could reach him. I realized that I would have to modify the classroom structure to discover and accommodate Adam's mode of learning. I, therefore, modified the way in which he completed writing assignments. Following the procedures of Allen (1976) and Manning, Manning, Long, and Wolfson (1987), I acted as Adam's scribe whenever I assigned extended writings, such as written retellings. I also customized Adam's mode of learning by allowing him to tape his assignments rather than write them, reducing the amount of his written assignments, and partnering him for assignments with other students he liked or those who could help him. I also tried to observe more carefully for things that he did well so I could give him positive recognition and affirmation in class.

As Adam participated in these modified assignments, I began to notice his strengths. For example, he had wonderful recall of details and provided outstanding insights into characters, conflict, and resolution in stories. Adam also outperformed many other students in his retellings, although only if these were oral retellings. About halfway into the school year, Adam demonstrated an enthusiastic retelling of Mwalimu's "Awful Aardvark" (1995) and included illustrations with his retelling (see Figure 9).

Adam's retelling had so many good qualities that I decided to make an overhead transparency similar to the one I had made of Judy's successful retelling. Again wanting the class to learn from a student's achievements, I used the overhead transparency of Adam's retelling in class. I asked the students to look for and point out good things in the retellings, although I also tried to guide the students to find specific good things. Because I had stressed how important it was for the students to concentrate and stay on the subject during their retellings, the students were quick to note that Adam had accomplished this in his retelling:

Peter:	He stayed on the subject.
Stewart:	Yes, he did. What else do you see that is good about his work?
Frances:	He told everything in the right way...like it happened in the story.
Stewart:	Do you mean he put in all the right parts of the story or that he told the story in the right order?

Figure 9
Adam's Retelling of "Awful Aardvark" (Mwalimu, 1995)

Awful Aardvark

Retold and Illustrated by Adam

Aardvark has a tree limb. He sleeps on it. It is smooth. He likes to sleep on it at night. He snores really **LOUD!**

One day Mongoose had a plan. His plan was to gather up all the animals for a meeting. The plan. was at night when Aardvark was sleeping they could disturb him . . . and they did a good job! (They **DID!**)

Rhinoceros bumped the tree. Aardvark almost fell off the limb!

(continued)

Figure 9 (continued)
Adam's Retelling of "Awful Aardvark" (Mwalimu, 1995)

Monkeys started screeching and screaming.

Aardvark woke up. He told the monkey to quit screeching and screaming. He said," **STOP THAT NONSENSE!**" And lion started growling under the branch. Then termites started eating on the roots of the tree. Aardvark fell off of the branch and hit the ground very hard . . . and then the Mongoose said it was none of them and pointed at the roots of the tree. Aardvark looked. He saw thousands of termites.

He threatened to eat them. He said he would eat them all. They started running to mud and dirt holes. He chased them down in their holes. He stuck his nose in the hole and tried to get some of the termites.

From that day on, he started sleeping in the day so at night he could catch termites trying to eat trees!

Frances:	Well, he did both!
Stewart:	You're right. He put in everything important from Mwalimu's version, and he told all those things in the right order. Good for you for noticing, Frances.

Because Judy had not included illustrations with her retelling, I made sure to point out this unique feature of Adam's retelling.

Stewart:	What about his pictures?
Jessica:	Well, he made some really good pictures.
Stewart:	What do you mean, some "really good" pictures?
Jessica:	His pictures were a lot like the ones in the book. I can kinda [sic] remember the book ones when I look at Adam's.
Cathy:	I think...I like 'em. I think his story is better because he put the pictures.
Stewart:	[pushing for more information] In other words, you think his pictures made the story stronger?
Cathy:	Yeah.
Stewart:	I think so, too. They helped me remember what I felt when I read Mwalimu's story and looked at the pictures. Adam, your pictures are really important for your story and...they're really good!
Adam:	Yeah. I like 'em. [He looks proudly at the group of students.]

After discussing Adam's pictures, I moved the students' discussion toward Adam's choice of words in his retelling. I told the students to look for words that were both in the book and in Adam's retelling. Many students were quick to offer information, although I again use this instance to support the students' learning by bringing their attention to a good thing:

Jimmy:	*Meeting, threatened...*
Matthew:	*Disturb...*
Janice:	*Branch...*

Stewart: Jimmy said *threatened*. That reminds me...when Adam was telling me the story...he said, "He said he was going to eat them." Then he went back and said, "No. Stop the tape. Do that over. He *threatened* to eat them." That was a really smart thing Adam did. Who knows why that was so smart?

Jimmy: Well, he wanted to use a better word. He started with a regular word. Then he thought of a better one.

Stewart: [smiling] You're exactly right! What Adam did wasn't a mistake. It was important. It was what good writers do. He told his story one way, then he thought of something to make it stronger, so he went back and fixed it. You can do that when you're telling a story or writing a story or reading a story. You can just go back and fix it when you think of a better way. In writing that's called "revising." Good authors *revise* their work to make it better, and to make it clearer and stronger.

I pointed out many other good things that Adam had done in his retelling, such as use "storybook language," which is another name for the type of figurative language used especially in storybooks (e.g., *once upon a time, from that day on*, etc.). Finally, I wanted to stimulate students' learning while also recognizing the good things Adam did. Focusing the students' attention on Adam's vocabulary in his retelling—especially the "noise words"—allowed me to do both. Even Adam became actively involved in learning from his retelling:

Stewart: OK, now let's look at some of the words in Adam's story that let us know about how noisy it was.... Who can name some?

Arthur: *Loud, screeching, screaming...*

Jessica: *Growling.*

Jimmy: *STOP THAT NONSENSE!*

Matthew: *HHHRRR—ZZZZ.*

Stewart: Why are they important to the story?

Adam: Well, they was lots of noise because them animals
          was mad, and they wanted to get Aardvark to stop!
          They had to let him know!

Stewart: You're right. The noise was very important to give
          us a "feel" for what was going on with all the ani-
          mals, wasn't it?

I concluded this "lesson" by telling Adam how much I loved his
retelling, although I also ended it with a request: write his next story
by himself. And he did, sitting next to me for confidence!

Because I first allowed Adam to use multiple modes of representation, he was able to complete his work, and I was able to share it
with the class. The students and I affirmed Adam as a writer-
storyteller-illustrator and as a person. And the students clearly enjoyed
Adam's work, which was evident in their lively participation in helping to point out the good things Adam had done. As I reflected on field
notes I had taken and videotapes I had made of similar lessons, I consciously noted happy expressions on students' faces. These lessons
illustrated shared enjoyment—a silent communication of joy between
the students and me and the students and one another—which was a
powerful factor in the growing sense of community in our classroom.
The students' smiles seemed spontaneous and genuine, not forced. In
critiquing my research writing, some of my peers warned me not to
mention so much smiling. They explain that hearing these Pollyanna
stories from my classroom may offend readers who are dealing with
difficulties in their own classrooms. I have included these stories any-
way because I hope that readers will recognize students from their
own classrooms with whom they have shared smiles or moments of
delight over some small triumph or inside joke. My students' spontaneous grins and spurts of laughter greatly contributed to making our
classroom the safe, relaxed place it was. I looked for those moments
of personal connection and celebrated them with my students.

Adam's work provided the students and me with a literacy event
to celebrate his accomplishment while strengthening our classroom
community. The supportive comments that the students and I made
about Adam's retelling also strengthened our language literacy
because we were able to recognize which writing strategies worked
best. The students and Adam took on the reciprocal roles of author and

responsive audience as they shared comments about Adam's work. Yet again, a student's work provided another opportunity to integrate needed strategy lessons in an authentic manner that made them relevant for all the students.

Balancing Forms and Styles

Another essential element of teaching is knowing how to balance the different forms and styles of student work. For example, I had shared Adam's exemplary oral retelling with the class, which he had dictated and I had typed. Because I did not want other students to get the idea that only typed pieces were acceptable for presenting to the class, I also chose to use James's handwritten retelling of "Awful Aardvark" (Mwalimu, 1995). James was a capable student who liked to read, and he wrote without complaint. James's work, already strong by beginning of second-grade comparisons, had improved a great deal by midyear and was almost conventional, as he learned to expand his ideas and focus his writing. I presented James's handwritten retelling to the class during a writing workshop minilesson based on the writing process and writing workshop strategies suggested by Graves (1983) and Calkins (1986). After the discussion of Adam's work, I asked the children to look at James's retelling and select the good things about his work (see Figure 10 for an example of James's written retelling).

I wanted to emphasize that even though Adam and James had used different processes to complete their retellings, each retelling had equally positive qualities as the other. I started the in-class discussion by explaining the differences between oral and written retellings, although I made sure not to stress that one was better than the other. Balancing forms and styles means acknowledging that each style is good in and of itself, not valuing one style over another. Therefore, I noted that writing a retelling requires a lot of concentration because the writer has to remember everything and write down everything he or she can remember. Because the children had already evaluated the good things in Judy's and Adam's retelling, they were more experienced and pointed out these things more easily than they previously had:

Judy: It's real neat and easy to read.

Figure 10
James's Written Retelling of "Awful Aardvark"
(Mwalimu, 1995)

Awful Aardvark
Retold by James
Aardvark Has loud snoreing.
HHHRRR — zzzz. He lived
in an old tree that was
dry and had a smooth
branch on it and Aardvark
loved to sleep on it.
Mongoose hated Aardvarks
snoreing. So he had a meeting
with the monkeys. And then
he talked to lion. And then
Rhinoceros. And that
night Mongoose called
the monkeys. The monkeys
shook the tree. And then
lion came and scratched the

(continued)

tree. Rhinoceros bumped the tree with his fat bottom. Aardvark nerly fell off the branch. There was a crack in the roots of the tree. The tree fell over. Aardvark was angry. He saw the termites. He said "I'm going to gobble you up!" and he did. From now on Aardvark sleeps in the day and eats termites at night.

Arthur:	It stayed on the subject, too.

Arthur: It stayed on the subject, too.

Jessica: I like his spelling. He did a good job on that.

Stewart: Right. He really did do a good job of his spelling. He has most of the words spelled like they would be spelled in a book, doesn't he?

Adam: Look! He got the snoring sound spelled just like it is here in our story!

Stewart: Right, but I want you to look at his spelling some more. Look at the hard words he tried to spell. Which ones did he try that were hard?

Adam: *Snoring, rhinoceros, mongoose.* [At the time, I noted that this was good work by Adam because he was not particularly good at spelling, although looking at the work of others was helping to improve this skill.]

Jimmy: *Monkeys...scratched.*

Peter: *Bumped, nearly.*

Jeff: *Crack.*

Stewart: I want you to know that all the words you mentioned are spelled like they would be spelled in a book except two—*snoring* and *nearly*—and look at how many letters he got right in those. [James had spelled them as "snoreing" and "nerly" so I wrote the correct spellings on the board.] Did James worry about whether he could spell those hard words? No, he just knew they were good words to use to tell his story and spelled them the best way he could. He tried to get his ideas on the paper first. James did you have to go back and fix any of your words?

James: A few.

Stewart: How did you do that?

James: Well, when I got finished I read what I wrote. Then I thought about if I had spelled 'em right. You know, I listened to the sounds.

Stewart: Well, that was a really smart way to go about it because you got your ideas right first, then worried about your spelling. [I am quite proud of James and want him to know it so I smile at him.] Well, you did a great job! You know what else you did that was great? You put quotation marks around the words that came out of Aardvark's mouth! That makes me so happy and excited. I can't believe you remembered to do that all by yourself! Does anybody see anything else?

After I highlighted how James attended to the *content* of his writing before the *conventions* of writing, the students were quick to point out other instances of this. For example, the students praised the use of initial capital letters at the beginning of sentences, correct punctuation at the end of sentences, the chronological order that closely matched that of the original story, and inclusion of many of the story's details. After catching all these positive elements in James's retelling, the students began to realize that there was *more than one right way* to do things. One student, Jimmy, suggested putting both the students' retellings in the hallway so everyone in the school could see them. After I had done this, students frequently stopped by our hallway display to enjoy those two retellings and requested that we display more.

The students and I spent much time that day studying Adam's and James's retellings and looking for constructive errors. Like Ferreiro and Teberosky (1979/1994), "We are not interested in defining children's responses in terms of what they lack in skills or maturity. On the contrary, we are attempting to expose positive aspects of what they know" (p. 20). In our attempts to discover strengths in students' work, we also focused on areas that might be strengthened. During the class discussion, I saw the two boys swell with pride because everyone had noted how well each of them had done.

James already thought of himself as a writer, but because we had focused on both oral and written retellings, Adam—as well as the other students—seemed to think of himself as a writer, too. This validation from the class allowed Adam to see himself differently and affect a change in his role as writer. Although Adam told me at a later session that I was his "designated writer" (his term, not mine), I noticed that he began to attempt more writing on his own. From then on, I consciously tried to diminish my role as his "designated writer" to make him assume more responsibility for his own writing.

There were many other instances—before and after this one—in which I served to direct attention to particular students and features of their work. This is just one example of how my role as artist helped the class to focus on literacy pieces, paying attention to language from multiple perspectives, as readers, writers, and tellers of tales. We attended not only to the semantic, syntactic, and graphophonic systems (Goodman, Watson, et al., 1987), but also to two class members and the ways they strengthened our literacy learning and our sense of community.

Conclusion

Because I opened the chapter with a 1986 quote from Calkins, it seemed fitting to conclude the chapter with a 2001 quote from Calkins, in which she continues to compare a teacher to an artist. Calkins carries through with her original idea that teachers must maintain an organizing vision as they negotiate ongoing aspects of schooling:

> The problem is that if our teaching is to be an art, we need an organizing vision that brings together all of these separate components into something graceful and vital and significant. It is not the number of good ideas that turns our work into art, but the selection, balance, coherence and design of those ideas.
>
> Artists know this. Artistry does not come from the quantity of red and yellow paint or from the amount of clay or marble but from the organizing vision that shapes the use of these materials. It comes from a sense of priority and purpose (Calkins, 1994). That sense of priority and purpose must come from a teacher who authors a vision for teaching. If our teaching is to be an art, we need to do more than compile materials and methods; we also need to infuse them with a sense of priority and vision, passion and grace. (p. 4)

The interactions between the students and me illustrate my priorities and vision in this particular second-grade classroom. I believe these interactions are essential to every classroom, although each teacher must find his or her own priorities and visions for the classroom. One way for teachers to do this is to become skilled in "kidwatching," which Goodman (1985) describes as the in-depth and professionally knowledgeable art of observing and learning from children. Expertise in the area of kidwatching is central to the artistic role of teachers because it is only through this careful observation of students that teachers can discover what is essential for each of their students.

Teaching demands serious observation of students. Just as medical doctors examine patients to find out how to administer to their specific needs, so must teachers to their students. Jaggar (1985) calls for observation in which watching, listening, and reflecting serve as critical links between theory and practice; that is, teachers should use knowledge of children and language to create learning environments and meaningful interactions with students. Feldman (1970) expands on the idea of teaching as an art:

> A central task of teaching is to imagine yourself into the minds of the people you teach. In this respect, a teacher is like the artist or novelist who enters the existence of his invented characters. Teachers "invent" their pupils, too, continuously correcting their artificial constructions in the light of what they see and know about them as real people. This artistic element in teaching, with its sensitive perception of the qualities in people, its subtle powers of self-correction, will defy simulation by computer for a long time. (p. 43)

Teaching is "a process of social interaction and critical communication" in which teachers discuss with their students the meanings and values of students' work—drawings, words, and other creations that might be called their "art"—and help shape the direction of both "the discussion and its implications for the further creation of art" (Feldman, 1971, p. 614).

The artistic role of teaching appears to be self-extending: Teachers step back to reflect on the patterns of classroom learning to define and highlight each student's strengths. Students learn from the actions of their teachers; students can also become artists. Therefore, students and teachers collaborate as artists who construct a classroom community that is built on what is essential for that particular space and time and for those particular students. As artists, teachers gain knowledge of themselves as they work with and gain knowledge of their students. Banner and Cannon (1997) express this well:

Self knowledge is the missing dimension of our preparation and growth as teachers in part because acknowledging its importance would require acknowledging another fact that is at the root of the mystery of teaching—that teaching is an art, not a science.

Like any art, of course, we can isolate its components. For painting, for instance, we can specify ground, medium, color, form, and tools—those elements that seem to make up a finished canvas. Yet it is the painters' unique selves, not their paintbrushes or the kinds of paint they use, that animate those components of their craft and make those components into what has never before been seen—works of art. Similarly, just as the various components of a work of art do not make art, neither do intellectual content and instructional method alone make teaching. Original acts of teaching, like those of art, cannot be replicated. They are unique. (p. 3)

CHAPTER 5

The Students' Complementary Roles as "Architects"

When given the opportunity, students influence the structure of the classroom just as much as teachers do. Although teachers ultimately are responsible for the structure, the expectations, and the outcomes of school spaces and activities, students also influence the design of those things, thus affecting teaching outcomes. Indeed, teachers often must adjust the classroom structure to fit the students' ever-changing needs. This chapter focuses on several students in my second-grade classroom who were architects—students who were both "dreamers" and "doers" (Feldman, 1970) creating their own spaces to thrive and grow.

I use real scenarios from the classroom to highlight the emerging subthemes from my data. For example, I use Jessica's book *My Vacation* to examine the place of *story* and *meaning making*, especially the role of approximations in literacy processes. Janice's note-taking experience illustrates *authentic experience*. Other scenarios within the classroom that involve the literacy efforts of groups—as well as individuals—help demonstrate the importance of group competition, talk, friendship, collaboration, reciprocal roles (in which students were both the helper and the helped, as well as the composer and member of the audience), choice, sharing, and empowerment. Each subtheme presented in this chapter was integral in the design of our literacy learning and our literacy community.

The Power of Story

Jessica was a vivacious, inquisitive student who undertook each project with a positive and optimistic attitude. Jessica's family vacation to Fontana, North Carolina, USA, was such an important part of her outside-of-school experiences that it was the focus of many of the writings she shared with the class. This important experience later became the basis for her favorite self-created book, *My Vacation*. This book was Jessica's idea from the beginning and grew out of her writing-workshop efforts. Jessica first mentioned her family vacation to Fontana in her first journal entry at the beginning of the school year. I assessed each student's journal entry in my beginning-of-the-year notebook by documenting strengths and needs of each student's writing. (Figure 11 shows Jessica's first journal entry, as well as my informal assessment of her journal entry.) Even at this early point in the year, Jessica included the element of *story* in her writing. Jessica was confident in her writing abilities and was always one of the first students to volunteer to share her writings with the class. Her sense of story and her willingness to share became catalysts for other students to share their own writings with the class.

Caulfield (1996) speaks of story and its power to change students' lives: I saw this power in our classroom through students' shared stories. As students wrote, told, and listened to one another's stories, they made important literacy connections, and perhaps more important, they made personal connections important in developing a classroom community. As Caulfield notes,

> Story has great power in our lives. It has the power to connect us to ourselves and to others. Students who at other times are restless will lean forward and become captivated when told a story. When stories are acknowledged and included within the school culture, a powerful message is sent to students. Celebrating both formal narratives and informal family stories encourages students to take the next step to become storytellers themselves. (p. 51)

Many times, I saw students take that "next step" as they became storytellers themselves. Jessica's readings from *My Vacation* encouraged other students to share their stories, too. Through examination of Jessica's drafts of *My Vacation*, I saw how the other students became captivated by Jessica's storytelling and why they were encouraged to

Figure 11
Jessica's First Journal Entry and My Informal
Assessment of Her Entry

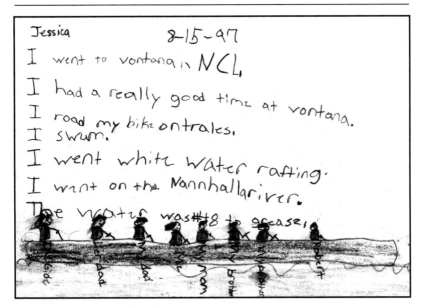

Student #8 ("Jessica")

Strengths:

+ Includes element of story in her entry
+ Starts sentences with capitals
+ Uses a capital for the word "I"
+ Ends sentences with periods
+ Uses mostly conventional spelling
+ Is willing to take risks in her writing: *trales* (trails), *Nannhalla* (Nantahala), *to grease* (degrees)
+ Has beginning, middle, and ending sounds
+ Uses illustration to enhance story line
+ Is aware of abbreviations but not yet conventional
+ Writes first and last name correctly
+ Can copy date correctly in number format

8-15-97 (from journal entry)

Needs:

- Work on abbreviations
- Show sources for spelling: *trales* (trails), *Nannhalla* (Nantahala), *to grease* (degrees)
- Work on past tense - *swum* (swam)
- Work on capitalizing city, state
- Work on proper nouns (Nantahala River)
- Work on homonyms (*road* / rode)

become storytellers themselves. For example, when Jessica read her book to the class, she sang the last two lines of a page on which there was a tune of a song (see Figure 12). The other children asked Jessica to read and sing that page over and over again as they joined in with her.

Figure 12
Jessica's Musical Conclusion of *My Vacation*

On the day when Jessica read her story to the class, I praised her for her ingenious writing device:

Stewart: Jessica, I *love* this page! Tell me about your song. I want to hear how this tune sounds again. [Jessica sings her refrain again.] That's wonderful. And look at your song coming from your mouth in that little cloud.... How did you know to show those notes like that?

Jessica: Well, it's supposed to be music, you know, and so I looked around and saw your Smurfs on the wall with those notes coming out of their mouths...so I made 'em sort of like that.

Stewart: Have you ever taken music lessons?

Jessica: [grinning] No. I just thought they needed to look like that.

Stewart: That's fantastic, Jessica. You were so smart to look around to find a way to make your picture show exactly what you wanted it to show. That's what good illustrators do. It made your story so much stronger. It really lets me see how you feel about going back to Fontana.

When Jessica's book was published in its final form, she read it to the class during the sharing portion of one of our writing workshops. When she sang her last page, the students once again pleaded, "Oh, do that page again." She read it again, and the other children spontaneously joined her in singing the ending. Jessica's book started a reading-and-writing revolution in our classroom because it was teaching the students how to employ new ideas in their writing, by using it to bring their lives outside of school into our joint school experience. The students began borrowing Jessica's book, using it to read to themselves or a friend or to look for ideas. After reading Jessica's book, students started to write books about personal experiences of their own, which ran the gamut from trips to parties to family stories. Sharing personal stories through this format seemed to bond our class into a community more than any other thing. Barton and Booth (1990) agree with this assertion, noting that the spoken word has implications for personal interactions and relationships:

Storytelling is about communities. Although reading is a great delight, it is often a solitary event. Telling stories, either personal or formal, is one of the most powerful social interactions that we experience. Storytelling, by its very nature, is an interconnecting event:

[I]t takes at least two people.... The ability to communicate and to respond to one another in person is part of the essence of our humanity. It brings us into communities as beings with interactive skills and common stories to bind us together. It is one important facet of personal connection that must not be lost.... An important part of all this is students' ability and willingness to make connections with their audience—be it only one person. They are taking a risk to share themselves, their learning, and their insights. (pp. 62–63)

Meaning Making

Stressing meaning through accepting approximations emerged as an important subtheme of our literacy community. As I reflected on Jessica's first draft of *My Vacation*, which was written during writing workshop in the early October, I began to see her work as one example of *meaning making*. Her story originally was included in a collection of many stories that she kept in her writing folder. (Another expectation I had was that each student would keep his or her stories in one writing folder so the stories were easy to access.) When I asked Jessica in early November to choose a story to turn into a published book, she selected *My Vacation*. Her first draft had many strengths, but the errors might have detracted from the story for anyone who was not used to looking for constructive errors (Ferreiro & Teberosky, 1979/1994).

I asked Jessica to find and correct everything she could so all her readers could appreciate the meaning of the story (see Jessica's marked-up first draft in Figure 13). She had learned, from our group editing of class stories, that it was acceptable to use some basic editing strategies, so she confidently lined out errors, circled confusing words, and used carets to show where material should be inserted. Jessica also devised her own system to let me know where I should leave page breaks in typing her stories by drawing lines across her text. These lines indicated that I should leave space to include photographs of her trip. Jessica's invented system became a workable system that all the students eventually used in their story drafts. Even

Figure 13
Jessica's Marked-Up First Draft of *My Vacation*

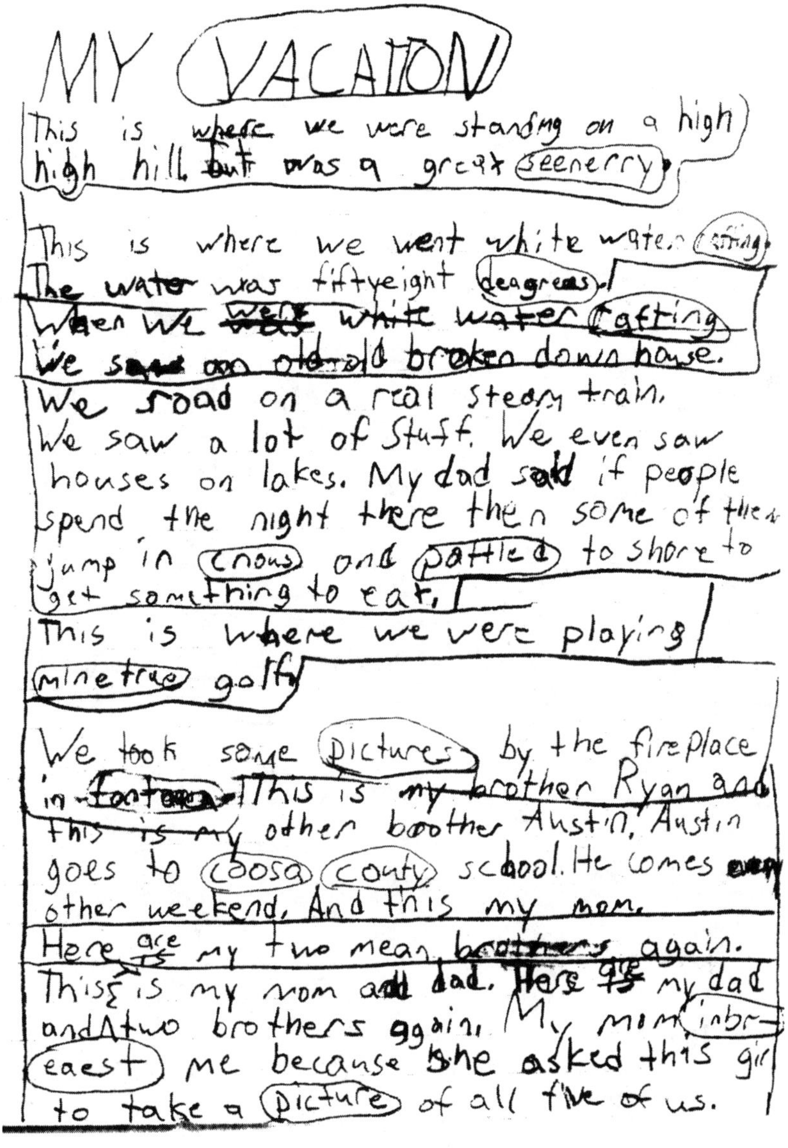

MY VACATION

This is where we were standing on a high
high hill but was a great seenerry.

This is where we went white water rafting
The water was fiftyeight deagrees.
When we were white water rafting
We saw an old old broken down house.
We road on a real steam train.
We saw a lot of stuff. We even saw
houses on lakes. My dad said if people
spend the night there then some of them
jump in cnows and pattled to shore to
get something to eat.
This is where we were playing
minetrue golf.

We took some pictures by the fireplace
in fontana. This is my brother Ryan and
this is my other boother Austin. Austin
goes to coosa couty school. He comes every
other weekend. And this my mom.
Here are my two mean brothers again.
This is my mom and dad. Here is my dad
and two brothers again. My mom inbreaest me because she asked this girl
to take a picture of all five of us.

(continued)

137

Figure 13 (continued)
Jessica's Marked-Up First Draft of *My Vacation*

Here are me and my mom.
Here are Ryan, Austin, and me again.

This is where we were standing above the outdoor pool. Fontana has two pools. It has an indoor pool and an outdoor pool. The second time we went to Fontana the water in the outdoor pool was freezing. My dad came and jumped into the freezing pool and said "the water isn't freezing" but then I said "I know the water isn't freezing" I was just teezing him.

This is where my mom took a picture of me, Ryan, and Austin in front of our van we came in.

I took a picture of the front of the train.

I think we're going to Fontana this year for vacation. Da da na ttt dana da na na na...

though it made their drafts look messy, these lines served a worthwhile and authentic purpose.

Jessica's final draft (see Figure 14) illustrates how she had worked through the writing process to correct her errors and make her writing conventionally correct and "publication ready." (Notice that the dividing lines are also present in Jessica's final draft.) I typed only stories that had been taken through this process to a final-draft stage. Many times, I had the students produce their books themselves, but I typed and printed what I considered to be very special pieces. I let the students assemble the book and add illustrations before I laminated the final product for them. Students took a very active role in the production of their books: They trimmed the laminated pages, punched the pages for binding, and inserted binding combs. Because of the elaborate process, the students invested this project with more importance than those books that were published in less elaborate ways.

The process of revision gave Jessica an aura of confidence as a writer. Jessica's writing illustrated how she was willing to take risks with her writing and make spelling approximations. She seemed to feel no threat about sharing her story with others; in fact, I believe her willingness to approximate gave strength to her work. Accepting approximations is a cornerstone of Cambourne's "Conditions of Learning" (1988) and a valued component of other language acquisition research (Ferreiro & Teberosky, 1979/1994; Peterson & Eeds, 1990). According to Peterson and Eeds (1990), "Competence is achieved over time, and we concern ourselves with the *direction* of the responses children make to literature every bit as much as the specific content of those responses" (p. 23).

Jessica used many good spelling approximations in her first draft:

- "seenerry" for *scenery*
- "deagreas" for *degrees*
- "cnous" for *canoes*
- "pattled" for *paddled*
- "minetrue" for *miniature*
- "inbreaest" for *embarrassed*
- "teezing" for *teasing*

Figure 14
Jessica's Final Draft of *My Vacation*

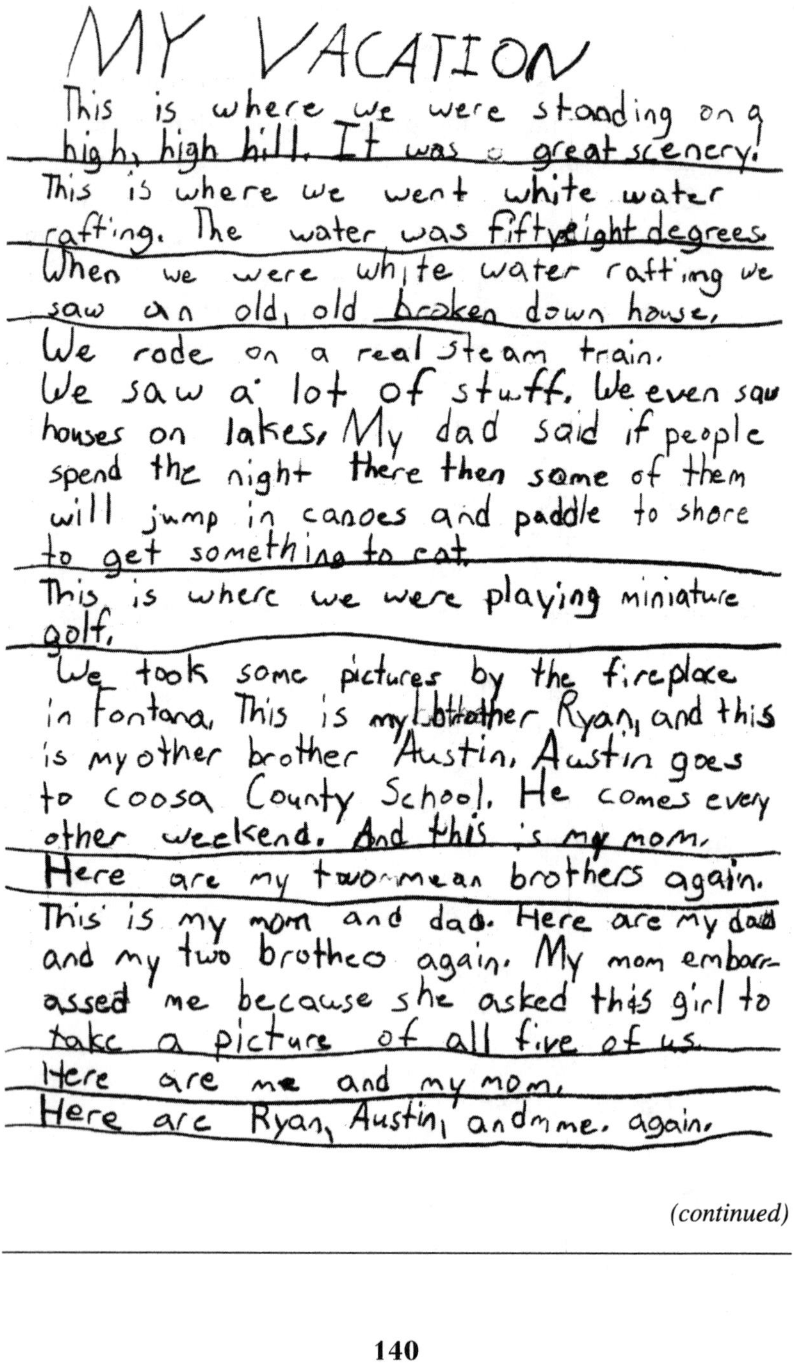

MY VACATION

This is where we were standing on a high, high hill. It was a great scenery!
This is where we went white water rafting. The water was fifty eight degrees.
When we were white water rafting we saw an old, old broken down house.
We rode on a real steam train.
We saw a lot of stuff. We even saw houses on lakes. My dad said if people spend the night there then some of them will jump in canoes and paddle to shore to get something to eat.
This is where we were playing miniature golf.
We took some pictures by the fireplace in Fontana. This is my brother Ryan, and this is my other brother Austin. Austin goes to Coosa County School. He comes every other weekend. And this is my mom.
Here are my two mean brothers again.
This is my mom and dad. Here are my dad and my two brothes again. My mom embarrassed me because she asked this girl to take a picture of all five of us.
Here are me and my mom.
Here are Ryan, Austin, and me. again.

(continued)

Figure 14 (continued)
Jessica's Final Draft of *My Vacation*

This is where we were standing above the outdoor pool. Fontana has two pools. It has an indoor pool and an outdoor pool. The second time we went to Fontana the water was freezing. My dad came and jumped into the freezing pool and said, "The water isn't freezing" but then I said, "I know the water isn't freezing." I was just teasing him.

This is where my mom took a picture of me, Ryan, and Austin in front of our van we came in.

I took a picture of the front of the train we rode.

I think we're going to Fontana this summer

Da da na ttt dana da na na na . . .

Her high-risk spellings in her first draft showed her comfort level in her abilities as a writer and with us as her audience. Because Jessica was not afraid to use challenging words to express her thoughts, she seemed to have internalized the fact that this was a working draft in which ideas were more important than spellings.

The revision process that Jessica used for *My Vacation* demonstrates how one student took *responsibility* for her learning. Jessica showed other students that they could be responsible for their own learning as well. As seen in Figure 13, Jessica confidently wrote her ideas in rough-draft form, then she returned to this draft, circling words that she thought might be spelled differently than they would be spelled in a book. She also crossed out verbs used incorrectly, "cut" her story into pages by drawing dividing lines to guide me in typing her story, and left spaces in the story so that she could place her photographs on the appropriate pages. She even looked in the dictionary for words she questioned and replaced incorrect spellings with correct ones. Jessica's confidence in using approximations was also evidenced by the invented spelling of her musical refrain at the end of her story. The approximations Jessica used for the musical tune were perfectly satisfactory for me, as well as the students, who chose to sing along with Jessica and reread Jessica's book over and over. The students and I understood her spellings, which were close approximations of the song she sang. Because the design of the class allowed Jessica to use approximations freely in her first draft, she focused on how to get her ideas across through her writing.

Authentic Experience

Authentic experience also appeared to be a subtheme of the students' complementary roles as architects. The students and I repeatedly stressed the connections between life in and out of school. Students created many opportunities to discuss or write about experiences they had outside of the classroom. *My Vacation* was the first elaborate example of this connection between out-of-school and in-school events because Jessica used her in-class writing time to create a project about her family's vacation experience. Although it is possible to explain all the subthemes through Jessica's book, I portray other students and literacy events to show that many students illustrated these subthemes throughout the school year. Many students' creations—books, journal entries, stories—showed the dominance of authentic experience in daily class life. One instance involving a student, Janice, shows the impact of authentic experience.

While traveling to a field trip by bus, I noticed that Janice was busily taking notes about the different types of transportation she saw (see Figure 15 for Janice's list). Because of the importance I had placed on taking notes during Elsewhere Expeditions, I was ecstatic when I noticed that she had filled a page of her small spiral-bound notebook with the types of transportation she observed. The students and I had been studying transportation, and I had told them just before our trip, "You will need to watch for the types of transportation we pass as we travel. We'll probably see many different kinds." Perhaps that statement was the catalyst for Janice's list, but it was Janice who had decided on her own to bring her notebook and a pencil and to take notes—she had brought the design of the class outside the classroom.

Adam had been first to point out what Janice was doing, saying, "Hey, Mrs. Stewart. Look at Janice! She's makin' a list. She's writin' down every kinda [sic] transportation we see!" Adam started asking Janice if she had seen certain types of transportation. Other children soon chimed in—Did you see that ambulance? Did you see that fire truck? Did you see that big wrecker?—until Janice finally got frustrated and closed her notebook.

On further assessing Janice's list, I noticed that she had tried to spell the best she could as she listed the different types of transportation. Janice initially used checkmarks to indicate multiple entries of the same type of transportation but later gave that up as impossible. She continued with her list until the boys got overexcited about seeing a police motorcycle and squad car. At that point, Janice tore out her list (which was covered on the front and back with kinds of transportation), threw it on the floor, firmly put her foot on it, and told the students, "Leave me alone." Noting Janice's exasperation, I asked her if I could have the list: "Janice, do you want to keep your list, or may I have it?" Janice told me that I could have it because the boys would not leave her alone. The following dialogue shows how I tried to convey to Janice the importance of her action:

Figure 15
Janice's List of Types of Transportation Seen on Bus Ride

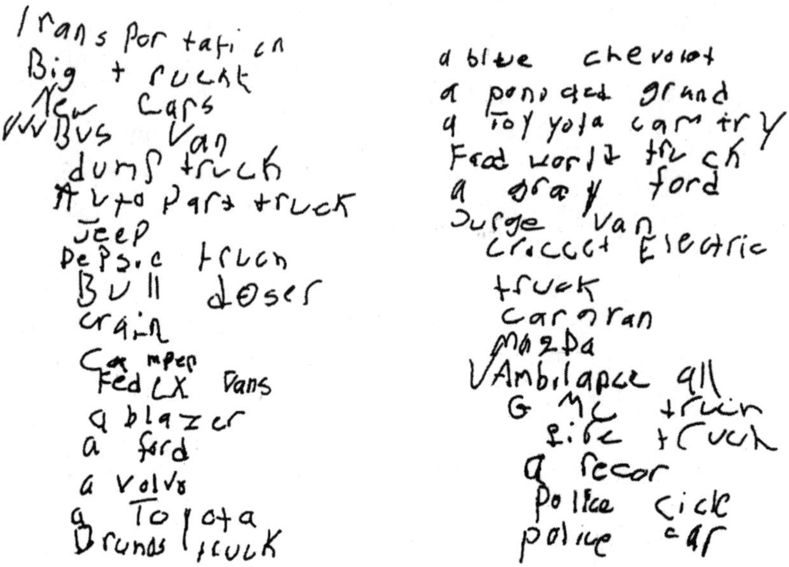

Translation of Janice's list:

Transportation

Big truck

New cars [on a transporter]

Bus   Van

dump truck

Auto Parts truck

Jeep

Pepsi truck

bulldozer

crane

camper

FedEx vans

a blazer

a ford

a Volvo

a Toyota

Bruno's truck [local grocery]

a blue Chevrolet

a Pontiac Grand Am

a Toyota Camry

Food World truck [local grocery]

a gray ford

Surge van

Crockett Electric [local company]

truck

caravan

Mazda

Ambulance 911

GMC truck

fire truck

a wrecker

police cycle [motorcycle]

police car

144

Stewart:	Well, I want it; it's a great list. [She hands it to me, and I begin to look over it.] I'm so glad you had the idea to take notes about the kinds of transportation you saw. We'll take this back to class and use it when we write about our trip. [She smiles and seems to relax.] How did you know how to spell all these hard words?
Janice:	I just looked on the cars—you know, they usually have their names on the back.
Stewart:	That's really using your brain. You are very smart, Janice.

I was thrilled that Janice had gone to the trouble to make her list as we traveled on another Elsewhere Expedition. The habit of taking notes seemed to be so ingrained in Janice that she did not want to let this opportunity pass to document our trip. Janice embodied the role of architect as she bridged the gap between school and the outside world.

Group Competition

One literacy event that deeply affected the development of our classroom community and the students' literacy learning was the "Train Contest." The Train Contest evolved when the principal and the librarian had written a grant to purchase two trunks of books, as well as several videos about all kinds of trains. One of the trunks was filled with books appropriate for grades K–3; the other, for grades 4–6. Each class had a turn to keep the trunk in the classroom for a period of time. There was to be a schoolwide contest in which students in each class tried to read more books about trains than the students in other classes could read. The rules of the contest were that (a) each child who read a book about trains could put his or her name in a cutout of a train car and have it signed by his or her parent or teacher as verification, and (b) students could do projects based on a book or video about trains that their teacher read or showed in class, and these projects would count toward the contest. For 7 days around Christmastime, it was our turn to have the "Train Trunk" in our classroom. Because the students knew how many books had been read by the class that had the Train Trunk before us, they were very excited about trying to beat that class and read as many books as they could. As a teacher, I thought the project was worthwhile because it stressed reading and because I could see possibilities for other projects. I also really wanted the children to win the contest, for which the reward was to be an all-day field trip to a train museum in a small town about an hour's bus ride away from school—an excellent opportunity for an outside-of-school Elsewhere Expedition. The students were excited about this trip as well, because they knew at the museum that there was a real train they could ride, a new experience for many of them.

Reflecting on the Train Contest, I saw that it played a central role in strengthening our classroom community because it involved *group competition*. The contest really pulled the whole class together. For example, I allowed more time than usual for reading and writing during the 7 days in which we had the "Train Trunk." I also read books to the students and had them complete written projects to explain what they had learned. For their parts, the students worked individually and in groups to help one another read and to plan and execute projects together. When the contest ended in March, I was overwhelmed with what my class had accomplished. Not only had my students read 164 books, but they also had completed 78 written projects, which were filled with amazingly detailed artwork and writing. From a learning standpoint, the students' work paid off: They learned a great deal about trains and were able to express what they knew in oral and written formats.

Teachers and students were told which day the judges were scheduled to select the contest winners. The students' projects were to be organized in either folders or compiled into some type of display so the judges could easily see what the students had accomplished. I decided it also would be productive for the students to realize their accomplishments, so I had my class create a large hallway display of our contest entries. Four days before the judges arrived, I began cutting long pieces of paper for the students to glue their work onto for the display. When we finished, the students and I were excited to find out just how much space our display would take up, but we did not want to hang it up because we thought another class might see what we had done and try to beat us by reading more books or completing more projects. We, therefore, kept our display papers (which were about 7 feet long by 3 feet wide) stacked on top of each other in a corner of our room until the day of judging arrived. After the students and I finished putting up our display, we were amazed at the space it covered—approximately 30 feet—and we began to think we really might win the contest. As it turned out, we did win, and were one of four classes who got to go on the field trip.

Not only did we gain benefits from the intensive reading, writing, and studying of trains, but we also had an opportunity to participate in an authentic experience that would be etched in our collective memory. The field trip/Elsewhere Expedition to the train museum was an exciting, fun-filled, and educational experience for the students. When we were on the train, the conductor allowed the children and their respective chaperones to explore every train car, stand directly behind the steam engine, and watch everything that was happening on the train at close range. What made the day even more special, though, was the fact that the students had earned their trip together. The students' participation in the contest truly was a group effort, which served to bond the group and provide them with literacy events and literacy learning.

Before we even went on our field trip/Elsewhere Expedition, the students predicted, "We know you're gonna [sic] make us write about our trip." I grinned and told them, "You've got it. Of course I will, so you'd better pay attention and take lots of pictures!" Using a Polaroid camera and a 35-millimeter camera, the students and I took many pictures to document our experience. We spent the next several school days sorting the photographs and using them to write about our shared experience in our daily writing workshops. From these writings, the students constructed our class Big Book about the trip to the train museum, although this was not until April. While the students were illustrating the Big Book and dictating pages for me to type, Adam walked into the hall with his notebook and said, "I'm gonna [sic] count what we did. I'll be right back." When Adam returned, he handed me a piece of notebook paper with a list of numbers written one above the other and explained that each number indicated how many entries there were for a particular book or video about trains. Then he asked for his paper, returned to his desk, and added the numbers. The other students thought this was really smart and insisted that we put

Adam's numbers into our finalized Big Book. Once again, Adam influenced our literacy community.

The whole experience of the Train Contest was definitely a case in which the shared community experience had a great influence on literacy processes and products over an extended period of time. As the students and I read, discussed, planned, wrote, shared, and reflected on trains, we learned much about literacy and grew as a community. Before this teacher-research study, I had thought there was little place for competition in creating a community of learners. The Train Contest helped me to realize that, although I prefer to encourage collaboration within the classroom community, group competition can also help to strengthen classroom bonds. Through this competition, the students and I supported one another as learners and as friends. I would like to think that we might have read as many books and completed as many projects without the contest, but we probably would not have had the opportunity to create a display of what we had accomplished. Creating the display—putting their efforts in a tangible form—invested the students with a sense of pride and ownership in the work they had done. There can be benefit to competition if it is handled in the right way and if children within the group are not pitted against one another. This Train Contest epitomizes *how I learned* from my students.

Talk, Friendship, Collaboration, and Reciprocal Roles

The subthemes of *talk, friendship, collaboration,* and *reciprocal roles* emerged in one scenario that happened in late February as I was conferencing with a new student, Susan, who had been in our class only a few weeks. Susan had extreme difficulty reading even the simplest books. One day, Adam seated himself beside Susan and me to work. I suggested that he might be distracted by what we were doing, but he said, "You know how much better I work when I'm near a grown-up." I decided to allow him to work near us and discovered that Adam was an insightful teacher of reading, as he began helping me teach Susan some strategies to make her reading more meaningful. Adam drew from the strategies that I had used with students in my class that year and shared them with Susan in his own way. Judy, who was another struggling reader, also decided to join Adam and me that day to help tutor Susan. For example, Judy often wanted to tell Susan words as Susan was working to read her book. Time and again, Adam admonished Judy to give Susan time to think because he wanted Susan to have time to use her new strategies to unlock the meaning. I was thrilled with Adam's and Judy's "teaching"; I could not have done a better job myself. This conference bonded Susan, Adam, and Judy and supported Susan as a reader. Adam and Judy's joint effort positively affected Susan's literacy learning: She had read five simple books, which she eagerly awaited to take home to read to her parents. Adam and Judy concluded the session by hugging Susan and each other; they also seemed to be elated with their success as teachers. This was an example of what Peterson (1992) calls an "incorporation rite" (p. 33)—the students accepted one another as they were, and Adam and Judy helped Susan make changes they all valued. I noticed Judy and Susan at a table during snack time, engrossed in reading another book together and showing confidence as readers.

Indeed, most of my students were beginning to see themselves as writers and readers and scientists and mathematicians; they were making strides in becoming autonomous learners as they became more confident and daring in the choices they made. We were building a community in which students were mediating knowledge for one another. Students further revealed these collaborative efforts in shared student-authored books, with efforts extended across days and sometimes weeks. I learned that "just as the role of language in a constructivist environment is to mediate between the learner and the world, the role of collaborative work is to allow learners to mediate for one another" (St. Pierre-Hirtle, 1996, p. 90).

The students also engaged in collaborative work in the many instances throughout the year when the students and I wrote stories as a whole group, especially at the beginning of the year when I tried to help the students learn writing strategies to carry over to their own writing. During those times of group writing, I modeled my thinking processes and wrote down exactly what the students dictated, which allowed the students to go through the process of spotting their own errors. I modeled various processes and strategies for correcting errors, which have been explained by other researchers (e.g., Atwell, 1990; Calkins, 1986; Clay, 1979; Goodman, Smith, et al., 1987; Graves,

1983, 1994; Manning et al., 1989; Weaver, 1994). This modeling of both thinking strategies and the processes of writing let the students carry these strategies and processes into other types of writing. For example, I noticed that some strategies were being used when students were working either in small groups or on topics of their own choosing. In those situations, there was need for cooperation, negotiation, and compromise.

One particular scenario that involved Adam, Judy, and Frances showed how the students had their own interpretations of group writing. Adam, Judy, and Frances had formed a group and decided to work together to create a story. As was my practice, I walked around the room and stopped by each group to conference with individuals. Conferencing was helpful in knowing how the groups were processing; it was also useful in preventing group squabbles from escalating into major difficulties. In my first pass around the room, the three students made the following comments as they negotiated for roles within the group:

Frances: I could write the story.

Judy: We'll say the sentences and get Frances to write it down.

Adam: We can talk about it and let Frances write it. Is that OK with you, Frances?

Frances: Yes.

In my second pass around the room, most of the students were trying to think about what they would write. Frances had started writing the first draft, but Adam and Judy were complaining about her sloppy writing. The group negotiated about how their draft, which they had to show me at the end of the writing workshop, should be:

Frances: It's a first draft. All first drafts are ugly.

Judy: Well, I'm gonna [sic] write a second first draft so we won't have to write it over.

Adam: Well, why don't you both write, and I'll pick which one we'll turn in.

Frances: Well, it has to be right, and it has to make sense.

Later that morning, I stopped by each group, asked the members three questions, and wrote down their answers in my field notes. The questions were (1) Did it help you to work in a group? Why or why not? (2) What did you like about it? and (3) What made it harder? These questions called for the students to reflect about what they were doing. The students were used to such questions—although the questions varied from situation to situation—because I had made reflection a routine part of their learning. The following is my dialogue with Adam, Judy, and Frances's group as I asked these questions:

Stewart: Did it help you to work in a group?

[Adam, Frances, and Judy each nod their approval.]

Stewart: Why?

Adam: It was quicker with a group.

Stewart: What did you like about it?

Judy: Having somebody to write the story.

Stewart: What made it harder?

Frances: [answering quickly] Too much talking.

Adam: We were playing a little.

Frances: Then I made some rules, and they settled a little bit. I said, "Don't talk when I'm writing, or I'll go back to my seat to write. Don't talk over each other. Don't go 'Ahhhhh' when I have to put your part in another place."

My conversation with these students illustrates how negotiations are made in group work and how each group must decide what works best for the group. Note in the above reflection on this collaborative effort the important subthemes of talk, friendship, collaboration, and reciprocal roles. It also illustrates the subthemes of *choice, sharing,* and *empowerment*: The group made its choice of topic, genre, and format for their writing; shared in the construction and ownership of the book; and was empowered by its investment in both the process and the product of the group effort.

Choice, Sharing, and Empowerment in the Classroom Community

The final three subthemes of choice, sharing, and empowerment were mainly supported by our classroom community as a whole. These subthemes were integral components of literacy events such as reading workshops, writing workshops, Elsewhere Expeditions, and shared story times. Choice seemed crucial to the events within this classroom and beyond. An excerpt from my field notes depicts Janice's perspective concerning choice:

> I ask Janice, "What do you think is important in our room?"
>
> She tells me, "Well, hmmm...I really think it's important that we get to choose so much in here. You know, like when we can choose our books to read...and we can choose what to write about...and sometimes we can choose where to sit...."
>
> "Anything else?" I ask her.
>
> She continues, "Yes, well, you know...sometimes we vote on our work and sometimes, we have to do a kind of work, but we can pick what part we want to do or maybe how we do it...."
>
> I interrupt, "Well, what about—" But she tells me with a broad smile, "I'm not through yet!" Then she continues, "We get to pick who we work with sometimes, too. I like to get to pick all those things. It kinda [*sic*] makes it more interesting—you know, not so boring. I think all the kids like it in here because of that." (Stewart, 1998)

A variety of research is available on the effect of early experience and oral language on children's early stages of reading and writing instruction (e.g., Delpit, 1990, 1991; Goodman, 1986; Graves, 1978; Heath, 1983; Newman, 1985; Smith, 1978). Teacher-researchers give student reflection as prominent a place as teacher reflection (Fedele, 1996). In my classroom, I saw the powerful results of group sharing and reflection as the students studied and discussed their written pieces in a community of friends. This freedom of expression supported the students' efforts and allowed their ideas to expand and their work to improve. The students gained from this supportive classroom climate, as did I. On the many occasions when I wrote with the students and shared my own writings with them, they showed as much genuine interest in my writing as they did with other students' writing. We were a mutually supportive community of readers, writers, listeners, and thinkers who shared ideas and learned from one another. It is important for students—as well as their teachers—to be as concerned with sharing, reflection, and consideration of the "whys" as they are with the "hows" of learning, particularly in language learning. Heath and Mangiola (1991) assert that it is important for students as tutors to be able to step back and reflect about what they and their tutees are doing so they are acquiring "fundamental characteristics of literate behaviors" (p. 23). When students and their teachers can reflect about what they are doing regarding literacy events and efforts, they also begin to acquire "fundamental characteristics of literate behaviors."

Conclusion

The subthemes discussed in this chapter show how the students' different perspectives led them to actively participate in the design of their lives at school. Students are also teachers—active in adjusting the classroom structure to fit their own needs and the needs of other students. Although the subthemes were separated here for the sake of discussion, they were reciprocal elements integrated throughout the study.

I think it is important for children to have a voice in the design of their classrooms. Many powerful results come from students' involvement in creating the structure of their learning spaces and designing much of what happens there. Students who act as architects feel free to change the configuration of the classroom to accommodate their learning needs, such as finding a quiet space when they want to read or write without distractions. They also are empowered to create, with their fellow classmates, spaces that allow them to collaborate, discuss, and carry out their learning experiences. Students who are architects design more than spaces and activities because they also create new techniques and procedures to make existing forms of learning better for that particular purpose and time. As a teacher who is also a researcher, I am constantly amazed at the variety and quality of students' architectural conceptions.

CHAPTER 6

The Students' Complementary Roles as "Artists"

Students also act as artists as they contribute ideas and insights about *their* visions of what classrooms should be. Students who are given opportunities to explore multiple ways of knowing and to discover their own best strategies for building understanding gain insight into elements essential to their most productive learning. While creating their own learning environments, these student-artists also influence the learning of their peers, as well as their teachers. Teachers who are aware of these possibilities build a classroom structure that enables students' contributions to learning. This synergism of teachers' and students' ideas creates a classroom structure that is more dynamic than a classroom structure created solely by the teacher. This chapter provides vignettes of students in the classroom who created their own vision of what was essential for learning.

Adam as Artist: Importance of Respect, Observation, and Advocacy

Throughout the year, Adam had taught the other students and me a lot—the importance of respect for others and their work, keen observation, reflection, involvement, caring, and advocacy. Adam's interpretation of classroom events changed my perceptions as teacher, allowing me to envision the classroom in a new way. The following dialogue occurred among Adam, James, and me on our bus trip to the train museum. This dialogue epitomizes Adam's role as artist.

Through Adam's vision, even the students knew that James, in his own way, also had been a teacher:

Adam: [sitting next to me] Why do you like to teach?

Stewart: Because I love children, and I enjoy watching them learn.

Adam: I knew that [nodding].

[Adam's comment warmed me because I had never explicitly told the children I liked teaching, although I had told them (and tried to show them) that I liked—even loved—each of them individually and as a member of the class.]

Adam: You've taught us a lot. We've taught you a lot, too! [grinning]

Stewart: You certainly have. [We both laugh.]

Adam: You remember, James taught you something you never knew.

Stewart: Yes, he did! He taught me a new word, didn't he?

Adam: Yeah. You know—the person who studies snakes.

Stewart: Yeah. He taught me *herpetologist*.

Stewart: [leaning back to James, who is sitting behind me and across the aisle on the bus] James, is the word *herpetologist* someone who studies snakes?

James: [grinning] Yes, but it's not just snakes, it's all reptiles and amphibians.

Adam had first influenced my perceptions on the day that he was having his own story typed. Adam, who was sitting next to me as I typed his latest story, leaned over, looked up at me, and teased, "I know somebody in here who knows something *you* don't know." When I asked him what he meant, he got up, went over to James, and asked James to come over and talk to me to ask me if I knew "that word."

James: Well...I'm going to be a herpnentologist [his word for *herpetologist*] when I grow up.

Adam: [grinning] Do you know what that word is?

Stewart:	Well, you've got me! I've never heard of it. What does that mean?
James:	[smiling shyly and looking at Adam] It means that I'll be an expert on reptiles and amphibians. In fact, I already *am* one. You know that book I'm writing about snakes? Do you want to see it?
Stewart:	Of course I do!
Adam:	See? What'd I tell you? He knows something you don't know!

The previous scenario with James shows how Adam acted as artist: Adam enabled me to discover James's literacy creation, as well as James's artistic role as he crafted his nonfiction book.

Adam interpreted people and situations in the classroom, and he often helped to provide interpretations for the other students. On the first day of school that year, I had the students write group stories that I believed would quickly set into place some strategies for writing without my having to lecture. A group story is jointly composed by the children as a group, with the teacher acting as facilitator and scribe. (See Stewart, in press, for a complete description of a group story.) I also had brought in several drawstring bags that were all very different looking—some were velvet, some were quilted, some were made out of rough fabric and covered with brightly colored question marks, some were glittery and golden, and some had soft floral prints on them. Before we wrote our group story, I asked one student, Terrie, to demonstrate opening and closing one of the bags. I then compared stories to the drawstring bags: We would have to "open" our story with a sentence or two that would invite readers to "look inside" to see our story, and we would have to write a sentence or two at the end of our story to "draw" it to a close (Stewart, in press).

As the students and I talked about the possible stories we could write that day, we also discussed that—even though all the bags were drawstring bags—each of the bags was different. This allowed the students to talk easily about the different kinds of stories we could write. The students noted that some bags were soft, whereas others were hard and rough. Then they remarked that some stories were informational or contained mysteries like the bag with the question marks.

The students and I finally decided to write a story about our first day in second grade. To begin, I gave all the students some paper and asked them to make illustrations of their own perspectives. (I have found that students wait more patiently for their turn to add a sentence when they are working on these illustrations.) Adam was eager to start our story; his first statement allowed the other students to understand the metaphor of our stories as drawstring bags.

Adam: I have a good way to open our bag: Today was our first day in second grade.

Stewart: Great, Adam! Do you know what you just did with that beginning sentence?

Adam: I opened our bag?

Stewart: Yes, you did. Do you know *how* you did that?

Adam: I guess it was that I put the people in our story. You know, the people who will read it—let them know what was happening.

Stewart: That's right.... Why is that important for the people who read our story? [I look at the other students when I ask this question.]

Adam: [seems unsure] So they understand it's our first day in here?

Stewart: Yes. Why is that something they need to know?

Adam: Because they'll know everything is new to us. They'll know where we are...who we are.

By his taking the lead in directing the joint attention of the class to this strategy, Adam helped all the students to become more conscious of the importance of having a lead-in sentence to invite readers into the story. Adam knew what the students needed and guided them in the right direction.

After Adam's good beginning, which *supported* the students' learning, I was able to use questioning to guide the sequence of the students' sentences as we built the story together. As I came to the bottom of the chart paper on which I had been writing the story, I told the students we were running out of space and needed to draw our story to a close. Because of our earlier discussion about the drawstring bags, they understood what I was saying. With a little guidance from me, the students were able to come up with a sentence that made sense to us to end our story.

This process of group writing was an easy-to-use strategy to immerse the students in writing and reading their own stories; it was also effective in helping students refrain from topic-hopping. By the time the students had written enough stories to fill the available space on our classroom window shades, they understood that they *could* write stories; were expected to make revisions (e.g., make their ideas stronger, cross out changes, insert words, and circle questioned spellings); and were allowed to write with other students if necessary.

The class and I wrote whole-group stories for several days after that until I noticed that some students had started to take over the direction of our stories; therefore, I started asking the students to form small groups to write stories. Sometimes the students formed groups according to the topic the students wanted to write about, although other times students formed groups of their friends and voted on what topic the group would write about. I helped them form a variety of combinations of groups so that each student would be able to contribute to a story, and therefore, know that he or she had something worthwhile to add to group stories. Adam was also a leader in gathering groups to write group stories. Through his enjoyment of each story and each group member's contribution to the story, he helped other students focus on the positive aspects of creating stories together. An excerpt from the audiotape of Adam's end-of-year interview shows the position that storytelling held from the students' views. This excerpt also illustrates how Adam actively helped other members of the class in their learning:

Stewart:	What can you tell me about reading, writing, or telling stories?
Adam:	I like telling stories because it just interests me....
Stewart:	Is it easier for you to tell stories, write them, or read them?
Adam:	Tell them.
Stewart:	Why?

Adam:	Because they're fresh on my mind, and it takes me too long to write it. So I have to tell it, just like I am on the tape right now.
Stewart:	Tell me more.
Adam:	I like saying retelling on a tape—like I said—for writing workshops. It's because it's fresh on my mind, and I gotta [sic] write it. If I write it, then I lose it 'cause it takes me so long. But when you help me, like when we're writing those stories together that we put on the shades, that helps too.
Stewart:	How does that help?
Adam:	Well, that's real easy because we got a group...you know, a group of friends...and we get to tell our stories together, and you write 'em on them [sic] charts for us....
Stewart:	That's right. You really help when we write stories together, Adam. Do you know what you do that helps?
Adam:	Well, I can think of something I'm really good at....
Stewart:	What?
Adam:	What I'm doing right now—telling!
Stewart:	Telling! Yes, you are! What else are you good at?
Adam:	Um...I can't think of any of that...
Stewart:	Oh, yes...you're a good thinker. You come up with the best ideas! Have you ever realized that?
Adam:	Yeah.
Stewart:	I thought...
Adam:	...'cause that right there [pointing to a story on one of the window shades]...I just figure out what needs to happen next when we're telling a story...and if somebody else don't come up with a good idea, I just help 'em think of it.

If I were not doing reflective practitioner research, I doubt that I would have known this side of Adam. I definitely would have been aware of the loud and bouncy Adam who rarely finished his written assignments, who found every excuse to refrain from putting pencil to paper. But I would not have known this thoughtful and reflective side of Adam—the boy who tried to sit across from me at lunch as often as possible, and the boy who came to me to discuss his questions and share his ideas. This side of Adam was known to me only because there was time and opportunity for us to interact on many levels. Time and opportunity are two of Cambourne's (1988) conditions of learning that I worked to establish in our learning community. As Cambourne notes, "Learners need time and opportunity to use, employ, practise [sic] their developing control in functional, realistic, non-artificial ways" (p. 33). I deliberately looked for time when I could interact with students as they were thinking about, talking about, and carrying out their work. I tried to get to know each student on a deeper-than-surface level. Even though, as a good teacher, I would have looked for this time and opportunity whether or not I had been conducting teacher research, I probably would not have taken the time to document these occurrences and reflect on the data collected. Had I not been involved in teacher research, I would not have known Adam—a caring, intuitive, and persevering child—at this deeper level. Adam and I knew each other as teacher and student, sharing reflections about books, stories, words, and pictures. We knew each other as friends, sharing reflections about family, classmates, and class problems and solutions. I will always feel a connection with Adam because I got to know him as both student and individual.

James as Artist: Importance of Classroom Community

James's own creative vision of his book allowed me to demonstrate to the students a new concept. As previously noted, Adam had first brought James's book to my attention. After looking at James's book, I realized that James was writing a nonfiction book with illustrations that would have captions and labels. I became interested in keeping a copy because I had emphasized to the students that they should read all illustrations, charts, and graphs—including captions and labels—in nonfiction books in order not to miss any information. As students began their own writing, I likewise encouraged them to use illustration as an information-giving strategy in their own books. James's book was a perfect example of the kind of nonfiction book I wanted the students to write (see Figure 16 for an example of an illustration from James's book).

Figure 16
Example of an Illustration From James's
Nonfiction Book on Snakes

All snakes that have fangs are poisonous.

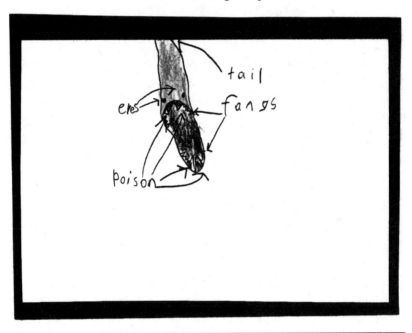

After reading James's book, I made sure to praise his illustrations—as well as the captions and labels—and I asked him how he had learned so many facts about snakes. James told me that he learned about snakes through reading books, especially one book titled *Eyes on Nature: Snakes* (Resnick, 1996). Seeing an opportunity to teach the other students about a new strategy to use when writing their books, I engaged James in the following conversation:

Stewart:	Well, if you got some of your ideas from that book, you have to give credit to the author because you used her ideas. Go get the book, and let me look at it. [James gets the book.] Who is the author?
James:	Um...Let's see... [He looks at the book's title page.] Jane P. Resnick.
Stewart:	What year was it published?
James:	Just let me look. Um...1996.
Stewart:	OK. Now, what you have to do is to include a reference page in your book. When Adam and I finish up here, I'll show you how to do that.

Because this was the first time anyone in this class was going to use a reference page, it started a wave of interest in the others students, who immediately wanted to include reference pages in their own books. James reference was as follows: "Resnick, Jane P. (1996). Eyes on Nature: Snakes. Chicago, IL: Kidsbooks, Inc." Although the reference was short, James was proud of his contribution to the design of our class. Students began patterning their texts on James's nonfiction work and including reference pages as standard elements of their books. I noticed that children began to concentrate carefully on title pages in the books they were using as references. Over time, children began not only using, but also documenting more than one source of information.

The routine inclusion of author pages at the end of the children's self-authored books is another example of how James influenced our classroom design. With no help from me (but following my help in setting up his reference page, thereby showing him the importance of citing sources), James created an author page for his *Snakes Book* (see Figure 17). I never explicitly told the children to include author pages in their books; although, in reading aloud nonfiction and fiction to them, I routinely read the information about the author from the books' jackets or back pages. However, almost all the students created their own author pages for their published books. The students' author pages were different with each of their published pieces, as they personalized them for each book. James's page included the usual information that was included on most author pages, as he introduced himself and revealed something personal about his life. His author page was exemplary, however, because it included the following rich information:

- Personal connection
- Scientific vocabulary
- Reference to his informational source
- A conclusion that tied in this work and his recognition of purposeful work in school, particularly in collaboration with his best friend, Peter

James also chose to include a photograph of himself on the bottom of his author page. The photograph James wanted to include was the one that I took of him on the first day of school. He had asked me if he

Figure 17
James's Author Page

About the Author

Hi! I am James, the author of this book. I like snakes a lot. That is why I wrote this book. I want to be a herpetologist when I grow up. (A herpetologist is a scientist that studies reptiles.)

If you want to know more about snakes, read <u>Snakes</u>, written by Jane P. Resnick.

I like writing in school. I always use my imagination in writing. I sometimes learn more information from books to help me with my writing. Peter sometimes helps me learn. We like to work together on books.

could take it from his *All About Me* book, which he had written earlier. I was delighted that he wanted to include a picture of himself in order to model his author page after the ones he had seen in the various nonfiction and fiction texts in our classroom.

After seeing James's author page, students routinely added their own author pages to their nonfiction books—as well as to fiction books that they had done in the past—and tried to include something different in each one, unique to that book. James showed his confidence in his writing and his comfort working in a community of friends, as he shared his work with me and the other students.

Through James, I was able to see that our classroom community influenced small groups in many instances across our year together. One example emerged from my data as representative of our classroom community because it depicted the joint efforts of students as they worked in groups to accomplish written projects. Because the students and I already had established a climate of acceptance and regard for one another's stories, I had pushed the students to write nonfiction as well as fiction. One group of boys, James, Adam, and Peter, began writing about animals and their favorite topic was snakes. I overheard James, our self-proclaimed expert "herpnentologist," discussing his nonfiction book on snakes with several friends at lunch in March:

James: Hey, you guys...I need help when we get back from lunch. Mrs. Stewart wants me to make two sets of pictures for my *Snakes Book* so she can keep a copy. I have so many pictures I can't get 'em all done by myself. Adam, will you help?

Adam: Sure. I'm good at getting pictures right. We'll start while Mrs. Stewart is reading us our story. She won't care.

James was asking for help with the illustrations because I had told him I would like him to do two sets of illustrations—one for his book and one for me to share with other teachers and students. When James and his friends had finished the illustrations, they had so many that James asked me to make the duplicate set on the copier; all they would have to do now was color the duplicate set. James also asked me to type his book on the computer and told me that I could print a copy for myself. When James's project was complete, I printed out five copies—one for me, one for James, and one for each of his co-illustrators (which now included Jessica)—and copied an additional four sets of the illustrations. The writing process included taking notes, writing rough drafts, completing a final draft, and submitting the final version to me for typing. James's book assumed these major proportions during the 2 weeks it took them to finish their work in writing workshop. What began as one student's simple project became a group's massive undertaking because of our classroom community and the connections between these students.

Jimmy as Artist: Importance of Hard Work, Attention to Detail, Personal Style, and Sense of Humor

Jimmy's written retelling in January of *The Day Jimmy's Boa Ate the Wash* (Noble, 1980) serves as another example of a student's artistic contribution to the class (see Figure 18 for Jimmy's retelling). For Jimmy, hard work, attention to detail, personal style, and a sense of humor were essential elements in learning. At this midpoint in the year, the students had learned, from many episodes of hearing and comparing several versions of the same story, how to "balance" their retellings so that the retellings included elements from the original stories as well as the students' interpretations of the stories. Although Jimmy's retelling was based on a published story, he made the story his own by paraphrasing the words and ideas of the actual story. I had decided to use Jimmy's retelling as a teaching piece to demonstrate yet another example of a good retelling. (Jimmy had been an active participant when I previously shared Adam's, James's, and Judy's retellings with the class.)

One of the first good things that I noticed about Jimmy's retelling was the hard work that he had put into it to get the sense of the story right. Throughout Noble's (1980) story, a mother and daughter are discussing the daughter's class field trip to a farm. When the daughter comes home, the mother asks, "How was your class trip to the farm?" (p. 1). The daughter replies, "Oh...boring...kind of dull...until the cow

Figure 18
Jimmy's Retelling of
The Day Jimmy's Boa Ate the Wash (Noble, 1980)

The Day Jimmy's Boa Ate The Wash
Retold By Jimmy

How was your class trip to the farm?

Oh, boring... kind of dull--- until the cow started to cry. Why did she start crying? You see a hay stack fell on her. Oh come on hay stacks dotent just fall over. It would if a farmer ran over it with his tracter. A farmer wouldn't do that. He would if he were too busy yelling at the pigs to get off the bus. What were the pigs doing on the bus. Eating our lunches. Why were the pig eating yalls lunches? Because we threw there corn. Why did yall throw there corn? Because we ran out of eggs. EGGS Why were yall throwing eggs? / / / Jimmy's boa consticter. What was Jimmy's boa consticter doing on the farm? He came to show it, but the chickens didn't like it. You mean he took it in the hen house. Yeah... then the hens qackled around. Go on go on whot hapend. Well we heard the farmers whfe screaming. What hapend. We donit know. We sorter left in a herea. Jimmy must have ben sad for leaving is boa on the farm. No...We left in such a herea / pig did not get off the bus. Now he has a pet pig.

166

started crying" (p. 2). Notice in Figure 18 that Jimmy had written these details of the story almost verbatim. In Noble's story, which is written in dialogue that is distinguished only by its placement on the page and the proximity to the illustrations, the dialogue between the mother and daughter continues: "A cow...crying?" "Yeah, you see, a haystack fell on her." "But a haystack doesn't just fall over." "It does if a farmer crashes into it with his tractor." "Oh, come on, a farmer wouldn't do that" (pp. 3–5). Again, notice how Jimmy had the sense of Noble's story. Even though his wording was not exact, he did use combinations that occur in the book (e.g., "Oh come on" for *Oh, come on* and "It would if a farmer ran over it with his tracter [sic]" for *It does if a farmer crashes into it with his tractor*).

Jimmy demonstrated personal style in the unique format he chose for his retelling. Noble's story is written in picture-book format, with the pictures depicting the action of each sentence (or two or three sentences at most per page). Because I believed that this format made text more memorable for young children, I encouraged the students to use this format in many of their own writings. Jimmy acted as an artist because he chose *not* to use this format, but to string together all the dialogue, one line under another, so that he had to create only *one* illustration to show the gist of the story. Jimmy was not afraid to use a new and unique format, even though he knew his retelling might be shared with the class. His thoughtfulness in creating his retelling this way—as opposed to modeling his retelling in the picture-book format—allowed him to construct a strong retelling yet kept him from having to spend the tremendous amount of time and effort it would have taken to construct his retelling in the complex picture-book format. Jimmy specifically had preplanned to do his retelling this way because he wanted to make time to work with his friends on a collaborative project that they were in the midst of setting up. Jimmy took initiative and developed his own strategy so that he could complete one project and move on to another project in which he was more seriously invested. He truly acted as artist and did what was most essential for his learning.

When the students and I examined Jimmy's retelling on the overhead screen, we pointed out the good things in his work and occasionally made suggestions. For example, the students remembered that when Jimmy originally had shared his retelling with the class, he changed the tone of his voice to differentiate the story's characters. The students suggested that to differentiate between characters' speech in his written retelling, Jimmy could have used "speech balloons," written each character's speech on a different page as in a picture book, or used quotation marks as in our literature anthologies. The students also pointed out how Jimmy's illustration had captured the humor of the original story. Other strong points the students noticed about Jimmy's retelling were

- accuracy and completeness,
- use of many exact words from the original story,
- use of good ideas, and
- spelling approximations (e.g., "dotent" for *doesn't*, "consticter" for *constrictor*, "whyfe" for *wife*, "sortev" for *sort of*, and "herea" for *hurry*).

The students and I also talked about the fact that Jimmy had conformed a whole picture book into one full-page story by putting the story's entire conversation on one page. I told the students that the use of quotation marks would have made this conversation easier to read because the marks would allow them to tell who was speaking.

Jimmy's retelling also demonstrated his attention to detail. For example, his retelling included the story's main idea, sequence of events, dialogue, and illustrations. Jimmy also paid attention to mechanics—capitalization of the story's title, identification of the story's author, mostly conventionally correct punctuation, extension of sentences beyond the ends of lines, and spelling approximations. More specifically, Jimmy remembered that *THE BOA CONSTRICTOR!* appeared in the story in capital letters with an exclamation mark following it and came close to reproducing it in his retelling with *EGGS!!!* Remember, Jimmy had no book to support his retelling, and he had heard me read this story only twice. However, this is a book that Jimmy had read and reread because, as he told me, it was "hilarious! I laugh so much it makes my stomach hurt" (Stewart, 1998). Knowing how much he enjoyed *The Day Jimmy's Boa Ate the Wash* (Noble, 1980), I am sure that Jimmy read the book several times himself to support his learning. Comments from Jimmy's year-end interview showed me just what he had accomplished with this retelling:

Stewart:	What is the hardest thing about a retelling?
Jimmy:	The hardest thing is, you know, how you have to keep stuff in your mind and your mind is...it conducts your brain to remember and all that....
Stewart:	Yeah...and to try to remember it in the right order.... Yeah, that *is* hard. What's the *easiest* thing about doing a retelling?
Jimmy:	At the first of it you remember a lot of it.
Stewart:	OK. And then the further you go, what happens?
Jimmy:	The harder it gets!
Stewart:	Why?
Jimmy:	Because you have to remember *all* that stuff and...
Stewart:	[smiling] Plus, what's happening to your hand during that time?
Jimmy:	It's firing up! [He chuckles.] Blow up!
Stewart:	Getting tired, isn't it? [I laugh.]
Jimmy:	Feels like it's going to blow up!

Jimmy's comments showed that he was aware of his difficulties and the effort he had to put forth during a retelling. His ability and willingness to exert that effort encouraged other students to keep working on their own retellings.

The students and I were impressed with Jimmy's hard work after we had talked about all the strengths in his retelling. Jimmy was acting as artist because he had drawn from many good ideas demonstrated in other retellings and used new strategies to create a unique retelling. In-class reflection on retellings has many benefits for students: They use all the language arts in combination for intensive listening, speaking, reading, and writing about a particular topic because the sharing-and-comparing component of a retelling lesson involves multiple readings and rereadings of both the original text and the retelling (Brown & Cambourne, 1993). Brown and Cambourne observed students' growth through use of retellings in the following areas: "knowledge of text forms...[and] conventions, consciousness awareness of the processes involved in text construction, range and variety of text forms and conventions being employed in other writing tasks, control of vocabulary, reading flexibility, [and] confidence" (pp. 11–12). These benefits were present in our classroom throughout the year, as evidenced by the numerous sharing and comparing of retellings in which we participated.

The class assessment of Jimmy's retelling also made me notice that the students were developing their own ideas about class life and what was essential to learning. For example, students were taking a more serious approach to their work that was to be shared in class, and also were becoming more critical audience members for their peers. I initially had stressed the importance of the students' dual roles as authors/audience members, but the *students* were the ones who took responsibility to commit themselves to these roles. In the beginning of the year, students often left out words when they shared stories with the class; by midyear, however, students were trying to catch those problems with a partner or peer group before sharing their work with the whole class. In his year-end interview, Jimmy also seemed interested in getting his work to be the best it could be before sharing it with the class. He commented on how he consciously sought a peer audience to help him improve his work:

Stewart: Is it easier for you to tell stories or write them or read them?

Jimmy: Write 'em and read 'em and then tell 'em.

Stewart: Why?

Jimmy: 'Cause, you know, sometimes I tell 'em to Jessica to make sure I got 'em right. She'll tell me yes or no.

Stewart: OK, so you get a friend to listen for problems. Do you read it to her?

Jimmy: Yeah, I read the whole thing to her, and she'll listen, and she'll remember it...if I got something wrong— like if I forgot to put a period—she'll tell me to do it.

Stewart: What about if you get your ideas...if you leave out a word or you get your ideas mixed up?

Jimmy: When I was writin' that John Henry thing, I left out two words in it.

Stewart: [leaning toward Jimmy] And you didn't realize it till you read it to Jessica?

Jimmy: [shakes his head] No, I read it to my momma instead.

Jimmy's comments indicated that he was serious about his work and conscientious about trying to do his best on a writing piece before it was shared with the class. All the students seemed to sense that I would be looking for writing pieces to share with the class—writing pieces that showed good things. Not only did Jessica (previously mentioned in Chapter 5) and Jimmy want their work to *sound* right when they read it, but they also wanted an opportunity to *show* others what they had done. The students had created their own framework of how they wanted their work to appear in other students' eyes.

Janice as Artist: Importance of Personal High Expectations

Because I had designated purpose as an integral component to the classroom design, Elsewhere Expeditions became important backdrops to the students' literacy events. For example, our Elsewhere Expedition of the school lunchroom was a conscious attempt to give the students an experience that combined their interests with social studies learning (mandated study of community helpers and careers), observation, note taking, reflection, and writing.

After the Elsewhere Expedition to the lunchroom, the students wrote about their experience by writing thank-you letters to the lunchroom manager and by writing stories. Because friendly letters were also a required component of second-grade instruction, the students were able to combine a requirement with a nice gesture. I use one of these letters, by a student named Janice, to illustrate how the students' high expectations were becoming essential to their learning.

For several months, the students seemed to be driven primarily by *my* high expectations, which I specifically set up as part of the class design. Gradually, however, I noticed that the importance of my high expectations was being supplanted by *their* high expectations.

Janice's first-draft thank-you letter emerged from my data set as an instance in which a student's high expectations met the high expectations I had for the students (see Figure 19). Even though three periods and one capital letter were missing, Janice's letter was outstanding in its conventional correctness, especially because it was her first attempt at letter writing, which was a new form of writing for the class. Janice's letter demonstrated how her good use of correct vocabulary was not limited by her lower level of expertise in spelling. For example, her use of the word *sincerely* and its spelling was correct. Because of the classroom community we had established, Janice was confident in looking up words in the dictionary, as well as making approximations about spellings (e.g., "exiting" for *excited* and

Figure 19
Janice's First-Draft Thank-You Letter
to the Lunchroom Manager

803 Senna Ave.
Goodtown, AL. 35150
January 22, 1998

Dear Mrs. Smith,
Thank you for letting us tour the lunchroom yesterday I loved it so much.
I was exiting about those big pans. The best thing I liked was that colloer that was of it had ice on the floor. I liked those big pans. I like the tomato slicer I wish my dad had one of those.

Sincerely, Janice

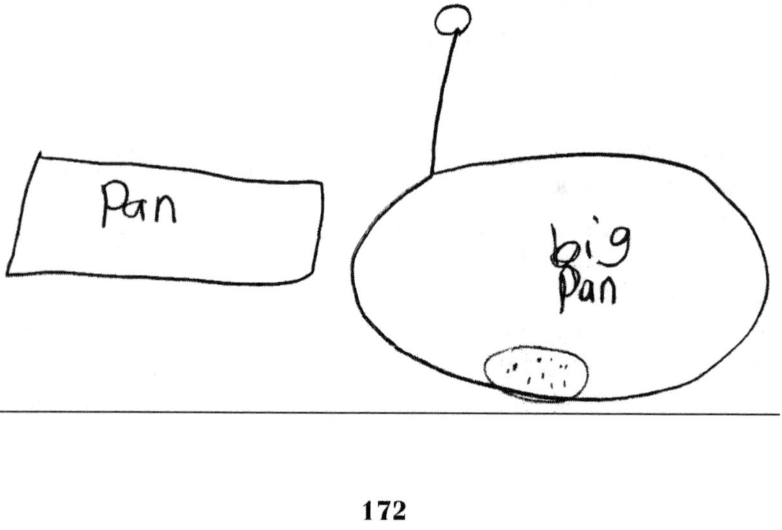

Pan

big Pan

"colloer" for *cooler*). Janice's letter also reflected that her prior knowledge of temperatures and thermometers—probably gathered from her classroom studies in science and math—carried over to this authentic writing activity (i.e., she distinguished between Fahrenheit and Celsius in her letter). Overall, I noted that Janice's letter was in good friendly letter form, held sound ideas, and stayed on the subject. As I evaluated the letter, it was clear that Janice had used her own expectations of herself to dictate the piece. Indeed, Janice had only minor corrections to make before finalizing her letter and delivering it to the lunchroom manager.

I eventually used Janice's thank-you letter as a teaching piece to demonstrate relevant strategies to the other students. More important, however, was the fact that I used it as a teaching piece to illustrate what happens when students set their own standards and high expectations.

The Students as Artists

Importance of Thinking Ahead, Planning, and Predicting

Thinking ahead, planning, and predicting emerged as learning essentials that all the students shared. The field trip to the potato chip factory, airport, and historical site exemplifies the importance of each of these essentials. Each second-grade class could take only one official school trip; therefore, all second-grade classes planned together for this trip, which would conclude several content units mandated by the school district. The students had studied goods and services and transportation in our most recent units. The field trip took place in a large city about 50 miles from our school where we would visit a well-known monument to manufacturing, a potato chip processing plant, and the large municipal airport.

As we were thinking ahead to our upcoming trip and planning what we would do, the students reminded me that we could make some prediction webs, which were simple diagrams that would allow us to predict what might happen on this field trip. The students specifically talked about the prediction webs we had made the previous fall, in preparation for an animal show that we were going to see in our gym, and told me that we should create new prediction webs for our approaching field trip. In the fall, I previously had explained to the class exactly how to construct such a web. That day, however, I asked one student, Peter, to help me as I created a blank web on the chalkboard. The web had a large central circle with five smaller circles attached to it. I asked Peter to tell me the name of one of the places we would visit on our field trip. After Peter told me to write the name of the monument in the large central circle, I asked the other students to help Peter and me predict what we would experience at the monument. Peter called on various students and then told me what to write in each of the five smaller circles. After we had completed this prediction web together, I erased it and asked the students to make three webs of their own (one for each place we would visit on our field trip). Adam and another student, Andrew, asked if we would play a guessing game, which they had created in the fall, when we later shared our webs. In this game, other students could guess what place each web was predicting: We would not be able to tell the others what was in the central circle, although we could reveal the information in the outer circles. (See Figure 20 for two examples of one student's prediction webs—one for the airport and one for the potato chip plant.)

After the field trip, the students and I reflected on the prediction webs to see if our predictions were accurate or inaccurate. The prediction webs became resources for the students as they wrote about what happened on our field trip. As a group, the students acted as artists because they refocused our attention on a past episode of our shared history, in which they had created a game based on a critical-thinking strategy that I originally had introduced to them. This strategy was helpful because it focused the students' attention before and during the field trip. By reminding me to include this as a part of pre-planning in anticipation of the long-awaited field trip, the students made the learning on the field trip *their own*.

Importance of Enjoyment

Enjoyment was one important condition that the students brought about in their roles as artists. One episode especially depicts enjoyment because the students used a shared group experience to create a new learning experience. The children routinely attended art class for 40 minutes each Tuesday. On one Tuesday in April, the school children were scheduled to do a performance for the Parent-Teacher Association that evening, in addition to a performance they already had given to the entire school that morning. Therefore, the children were wearing their special

Figure 20
Two Examples of One Student's Prediction Webs

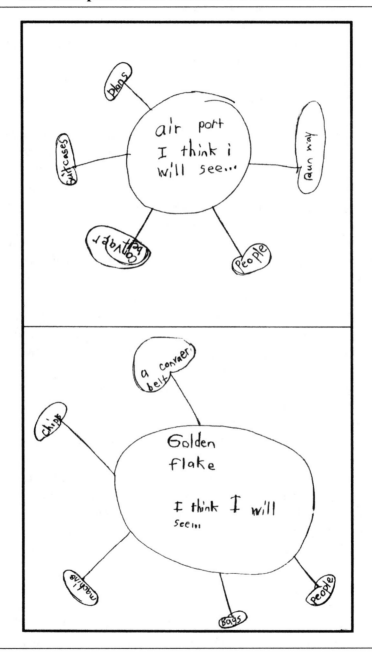

performance clothes that morning, which they would need to wear for that evening's performance as well. Because many of the students were economically disadvantaged, the teachers involved in overseeing the performance had decided that the children would wear blue jeans and solid-colored T-shirts (in a variety of colors) for their performances. Unfortunately for my second graders, this was also the day when the art teacher changed from her usual mode of using crayons as a medium of expression to using *paint*. The majority of my students returned from art class that day literally covered in paint. The students begged me to take them to the restrooms so that they could try to wash the paint out of their performance clothes, because the students wanted to be clean and dry before the performance. As my paint-soaked children led me down the hall to the restrooms, we must have been a spectacle to anyone else who saw us. We spent over an hour getting everyone cleaned up.

When we returned to the classroom, the children started laughing and could hardly contain themselves. Frances called the girls' bathroom "Stewart's Washerteria" and asked the boys if they had "Stewart's Washerteria" in their bathroom. Her comments started joyful hysteria in the classroom—every time the children looked at one another or at me, they began giggling. I laughed so hard that I had tears in my eyes. To anyone else, I doubt this would have been funny, but to us, the mental pictures of children struggling to wash clothes while wearing them and dry themselves under hand dryers were hilarious. Perhaps we enjoyed this as much as we did because it was a shared event in our bonded learning community. Frances, Adam, and Peter said that they knew I would want some stories about this event, so *they* asked if they could have in-class time to write these stories. Because the students specifically asked for writing time to devote to these stories, we made it possible to include time in our schedule for this. Some students eventually created plays called "Stewart's Washerteria." Rather than allowing themselves to be crushed by what could have been a potentially negative situation, the students, through their enjoyment as a group, made an amazing positive literacy learning experience out of this incident.

Conclusion

Children take different paths in their learning, as Clay (1998) reminds readers. It is important for teachers and students to recognize different learning paths that students take and value those paths. Teachers and students must affirm strengths of individuals as they struggle to find the right path into literacy learning. If teachers openly point out positive aspects of students and their work, students will do this also. As students move their focus to the importance and meaning of the work, less teacher attention is needed for managing the behavior of the students. Both teachers and students are able to give more attention to the real work of learning as they find daily enjoyment in the classroom community they have created.

Because culture and language are interrelated in classrooms, teachers must take stock of roles they take on, as well as their expectations and assumptions of students. Arguing for such reflective roles, Heath and Mangiola (1991) encourage teachers to view students' diverse backgrounds and personal experiences, not as differences to be repaired, but as ways to expand knowledge and use language. Indeed, I saw my students' learning grow as I treasured the unique gifts of each person and looked for his or her strengths. The students also began to value what they found in one another and in themselves. As artists, teachers and students call attention to particular details of the classroom, foregrounding important aspects of the classroom that support literacy and community. The students recognized their contributions to class life. Each student recognized in himself or herself—and in one another—artists who had new and valid ideas to help understand the world.

Other researchers seem to affirm the artistic role of teachers, although they do not specifically refer to it by that term. Authorities such as Dewey (1900, 1902/1990), Eisner (1981), and Feldman (1970, 1971) seem to value the artistic role of teachers, realizing that teachers are responsible for envisioning appropriate instruction for individual students. I want to take this thought a step further by asserting that as both *students* and teachers become artists in their own classrooms, they also determine what is affirmed—or has failed to be affirmed—and how that affirmation—or lack of it—is translated into daily classroom life. The classroom environment is determined by what the teacher and the students deem as essential.

CHAPTER 7

What Have We Learned?

My yearlong teacher-research study was important in two ways: (1) It described ways in which particulars of context influenced the interconnectedness of language literacy and classroom community, and (2) it illustrated the importance of reflective practitioner research. The bulk of this chapter describes those first important particulars. This chapter points out what works and what does not in the reality of this classroom, tries to make sense of what this means to teachers and learners, and tries to bridge the gap between theory and practice.

What and What Ways Will We Teach? Themes of the Study

Rather than polarizing literacy issues and forcing people to choose sides (Routman, 1996; Strickland, 1998a; Vacca, 1996), we must look at literacy in new and complex ways (Allington & Walmsley, 1995; Brown, 1991; Gambrell et al., 1999; Willinsky, 1990). We must focus on what *teachers* and *students* do in their quest for literacy learning for all learners.

My teacher research attends to some important aspects of teaching connected with addressing the discrepancy between pedagogy and pragmatics. I asked the following questions as I analyzed the teacher-research data:

- How did I structure my teaching so that the students engaged in active processes of learning; gained deep understandings; and were able to explain, apply, problem solve, and transfer what they learned?

- How did this class focus on literacy processes as well as products?
- How did this class structure social aspects of schooling to make learning most meaningful?
- How did this class become responsive to the condition of each individual learner *personally*?
- How did this class understand and practice *culturally relevant teaching* and *learning*?

Undergirding this classroom study are the beliefs and practices of the teacher-researcher. According to the popular catch phrase "success is in the eye of the beholder," we find what we set out to find; we reap the harvests of our expectations. This is especially true in classrooms in which teachers and students are bombarded with expectations and pressures from a variety of outside power brokers (i.e., politicians, administrators, corporate executives, and university and governmental researchers). As architect and artist, the teacher works to design and mold the structure of this classroom to the students' needs, not fit the students to the classroom structure. Reflection shows that both processes and products of literacy were taught through content of all subject areas, which fulfilled district mandates as well as the needs of individual learners. Students' roles as architects and artists complemented my roles in ways that enhanced the reciprocal relationship of which Gramsci (1971) speaks, so that I was continually a student and every student was continually a teacher.

This study shows how the students and I actively looked for ways to strengthen our connections with one another and our learning. I compare constructing our classroom connections to constructing a raft. The students no longer needed to float on the waters of school assignments, almost as individual corks, popping up here and there, receiving attention and resubmerging, only to pop up again. We used many different methods of binding ourselves together, wrapping and rewrapping our support around one another until we were joined, much as a raft would be joined. Our joining enabled us to float those sometimes-treacherous waters of learning together, supporting and guiding us as we moved toward a common direction. At times, our raft ran aground, and we had to start in a new direction to solve problems. Whereas other times, we were determined to stay in one spot until we understood our difficulties. Sometimes we drifted on the current of mandates. But there were those exciting times when we let our ideas and experiences carry us beyond our expectations to new learning destinations. Whatever our direction, our raft was strong because it was bound by common literacy experiences and events. In the attempt to explain the construction of this raft of learning, I offer the following discussion of the themes and subthemes of this study.

Talk

Talk, or discourse, emerged as one of the primary connections between students across their different backgrounds and experiences. This talk occurred between students, as well as between the students and me. Talk was the basis of our classroom community and the heart of our language learning as we read and discussed literature and our own writings. Shared talk moved the focus of the classroom from me as teacher to the students and me as a community of learners. Indeed, the discoveries we made and the learning we shared were made more powerful by talk that occurred between us. Many scaffolds were in place to support learners in our class, although talk was one of the most predominant (Bruner, 1978; Dorn et al., 1998; Rogoff, 1990).

Talk emerged from my research data in a variety of ways that also have been discussed by other researchers. The predominant form of talk in this teacher research was the use of talk between peers to understand one another and to communicate their thoughts. According to Piaget, this type of talk helps children *objectify* their knowledge (1955, 1977). There was also talk between novices and more experienced students that moved the novices forward in their thinking and their work; the novices were then able to do with help that which they could not accomplish by themselves (Vygotsky, 1934/1978). Talk was the link between our thoughts and our actions (Vygotsky, 1934/1997). Talk influenced students' learning because it provided them with opportunities to relate new information to their existing understanding (Barnes & Todd, 1995).

Talk was important in every aspect of our classroom as it transcended both age and culture (Pierce & Gilles, 1993). Talk gave us a personal way of knowing within our social setting, which made our classroom an inviting place that promoted our interactions (Watson, 1993). My teacher research demonstrates the power of talk for building a learning community (Barnes, 1971; Dickinson, 1993; Dyson, 1989, 1993; Short & Pierce, 1990). Because it was an integral and valid part of learning, talk empowered us as members of our learning community (Cree & Donaldson, 1996; Jones, 1996a, 1996b; Kirk, 1996; VonDras, 1993).

I created situations in which students felt comfortable opening up and expressing their feelings. By turning over much of the discussion to the students, I worked to avoid monopolizing classroom conversations in order to encourage student talk (Kincheloe, 1991). Class discussions facilitated students' learning by enabling them to refine and reorganize concepts as they discovered what things were and what they meant (King, 1985). Students built on their learning through reflection and explanation. Our classroom was a language learning environment in which we naturally used talk to support language (Jaggar, 1985), especially as we worked through the processes of reading about, writing about, and investigating science, social studies, and math. Verbal and written talk mediated our learning (Patterson, 1996).

The students and I used "the power tools" (Fraser & Skolnick, 1994, p. 145) of listening and talk to aid learning and the construction of knowledge within our learning community. Our talk served our learning community in many ways, especially our critical thinking and social interactions. The students created scaffolds through talk because "talking together lets students stand on each other's shoulders as they become joint creators of meaning" (Fraser & Skolnick, p. 158). Listening was also important to our learning community: Students had many opportunities to listen to literature being read to them, to listen to classmates' writing, and to listen to one another reflect on that literature and writing, questioning and searching for multiple responses and giving rationales for their answers. Students listened to me and to their peers, and we listened to them as well.

Peterson and Eeds (1990) note that in natural learning, "dialogue is a process of coproducing meaning. Dialogue partners need one another's patience, ideas, and encouragement. The give-and-take nature of the system depends on other participants to take up an idea, expand it, and add to it" (p. 21). I often used this "give-and-take system" within the classroom because I believe that "dialogue [is] the best pedagogy" (Peterson & Eeds, p. 21).

Discourse as Acquired and Learned Literacies

Looking at discourse within my classroom—both written and oral language—leads to discussion of the various literacies that children (and others) control and practice. Gee (1989) discusses discourses as power structures that embody values and viewpoints. Discourses involve "a socially accepted association among ways of using language, of thinking, and of acting that can be used to identify oneself as a member of a socially meaningful group or 'social network'" (Gee, p. 18). Various discourses were in evidence in my second-grade classroom. Primarily, there was the so-called "dominant discourse" of school standard English. For the most part, however, standard English was a "secondary discourse" for the majority of my students, because many did not speak totally standard English in their normal, everyday conversations. In his article, Gee makes a point to distinguish *acquisition* from *learning*—especially with regard to gaining control of discourse(s). Readers must understand that

> *Acquisition* is a process of acquiring something subconsciously by exposure to models and a process of trial and error, without a process of formal teaching. It happens in natural settings which are meaningful and functional in the sense that the acquirers know that they need to acquire something in order to function and they in fact want to so function. This is how most people come to control their first language.
>
> *Learning* is a process that involves conscious knowledge gained through teaching, though not necessarily from someone officially designated a teacher. This teaching involves explanation and analysis, that is, breaking down the thing to be learned into its analytic parts. It inherently involves attaining, along with the matter being taught, some degree of meta-knowledge about the matter. (Gee, p. 20)

Gee further separates acquisition and learning by explaining that they "are differential sources of power: acquirers usually beat learners at performance, while learners usually beat acquirers at talking about it, that is, at explication, explanation, analysis, and criticism" (1989, p. 21). In terms of my study, this means that the students were gaining control over their two discourses—their primary discourse, which was the language they brought with them from home, and their secondary discourse, which was the language of school, or standard English—in two very different ways. I believe that my students gained control over discourse by *acquiring* control over their discourse. Gee states two principles that he believes to be true about literacy learning. I used these principles to inform my teaching in the classroom and interpret data from my research:

Any discourse (primary or secondary) is for most people most of the time only mastered through acquisition, not learning. Thus, literacy is mastered through acquisition, not learning, that is, it requires exposure to models in natural, meaningful, and functional settings, and teaching is not liable to be very successful—it may even initially get in the way. Time spent on learning and not acquisition is time not well spent if the goal is mastery in performance.

There is also a principle having to do with learning that I think true: One cannot critique one discourse with another one (which is the only way to seriously criticize and thus change a discourse) unless one has meta-level knowledge in both discourses. And this meta-knowledge is best developed through learning, even when one has to a certain extent already acquired that discourse. Thus, powerful literacy, as defined above, almost always involves learning, and not just acquisition. (p. 23)

Acquisition and learning are ways to reach very different goals. For example, Gee (1989) explains that mainstream middle-class children appear to be *learning* literacies in school, although they are *acquiring* literacies through their home experiences, which—because of their control of that discourse—also prepares children to acquire literacies during school experiences. However,

children from non-mainstream homes [in the United States] often do not get the opportunity to acquire dominant secondary discourses—including those connected with the school—in their homes, due to their parents' lack of access to these discourses. At school they cannot practice what they haven't yet got and they are exposed mostly to a process of learning and not acquisition. Therefore, little acquisition goes on. (Gee, p. 24)

This means that they acquire little proficiency in actual performance of literacy. Research by Cook-Gumperz, Gumperz, and Heath (as cited in Gee, 1989) shows that many school-based secondary discourses are in conflict with discourses of the home and larger community. In fact, Gee bases his definition of "non-mainstream" on this conflict between these children's use and mastery of dominant secondary discourse (such as school discourse) and their "primary discourse [of the home] and their community-based secondary discourses" (p. 25).

Gee's theoretical remarks lead to several practical implications that he sets forth and that I have interpreted as important to understanding the data from my study:

- We must focus classrooms toward acquisition, not learning, if our goal is to help nonmainstream children attain mastery of literacies.
- We should value and build on the fact that mainstream children are actually using much of the classroom teaching and learning not to learn but to acquire as they practice their developing skills.
- We need to be aware that nonmainstream children often will have a more difficult time than mainstream children in using and mastering dominant discourses of school.

Our challenge is to develop "wider and more humane understanding[s] of mastery and its connections to gatekeeping" (Gee, 1989, p. 25). Gee notes that it is commonplace in the world of art to allow conflicts to give rise to new sorts of mastery; he suggests that we make it so in society at large. Data from my study suggest that children were engaging in literacy in many ways that were helpful to their acquisition of literacy—especially as they practiced story as a discourse— and to their learning of literacy—especially as they gained knowledge of the parts and processes of language.

Authentic Experiences

To parallel Dewey's (1938/1997) principle of continuity—which may also be called the "experiential continuum" (p. 33) in which experiences are linked cumulatively to each other—I planned for many of the second-grade students' activities to foster educational growth not only to enhance their present understandings, but also to enable and connect to future learning. Elaborating on educative and miseducative experiences, Dewey writes,

If an experience arouses curiosity, strengthens initiative, and sets up desires and purposes that are sufficiently intense to carry a person over dead places in the future, continuity works in a very different way. Every experience is a moving force. Its value can be judged only on the ground of what it moves toward and into. (p. 38)

I also tried to make our classroom experiences correspond to Dewey's (1938/1997) principle of interaction, in which transactions occur between students and their environment. In this sense, "environment" means "whatever conditions interact with personal needs, desires, purposes, and capacities to create the experience which is had" (Dewey, p. 44). According to Dewey, the two principles of continuity and interaction are not separate but work together "in active union" (p. 44) to provide the measure and value of an educative experience. In my role as architect of the classroom, I designed "educative experiences" (Dewey, p. 28) in which, according to Dewey, everything depends on two aspects of the quality of the experience—the "immediate agreeableness or disagreeableness" (p. 27) of the experience and its influence on future experiences. I, therefore, worked to encourage experiences that were both engaging at the time and thought-provoking enough to foster future inquiry and learning. With my students, I planned relevant, meaningful experiences as the center of our work. In my role as artist, I ascertained capacities and needs of individual students in order to ensure that the content of the experiences would "satisfy these needs and develop these capacities" (Dewey, 1938/1997, p. 65). My flexible classroom structure allowed each student to embrace his or her individuality yet provided focus to give all the students direction. Our learning process was also a social process in which we formed a community because,

> When education is based upon experience and educative experience is seen to be a social process, the situation changes radically. The teacher loses the position of external boss or dictator but takes on that of leader of group activities. (Dewey, 1938/1997, p. 66)

My students had an impact on their own teaching and learning because they were part of a community that encouraged their active participation.

One example of the students' shared authentic experiences is the daily Elsewhere Expeditions, which connected literacy and community through the overlap of shared experiences, processes, and products. Elsewhere Expeditions invested the various reciprocal themes and subthemes that emerged from the data set with relevance and purpose, binding together the students' lives in and out of the classroom.

Choice and Ownership

Choice was important to the students' literacy learning and their sense of community. Students invested themselves more completely in assignments when they were given some aspect of choice. For example, students seemed to have more interest in completing a piece of writing if they were able to choose the genre in which they could write, the length of the piece, or the topic of the piece.

Choices seemed to allow the children to feel ownership of literacy tasks. That ownership encouraged children to be more respectful of one another's work, especially when that work was being shared in class: Students listened to one another and participated in in-depth discussions about one another's work. This give-and-take environment grew over the school year. At first, I provided all the comments on students' pieces, but this eventually changed as the students began to talk about what they liked or about another person's work, ask questions about other students' work, or make suggestions to improve other students' work.

This choice in the classroom also gave students a sense of ownership of their writing. As this sense of ownership developed, students began to use peer audiences to help them make their writing pieces stronger. These peer audiences were usually self-selected by the students who wanted help in creating stronger pieces. Ownership empowered the students as literacy learners, much as it empowered the students described in Allen and Mason's *Risk Makers, Risk Takers, Risk Breakers: Reducing the Risks for Young Literacy Learners* (1989). I observed this ownership in many students' pieces, and the students, in their year-end interviews, often told me that they felt this ownership of their work. Pride of process and product in my classroom was possible because of the students' sense of ownership that developed over time.

Collaboration

Another important theme throughout my study was collaboration, because the classroom design provided many opportunities for collaborative interaction between the students. One powerful example of this collaborative interaction was group writing. As I analyzed the classroom data, I found three components that emerged during each episode of group writing: story, process, and negotiation. Students used various writing and thinking strategies when working in small groups; therefore, group members often needed to cooperate and compromise to reach their final goals.

Our communicative classroom environment was constantly constructed by participants as we collaborated in various ways, which supported prior research from an interactive sociolinguistic perspective (e.g., Goodman, 1986; Goodman, Smith, et al., 1987; Harste et al., 1984; Heath, 1983; Smith, 1973; Weade & Green, 1989). Social and cultural aspects emerged especially during collaborative interactions. Collaborative inquiry expanded the range of the students' roles and my role as teacher as we worked together to make sense of new ideas and experiences. Collaborative inquiry enhanced our learning and community as it similarly had enhanced learning and community in classrooms described by other researchers (e.g., Barnes & Todd, 1995; Dickinson, 1993; Katz & Chard, 1979; Nussbaum & Puckett, 1990; Peterson, 1992).

A Print-Rich Literacy Environment

A print-rich literacy environment also strengthened literacy and community in my classroom. For example, availability and use of literature created many connections between (a) student and student, (b) teacher and student, (c) teacher's roles and students' roles, (d) literacy and community, and (e) helper/helped and the composer/audience.

My second-grade students were quick to notice the number of books available everywhere in the classroom. In my field notes, I documented many students as they commented on the number of books in the classroom. Earlier in the year, one student, Peter, told me, "Well, I can tell you *really* like books. You've got 'em everywhere!" My goal in placing these books throughout the classroom was to try to get the students to notice that there were many books available to *them—* books of all shapes and sizes, books on many subjects, and books on many levels of difficulty.

The students and I often discussed the need for lots of books in our room. Even though we had hundreds of books in our classroom, we soon found ourselves going to the library or to other classrooms in search of books in a particular genre, by a particular author, or on a special subject.

After the students checked out library books, they often brought them to me so I could read them to the class. They eagerly wanted to share each new find and would tell me things such as, "You gotta [*sic*] read this one! The other kids will really like it!" Books were a vital part of our classroom and soon became a vital part of each student's life.

Students had immediate access to literature, which helped them to work in ways that integrated their literacy learning into various content areas. I made a range of levels of text available to support the needs of all levels of learners, and as students grew and their interests changed, I provided new literature to meet those needs. To fulfill those needs, for example, I made trips to the local library every 2 weeks to satisfy the students' requests for new books. Access to books has strong support in valued research. For example, Allington and Cunningham (1996) talk about the importance of providing students with easy access to books (i.e., having books available in easily accessible classroom libraries) and having a lot of easy reads available to them as well. McQuillan (1998) gives further evidence of the importance of this access, providing statistics that illustrate that "more reading leads to better reading achievement" (p. 69). Morrow and Smith (1990) also support the stance that children must consistently have immediate access to books. In our classroom, the students and I were not the only ones who realized the importance of our print-rich environment. Students' parents, administrators, adult helpers, and older students also commented on the amount of print available in my classroom, the ease with which the students accessed this print, and the students' interest and diligence in reading this print. The importance of a print-rich literacy environment is confirmed by various experts in the literacy acquisition research base (e.g., Bloome, 1983, 1989; Cambourne & Turbill, 1991; Cazden, 1981; Clay, 1993; Goodman, Smith, et al., 1987; Manning et al., 1989). Research shows that a rich literacy environment, with a variety of literature that causes a range of interactions, produces concepts and language made stronger through those literacy experiences (Edwards et al., 1979/1994; Flood, Heath, & Lapp, 1997; Goodman, 1985; Goodman & Burke, 1980; Goodman & Wilde, 1992; Wolf & Heath, 1992).

Interconnectedness of Literacy Elements

The interconnectedness of literacy also bonded my second-grade students. Rather than teaching reading, writing, and oral language as separate components of language, I chose to interweave them in my instruction and in the various contexts of the students' learning. I made clear to the students that reading, writing, and oral language were not separate tasks. This idea is validated by research that describes reading, writing, speaking, and listening as interdependent because each rests on a speech base (e.g., Goodman, Smith, et al., 1987; Holdaway, 1979; Nelson & Calfee, 1998). This research also stresses the importance of learning *all* aspects of language in real settings; therefore, I chose to integrate reading, writing, speaking, listening, spelling, and thinking for best results. In fact, it seemed impossible to separate literacy elements—no matter which element of language the students and I used, we found ourselves somehow engaged in all the others.

The students and I used content as the basis for our work with the elements of language. As we studied content, we used many elements of our language processing to strengthen our understandings of subject matter. We could not divorce our language from the real world of content and context, which enabled us to engage diligently in activities for long periods of time. Because we felt our activities had a purpose, we invested ourselves in them—we had real questions and inquired in authentic ways. This integration of all aspects of language made our learning interesting, focused, purposeful, and fun.

High Expectations

I originally used my high expectations to design the structure of the classroom, but the students' high expectations of themselves emerged as an important cord of the classroom environment. In my classroom—as in other literacy-based classrooms—I valued the processes and products of literacy efforts, as did the students.

I emphasized the significance of literacy processes to the students through daily reading and writing workshops. As suggested by Bissex (1980) and Newkirk (1989), I also encouraged spontaneous writing in the classroom so I could observe the range of the students' writing and call attention to writing possibilities that built on that spontaneity. Following Goodman's procedures (1985), I looked for development of language and knowledge in my students' reading and writing processes both across time and in different settings to see if my high expectations were being met.

As the students created their own books, stories, and projects, they learned to appreciate their literacy products. And as high expectations of themselves grew, the students were not satisfied to create products of inferior quality. In-class sharing of student work gave students the opportunity to see good things in other students' work as well as their own. This sharing helped them to ensure that their products indeed had good things.

Acceptance of Approximations

Acceptance of approximations connected my classroom as well. Acceptance of approximations is a cornerstone of much of the language acquisition literature (e.g., Brown & Cambourne, 1993; Edwards et al., 1979/1994; Ferreiro & Teberosky, 1979/1994; Peterson & Eeds, 1990). Because the students and I built an environment of acceptance—especially of approximations—students seemed to be willing to try new things in their writing, reading, speaking, and spelling because they did not fear ridicule of their peers. This willingness to approximate often gave strength to students' work because they focused more on expressing their ideas. Because the students were willing to take risks and express their ideas, they made essential connections between themselves and the literacy learning community as a whole.

Acceptance helped each student to become more tolerant of other students' differences in learning and respectful of the in-class contributions of other students. Students became more accepting of one another as we focused on the strengths of individual students. Although I at first feared that some students might be left out because of their learning difficulties I came to realize that in this environment of acceptance, students viewed one another's comments as equally important. For example, Susan was a student who was unable to perform the simplest tasks and could only read the easier-level books. Susan, however, worked very hard to be an active member of the class: She eagerly listened to other students as they talked in class, found partners to guide her through assignments, and worked hard until she was able to read books considered to be for emergent readers. The other students accepted her as a reader and writer because they saw her work and try hard; students were not concerned that she was working at a different level than they were. In her year-end interview, for example, Jessica cited Susan as one of the best readers in the class. I suspect this is because Jessica knew that Susan could read some books well, even though Jessica realized Susan had read only the easier books.

Susan demonstrated that students who have learning differences do benefit from being full and equal members of the learning community (Aldridge, Eddowes, & Kuby, 1998; Avery, 1987; Derman-Sparks & Phillips, 1997; Ladson-Billings, 1994; Mallory & New, 1994). Our predictable structure—our acceptance of approximations—provided a secure, rich language-filled environment, which enabled and supported the students' learning of communication skills. The students and I welcomed diverse learners into our learning community, which was a learning community that aided *all* students. The stimulation of language and literacy is as much the responsibility of schools as it is of families (Chall, Jacobs, & Baldwin, 1990).

Friendships

Friendships influenced the reciprocal relationships, such as helper/helped and composer/audience, within this learning community. Friendships built on mutual trust and caring emerged as a crucial component in building both literacy and community. The fact that there was virtually no teasing or put-downs as the students shared their ideas and work is remarkable because of the range of diversity within our classroom. Perhaps the students respected diversity because I set the tone for this atmosphere during that all-important first day of school by discussing with the children the importance of looking for "good things" in people, situations, and performance. But the students carried through with this respect by building trust with other students and making the classroom a safe, comfortable place to be. This trust was most evident when student work was shared with the class, as the students' intense listening and response to each other's work helped build a secure environment. Researchers support enabling caring relationships within literacy learning communities (e.g., Charney, 1996; Donoahue et al., 1996; Gandini, 1979/1994; Malaguzzi, 1979/1994; Nussbaum & Puckett, 1990; Wolf & Heath, 1992).

Sharing

By allowing students time and opportunity to practice shared literate behaviors in the classroom, I enabled the students to support one another as learners and friends. I integrated my content instruction with real and purposeful shared experiences, which were followed by discussions, reading, and writing. I believed this integration would afford the students time and opportunities to practice their growing literacy expertise and internalize the complex system of language. By taking consistent time and opportunity to share processes and products of literacy in the classroom, we built connections with literature and with one another. Key language acquisition literature (e.g., Brown & Cambourne, 1993; Chomsky, 1969; Clay, 1979; Ferreiro & Teberosky, 1979/1994; Goodman, Smith, et al., 1987; Graves, 1983; Heath, 1983) emphasizes time and opportunity as *crucial* for practicing literacy processes and creating literacy products. I assert that it is equally important to provide opportunities for sharing them.

Reciprocal Roles: Helper/Helped and Composer/Audience

Having a real audience and receiving feedback from that audience appeared to be crucial for my students' literacy learning. My students' need for an audience confirmed important research built on detailed investigations in classrooms, which asserts that the need for children to have an audience for their writing is important (e.g., Brown & Cambourne, 1993; Calkins, 1986, 2001; Dyson, 1989, 1993; Graves, 1983, 1994). For example, students often rushed to me or to other students to have us read what they had written, listen to their ideas, or just share enjoyment in their work. After sharing their work with an audience, students readily revised if they perceived a mismatch between what they meant to communicate and what their audience seemed to understand (Freedman, 1985). My students needed support of an external audience as they began internalizing responses and planning for ways to make their work more understandable for readers and listeners. Response and feedback, which Vygotsky's (1934/1978) research points out as important learning tools, also emerged as important learning tools in my classroom.

Enjoyment

Holdaway (1979) says that "learning to read and to write ought to be one of the most joyful and successful of human undertakings. Notoriously, it is not so" (p. 11). A little more than decade later, in his foreword to Fisher's *Joyful Learning: A Whole Language Kindergarten*

(1991), Holdaway acknowledged a different classroom perspective reflective of "purposeful accomplishments and joyful satisfactions of real thought and action..." (p. xi). That joy is missing from many classrooms because of the regrettable search for one "best practice," which approaches each student's learning in the same way. In my classroom, however, I observed and documented joy in my students, especially from shared literacy events and the literature itself. The students showed their joy in many ways through the expressions on their faces and in their drawings and writings.

The actual reading of literature produced spontaneous celebration, such as when someone giggled as he or she enjoyed reading a book. Humorous words and illustrations in books such as *The Day Jimmy's Boa Ate the Wash* (Noble, 1980), *Arthur's Pet Business* (Brown, 1993), *The Stupids Die* (Allard, 1981), and *The Stupids Have a Ball* (Allard, 1978) produced much spontaneous student laughter. Shel Silverstein's humorous drawings in *Where the Sidewalk Ends* (1974) and *A Light in the Attic* (1981) also brought great enjoyment to the students, especially the boys. Peterson and Eeds (1990) note, "One of our foremost goals in teaching about literature is to involve children in story and to see that they find enjoyment—that they take in joy through story" (p. 70). The students often selected these humorous books for shared in-class reading, but students also read these books to each other, to me, and by themselves. To recapture the earlier enjoyment of reading these humorous selections, students often asked to have these selections reread to the class. Our classroom community freely expressed and looked for joy through literature. The students and I tried to "pass on the joy of literacy" to one another (Brinkley, 1993, p. 211).

Meaning Making

My students searched for meaning in everything they did because I frequently asked, "Does that make sense?" I asked the Title I instructional assistant and the classroom volunteer to use that question with the students as well so that we could encourage meaning making in each classroom task. Early in the year, I noticed the impact of asking this question as the students began to ask themselves and their peers, "Does that make sense?" For example, if a student was reading and inadvertently made a miscue, it was common for that student to stop and question himself or herself. That student would then reread the same passage to search for what *did* make sense. If I was with a student when he or she made the miscue and corrected it, I asked, "What did you just do that a good reader does?" The student's answer, which usually came forth quite naturally, was, "I went back and read it again until it made sense."

Drawing from the three language cueing systems used in reading—semantic, syntactic, and graphophonic—I encouraged students to enter reading through the semantic system so that they could more easily understand what they were reading (Butler & Turbill, 1984; Goodman, Watson, et al., 1987). Making meaning was integral to students' success in reading, writing, and overall learning. King (1985) asserts that children learn more than words or principles for making grammatical constructions in social interactions involving people, objects, and routines; "They learn a system for making and sharing meaning" (p. 21). Meaning emerged as a central focus of our study as it has in other research (e.g., Knapp, 1995). Indeed, Knapp devoted an entire book, *Teaching for Meaning in High-Poverty Classrooms* (1995), to the importance of meaning in instruction. Harste et al. (1984), Patterson (1996), and Rosenblatt (1978/1994) view reading and learning as transactions between people and texts as they are experienced in multiple social and cultural settings. The students and I confirmed this as particular contexts and purposes of our transactions altered meanings.

Studies by Bussis et al. (1976) and Bussis, Chittenden, Amarel, and Klausner (1985) discuss the significant periods of time and variety of contexts in which teachers are able to observe and interact with students in an attempt to understand the meanings students bring to their learning. These researchers agree that the special relationship that develops between teachers and students enables teachers to share common understandings with the students as well as establish interpersonal understandings. I concur with this assessment, as this special relationship developed between my students and me. I also believe that young children need to be with the same teacher for the entire day to allow maximum development of these relationships.

Reflections on Teacher Research and Educational Goals

Perceptions of teachers can change over time in primary classrooms, especially from the perspective of the teacher-researcher who embodies the dual role of insider-outsider within his or her own classroom. Introspection and reflection are valued aspects of practitioner research that enable teachers to think about and express belief systems or philosophies of teaching while acknowledging that these philosophies will affect how, why, and what they teach.

As I reflect on the importance of reflective practitioner research, I realize that it has gained a prominent role in my thinking and in my research. My teacher research has changed me and the way that I teach. In the final analysis process, as I examined the data and struggled to synthesize them into a comprehensible unit, a model seemed to emerge that represented the importance of teacher research. This model (see Figure 21) views reflective practitioner research as both a learning process and a catalyst for change, in which specific changes occurred in perceptions, thinking, and in the classroom. I offer this model as a way for people to examine my research findings.

Figure 21
Model Representing the Importance
of Reflective Practitioner Research

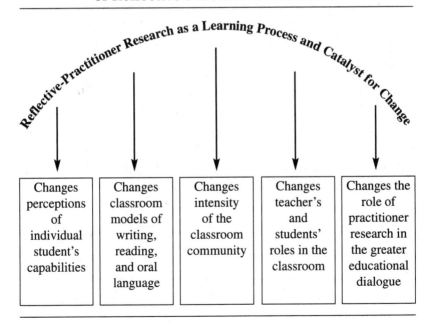

| Changes perceptions of individual student's capabilities | Changes classroom models of writing, reading, and oral language | Changes intensity of the classroom community | Changes teacher's and students' roles in the classroom | Changes the role of practitioner research in the greater educational dialogue |

Traditionally, there have been only two voices in the debate concerning educational issues and schools: (1) the strong, traditional voice of academicians who have debated primarily among themselves, and (2) the newer, more demanding voice of public and private researchers who often are funded by sources who have a vested interest in the outcomes of the debate and the research. I call for a third voice to contribute to these educational dialogues, which is the voice of the teacher-researcher. I use *dialogue* rather than *debate* because the term *dialogue* indicates an open exchange of ideas in which there usually is a multidirectional conversation to which *all* parties have a contribution to make. The term *debate* implies a reasoned argument in which each side tries to best the other's argument. In a debate, there are always winners and losers. A dialogue promises the possibility of compromise, which results because various parties are heard and understood. In a dialogue of peers, in which each participant acknowledges the value of other participants, there is a greater possibility for compromise and solutions. Although much work has been done by practitioner researchers in the last 30 years—and even more in the last 10 years—this qualitative research undertaken by practicing teachers is not always accorded the same respect as more traditional quantitative research. During this important time in educational decision making, teachers who are reflective practitioners and rigorous researchers must have a voice that is respected in the educational dialogue of the United States. As teachers, I believe we have a duty to help those on the outside of classrooms to see classrooms from the inside. Investigators must combine *all* research methods to spotlight important issues in education, such as diversity, power, pedagogy, and praxis, so that these issues can be understood more thoroughly.

Donoahue (1996) writes, "Teacher research often begins with one teacher working alone with his or her students, but its full power and influence is not felt until the community is extended beyond the classroom walls" (p. 102). With this in mind, my study attempts to present an alternative view of language construction to teachers who have never attempted holistic, process-oriented styles of teaching. In an effort to explain the importance of meaning making in the construction of language, I also try to contribute to the current body of research by presenting an in-depth picture of an early childhood process-centered language literacy environment. I have accommodated the qualitative aspect of this research by providing specific examples and details of classroom life. These details should enable readers to enter the study as insiders, to draw their own conclusions as they reflect on their own ideas, interpretations, and classroom practices. I have also provided specific methodology to connect my research to the broader issues of "best practice" in literacy. My research aimed to connect theory and practice. McFarland and Stansell (1993) encourage today's teacher-researchers to "eliminate the theory-to-practice gap.... Use what they learn from research to provide better learning opportunities for their students" (p. 17). Hursh (1995) speaks of the gap between theory and practice as

> two worlds. The university and the schools. The ivory tower and the trenches.... I have been concerned with the work of connecting both ends of education: the preparation and development of teachers, and the improvement in our understanding of educational theory and teaching practices. (p. 14)

Hursh's words have personal implications for me as I leave behind my 26 years in public school education and embark on a new career at the university level. I, too, hope to contribute to closing that "theory-to-practice gap" as I instruct and interact with preservice and inservice teachers. I am excited at the possibilities as I begin this endeavor with knowledge to share about my years of working with and learning from young children.

My teacher-research study also attempts to add to the current teacher-research literature. Teacher research is a well-established methodology that is supported by knowledgeable researchers (e.g., Atwell, 1987; Cochran-Smith & Lytle, 1990; Duckworth & the Experienced Teachers Group, 1997; Goff, 1996; Goswami & Stillman, 1987; Grover, 1990; Kamii, 1979, 1989, 1990; Mohr, 1987, 1996; Odell, 1987; Smith, 1980). Burnaford (1996), Elliott (1985), and Feldman and Atkin (1995) implore teachers who are researchers in their own classrooms to share insights gained through the research process. I hope that my study, which shows the possibilities of teacher research to change teaching perceptions, encourages other teachers to conduct research in their own classrooms. According to Stenhouse (1985), "The improvement of critique of classrooms and schools is central to the problem of quality in education, and it depends heavily upon practitioners extending vicariously their experience of schools and classrooms as cases" (p. 267).

There were many components that emerged from my study that mutually influenced language literacy and classroom community. I find it helpful to think of these components as being centered around the physical, social, and psychological environments of the classroom. We must be sure that the classroom environment acts as both a safety net and a launchpad for our students' learning. This environment includes support in literacy processes and products, as well as larger social supports such as talk, authentic experience, choice, responsibility, and sharing. This mutually supportive classroom environment also includes psychological supports such as value and affirmation of individuals and their efforts, tolerance of differences, acceptance of approximations, and joy in people and experiences.

My research concludes that students want and need the support of caring teachers and peers as they struggle to learn and grow. Teachers do matter. They cannot be replaced by prepackaged curricula. The elements of good teaching that I present here are not new, but they are needed now more than ever before. In our process of reaching to learn literacy, the students and I built a community. The elements of good teaching did not work separately in this community, but together to build the community. Teachers who engage in reflective practice examine and articulate praxis, or reflection on action. By looking, over time, at dynamic contexts of learning, these teacher-researchers, or reflective practitioners, explore the ways in which those contexts support and are supported by a community of learners. They view themselves and their students as reciprocal learners working together to construct both conditions and expectations for learning. These reflective practitioners investigate the ways in which they, informed by their theoretical beliefs, act as architects and artists who interact with students engaged in learning as architects and artists, also. Reflective practice forms the basis of a classroom community that is a multilayered and interactive whole (see Figure 22).

As reflective practitioners examine and articulate their reflections and actions, they find themselves looking in new ways at multiple layers of learning and interaction within their classrooms. This research is recursive and deepens as teacher-researchers strive to understand complex interactions in two ways: (1) They go deeper with each successive

Figure 22
Reflective Practice as an Interactive Whole

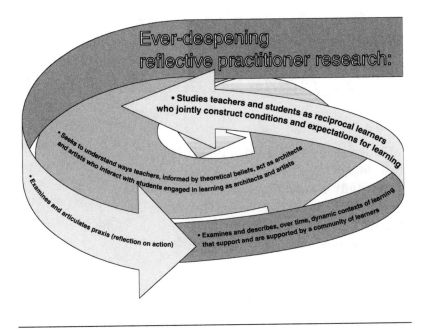

Ever-deepening reflective practitioner research:

• Studies teachers and students as reciprocal learners who jointly construct conditions and expectations for learning

• Seeks to understand ways teachers, informed by theoretical beliefs, act as architects and artists who interact with students engaged in learning as architects and artists

• Examines and articulates praxis (reflection on action)

• Examines and describes, over time, dynamic contexts of learning that support and are supported by a community of learners

reexamination of the data within a particular study, and (2) they go deeper in *seeing* and in *explaining* their findings with each successive study in which they engage. It is important during this era of attention to high-stakes testing and "scientifically replicable research" that *real* children in *real* contexts of schooling are not ignored. It is equally as important that the *voices of teachers* are heard, as they articulate their understandings gleaned from high-quality, rigorous research into their own practice and as they adjust their practice to best fit the needs of their students. This must be the basis of any form of "best practice"; that is, this practice must be tailored to the particular individuals involved.

Time Frame for the Study

Initiation of the Study: July–August 1997
(Selection of site and subjects; access and permission
for study granted)

Proposal to Doctoral Dissertation Committee	July 10
Approval of Dissertation Project Panel	July 21
Review and consent from school district superintendent	July 22
Review and consent from school principal	July 23
Approval of Institutional Review Board for Human Use	August 13
Consent of students' parents	August 14
Consent of students involved as participants	August 14
Consent of Title I instructional assistant as participant	August 14
Consent of classroom volunteer as participant	August 14

Exploratory Phase of Research: August–December 1997
(Data collection and analysis)

Spradley's (1980) ethnographic research cycle	August–December

- Began by asking broad ethnographic questions
- Collected ethnographic data
- Compiled ethnographic record using participant interviews, field notes, audiotapes, videotapes, photography, and classroom artifacts
- Analyzed data

- Investigated additional questions generated from data
- Continued the cycle

Glaser and Strauss's (1967) constant   August–December
  comparative method
- Collected and analyzed the data
  simultaneously
- Jotted down field notes daily
- Fleshed out field notes nightly
- Transcribed audiotapes and videotapes
  three times each week to reflect on patterns
  and meanings; noted personal comments
  and insights
- Coded emerging themes and subthemes as
  patterns emerged

Monthly retellings as integral part of our   August–December
  literacy experiences

Daily routines established and carried out   August–December
- Class meetings
- Daily news
- Reading and writing workshops
- Response journals
- Group stories
- Elsewhere Expeditions
- Group shared stories (postlunch)
- Shared reflections
- Lunch conversations

Qualitative Reading Inventories to gather   August
  baseline data

Introduction of note-taking strategies   September 2, 3, 5,
                                               8, 10

Extensive physical examination of data   October
  to ascertain patterns

Completion of draft of dissertation   November
  context chapter

Completion of draft of dissertation   December
  philosophy chapter

| Exploration of "Train Trunk" in classroom (intensive reading, writing, and discussion about trains) | December 16, 17, 18, 19 |

Medial Phase of Research: January–March 1998
(Continuation of data collection and analysis, with addition of formal interviews)

| Spradley's (1980) ethnographic research cycle | January–March |

- Continued asking broad ethnographic questions
- Collected ethnographic data
- Compiled ethnographic record using participant interviews, field notes, audiotapes, videotapes, photography, and classroom artifacts
- Analyzed data
- Investigated additional questions generated from data
- Continued the cycle

| Glaser and Strauss's (1967) constant comparative method | January–March |

- Collected and analyzed the data simultaneously
- Jotted down field notes daily
- Fleshed out field notes nightly
- Transcribed audiotapes and videotapes three times each week to reflect on patterns and meanings; noted personal comments and insights
- Coded emerging themes and subthemes as patterns emerged

Group writing projects	January–March
Audiotapes made of individuals' retellings	January–March
Audiotapes made of individuals' running records	January–March
Videotapes made of individual and group literacy events	January–March
Significant Elsewhere Expeditions	January–March
• Lunchroom tour	January 21

• Field trip to potato chip factory, airport, and historical site	March 9
Midyear portfolio evaluations and recording of miscue analysis on audiotapes	January
Formal interviews with key informants	January
Formal interviews with all participants of study	January
Extensive physical examination of data to ascertain patterns	January
Exploration of "Train Trunk" in classroom (intensive reading, writing, and discussion about trains)	January 5, 6, 7
Completion of draft of introductory dissertation chapter	February
Extensive physical examination of data to ascertain patterns	March
Completion of draft of specific events for dissertation data chapters	March
Organization of "Train Contest" projects for display	March 11
Student reflections about importance of Elsewhere Expeditions	March 16

Formal (Extensive) Phase of Research April–May 1998
(Continuation of all data-collection methods)

Spradley's (1980) ethnographic research cycle	April–May

- Continued investigating broad ethnographic questions
- Collected ethnographic data
- Compiled ethnographic record using participant interviews, field notes, audiotapes, videotapes, photography, and classroom artifacts
- Analyzed data
- Investigated additional questions generated from data
- Continued the cycle

Glaser and Strauss's (1967) constant   April–May
   comparative method
   • Collected and analyzed the data
     simultaneously
   • Jotted down field notes daily
   • Fleshed out field notes nightly
   • Transcribed audiotapes and videotapes
     three times each week to reflect on patterns
     and meanings; noted personal comments
     and insights
   • Coded emerging themes and subthemes
     as patterns emerged

Monthly retellings as integral part of our   April–May
   literacy experiences
Completion of draft of specific events for   April–May
   dissertation data chapters
In-depth contact with parents and administrators   April–May
Formal interviews with parents   April
Second formal interviews with students,   April
   Title I instructional assistant, and
   classroom volunteer
"Train Contest" winners announced   April 24
Year-end portfolio evaluations   May
Extensive physical examination of data
   to ascertain patterns   May
Third formal interviews with students   May 15

Concluding Phase of Research: June–August 1998
Formal reanalysis and completion of draft   June–July
   of all dissertation research
Formal year-end interviews with   June
   administrators, Title I instructional assistant,
   and classroom volunteer
Extensive physical examination of data   June
   to ascertain patterns
Defense of research   July
Final approval of dissertation by committee   July

Timeline of Important Elsewhere Expeditions and Related Activities

August 14	Elsewhere Expedition around school campus
September 2, 3, 5, 8, 10	Video shown to introduce note-taking strategies to help students write down Elsewhere Expedition observations (Taking notes helps build students' responsibility.)
September 11	Elsewhere Expedition around school campus (Students meet Mr. Randy.)
October 15	Elsewhere Expedition to see fire truck
November 5	Elsewhere Expedition to hear drug-prevention presentation by a student's father
December 16, 17, 18, 19; January 5, 6, 7	Exploration of "Train Trunk" in classroom (Preparation begins for possible Elsewhere Expedition to train museum if students win contest.)
January 21	Elsewhere Expedition to tour school lunchroom

January 22	Writing workshop about lunchroom tour (Students write thank-you notes to lunchroom manager and create books about their experience.)
February 23, 24	Elsewhere Expedition to magnolia tree outside classroom window
March 5	Students make predictions about Elsewhere Expedition/field trip to potato chip factory, airport, and historical site
March 9	Elsewhere Expedition/field trip to potato chip factory, airport, and historical site
March 10	Writing workshop about Elsewhere Expedition/field trip to potato chip factory, airport, and historical site
March 11	Organization of "Train Contest" projects for hall display
March 16	Student reflections about the importance of Elsewhere Expeditions
April 24	"Train Contest" winners (Competition helps to build literacy community and create authentic literacy experiences.)
April 27, 28	Creation of class Big Book about Elsewhere Expedition to train museum

References

Adams, M.J. (1990). *Beginning to read: Thinking and learning about print.* Cambridge, MA: MIT Press.

Adams, M.J. (1991). Why not phonics *and* whole language? In *Proceedings of the Orton Dyslexia Society Symposia: Whole language and phonics* (pp. 40–53). Baltimore: Orton Dyslexia Society.

Adams, M.J., & Bruck, M. (1993). Word recognition: The interface of educational policies and scientific research. *Reading and Writing: An Interdisciplinary Journal, 5,* 113–139.

Aldridge, J. (1991). Redefining learning for educational practice. *Journal of Instructional Psychology, 20,* 8–15.

Aldridge, J., Eddowes, E.A., & Kuby, P. (1998). *No easy answers: Children with attention and activity level differences.* Olney, MD: Association for Childhood Education International.

Aldridge, J., Kuby, P., & Strevy, D. (1992). Developing a metatheory of education. *Psychological Reports, 70,* 683–687.

Allen, J., & Mason, J.M. (1989). *Risk makers, risk takers, risk breakers: Reducing the risks for young literacy learners.* Portsmouth, NH: Heinemann.

Allen, R.V. (1976). *Language experiences in communication.* Boston: Houghton Mifflin.

Allington, R.L. (1998). The schools we have. The schools we need. In C. Weaver (Ed.), *Reconsidering a balanced approach to reading* (pp. 495–519). Urbana, IL: National Council of Teachers of English.

Allington, R.L. (2001). *What really matters for struggling readers: Designing research-based programs.* New York: Longman.

Allington, R.L., & Cunningham, P.M. (1996). *Schools that work: Where all children read and write.* New York: Longman.

Allington, R.L., & Walmsley, S.A. (Eds.). (1995). *No quick fix: Rethinking literacy programs in America's elementary schools.* New York: Teachers College Press; Newark, DE: International Reading Association.

Anderson, G.L., Herr, K., & Nihlen, A.S. (1994). *Studying your own school: An educator's guide to qualitative practitioner research*. Thousand Oaks, CA: Sage.

Apple, M. (1979). *Ideology and curriculum*. London: Routledge/Kegan Paul.

Atwell, N. (1987). *In the middle: Writing, reading, and learning with adolescents*. Portsmouth, NH: Boynton/Cook.

Atwell, N. (1990). *Coming to know: Writing to learn in the intermediate grades*. Portsmouth, NH: Heinemann.

Avery, C.S. (1987). Traci: A learning-disabled child in a writing-process classroom. In G.L. Bissex & R.H. Bullock (Eds.), *Seeing for ourselves: Case study research by teachers of writing* (pp. 59–75). Portsmouth, NH: Heinemann.

Banner, J.M., Jr. & Cannon, H.C. (1997, April 16). The "who" of teaching. *Education Week*, pp. 1–5. Retrieved February 13, 2002, from http://www.edweek.org/ew/ewstory.cfm?slug=29banner.h16&keywords=-teacher%20effec

Barnes, D. (1971). *Language, the learner and the school* (Rev. ed.). Baltimore: Penguin.

Barnes, D., & Todd, F. (1995). *Communication and learning revisited: Making meaning through talk*. Portsmouth, NH: Boynton/Cook.

Barton, B., & Booth, D. (1990). *Stories in the classroom: Storytelling, reading aloud and role-playing with children*. Markham, Ontario, Canada: Pembroke.

Beattie, M. (1995). New prospects for teacher education: Narrative ways of knowing teaching and teacher learning. *Educational Research, 37*(1), 53–70.

Berliner, D.C., & Biddle, B.J. (1995). *The manufactured crisis: Myth, fraud, and the attack on America's public schools*. Reading, MA: Addison-Wesley.

Bigelow, B., Christensen, L., Karp, S., Miner, B., & Peterson, B. (1994). *Rethinking our classrooms: Teaching for equity and justice*. Milwaukee, WI: Rethinking Schools.

Bissex, G.L. (1980). *Gnys at wrk: A child learns to write and read*. Cambridge, MA: Harvard University Press.

Bissex, G.L., & Bullock, R.H. (Eds.). (1987). *Seeing for ourselves: Case study research by teachers of writing*. Portsmouth, NH: Heinemann.

Bloome, D. (1983). Reading as a social process. In B. Hutson (Ed.), *Advances in reading/language research* (pp. 165–195). Stamford, CT: JAI Press.

Bloome, D. (1989). Locating the learning of reading and writing in classrooms: Beyond deficit, difference, and effectiveness models. In C. Emihovich (Ed.), *Locating learning: Ethnographic perspectives on classroom research* (pp. 87–114). Norwood, NJ: Ablex.

Bloome, D. (1993). Necessary indeterminacy and the microethnographic study of reading as a social process. *Journal of Research in Reading, 16,* 98–111.

Blumer, H. (1969). *Symbolic interactionism: Perspective and method.* Englewood Cliffs, NJ: Prentice Hall.

Bogdan, R.C., & Biklen, S.K. (1982). *Qualitative research for education: An introduction to theory and methods.* Boston: Allyn & Bacon.

Bogdan, R.C., & Biklen, S.K. (1998). *Qualitative research for education: An introduction to theory and methods* (3rd ed.). Boston: Allyn & Bacon.

Brandt, R. (1989). *Effective schools and school improvement.* Alexandria, VA: Association for Supervision and Curriculum Development.

Braunger, J., & Lewis, J.P. (1998). *Building a knowledge base in reading* (2nd ed.). Portland, OR: Northwest Regional Educational Laboratory; Urbana, IL: National Council of Teachers of English; Newark, DE: International Reading Association.

Brinkley, E.H. (1993). Passing on the joy of literacy: Students become writing teachers. In L. Patterson, C.M. Santa, K.G. Short, & K. Smith (Eds.), *Teachers are researchers: Reflection and action* (pp. 210–219). Newark, DE: International Reading Association.

Britton, J. (1987). A quiet form of research. In D. Goswami & P.R. Stillman (Eds.), *Reclaiming the classroom: Teacher research as an agency for change* (pp. 13–19). Portsmouth, NH: Boynton/Cook.

Brown, H., & Cambourne, B. (1993). *Read and retell: A strategy for the whole-language/natural learning classroom.* Portsmouth, NH: Heinemann.

Brown, R.G. (1991). *Schools of thought: How the politics of literacy shape thinking in the classroom.* San Francisco: Jossey-Bass.

Bruner, J.S. (1967). *Studies in cognitive growth: A collaboration at the Center for Cognitive Growth.* New York: Wiley.

Bruner, J.S. (1978). The role of dialogue in language acquisition. In A. Sinclair, R.J. Jarvella, & W.J.M. Levelt (Eds.), *The child's conception of language* (pp. 241–256). Berlin, Germany: Springer-Verlag.

Bruner, J.S. (1986a). *Actual minds, possible worlds.* Cambridge, MA: Harvard University Press.

Bruner, J.S. (1986b). Models of the learner. *Educational Horizons, 64,* 197–200.

Burnaford, G. (1996a). A life of its own: Teacher research and transforming the curriculum. In G. Burnaford, J. Fischer, & D. Hobson (Eds.), *Teachers doing research: Practical possibilities* (pp. 57–81). Hillsdale, NJ: Erlbaum.

Burnaford, G. (1996b). Supporting teacher research: Professional development and the reality of schools. In G. Burnaford, J. Fischer, & D. Hobson (Eds.), *Teachers doing research: Practical possibilities* (pp. 137–150). Hillsdale, NJ: Erlbaum.

Bussis, A.M., Chittenden, E.A., & Amarel, M. (1976). *Beyond surface curriculum*. Boulder, CO: Westview.

Bussis, A.M., Chittenden, E.A., Amarel, M., & Klausner, E. (1985). *Inquiry into meaning: An investigation of learning to read*. Hillsdale, NJ: Erlbaum.

Butler, A., & Turbill, J. (1984). *Towards a reading-writing classroom*. Portsmouth, NH: Heinemann.

Calkins, L.M. (1983). *Lessons from a child: On the teaching and learning of writing*. Portsmouth, NH: Heinemann.

Calkins, L.M. (1986). *The art of teaching writing*. Portsmouth, NH: Heinemann.

Calkins, L.M. (1994). *The art of teaching writing* (Rev. ed.). Portsmouth, NH: Heinemann.

Calkins, L.M. (2001). *The art of teaching reading*. New York: Longman.

Cambourne, B. (1988). *The whole story: Natural learning and the acquisition of literacy in the classroom*. Auckland, New Zealand: Ashton Scholastic.

Cambourne, B., & Turbill, J. (1991). *Coping with chaos*. Portsmouth, NH: Heinemann.

Carnine, D., & Meeder, H. (1997, September 3). Reading research into practice. *Education Week*, pp. 1–5. Retrieved February 24, 2000, from http://www.edweek.org/ew/vol-17/01carn.h17

Carnine, D.W., Silbert, J., & Kameenui, E.J. (1997). *Direct instruction reading* (3rd ed.). Englewood Cliffs, NJ: Merrill.

Caulfield, J. (1996). Students telling stories: Inquiry into the process of learning stories. In Z. Donoahue, M.A. Van Tassell, & L. Patterson (Eds.), *Research in the classroom: Talk, texts, and inquiry* (pp. 51–64). Newark, DE: International Reading Association.

Cazden, C.B. (Ed.). (1981). *Language in early childhood education*. Washington, DC: National Association for the Education of Young Children.

Chall, J.S. (1967). *Learning to read: The great debate*. New York: McGraw-Hill.

Chall, J.S. (1983). *Learning to read: The great debate* (Rev. ed.). New York: McGraw-Hill.

Chall, J.S. (1999). Some thoughts on reading research: Revisiting the first-grade studies. *Reading Research Quarterly, 34*, 8–10.

Chall, J.S., Jacobs, V.A., & Baldwin, L.E. (1990). *The reading crisis: Why poor children fall behind*. Cambridge, MA: Harvard University Press.

Chard, D.J., Simmons, D.C., & Kameenui, E.J. (1995). *Understanding the role of word recognition in reading the reading process: Synthesis of research on beginning reading* (Tech. Rep. No. 15). Eugene: University of Oregon, National Center to Improve the Tools of Educators.

Charney, R.S. (1996). *Teaching children to care: Management in the responsive classroom* (8th ed.). Greenfield, MA: Northeast Foundation for Children.

Children's literacy: Testimony before the House Committee on Education and the Workforce, 105th Cong., 1st Sess. (1997) (testimony of G. Reid Lyon, Ph.D.). Retrieved October 16, 1998, from http://www.apa.org/ppo/scippo/html

Chomsky, C. (1969). *The acquisition of syntax in children from 5 to 10.* Cambridge, MA: MIT Press.

Clark, C.M., & Peterson, P.L. (1986). Teachers' thought processes. In M.C. Wittrock (Ed.), *Handbook of research on teaching* (3rd ed., pp. 255–296). New York: Macmillan.

Clay, M.M. (1979). *The early detection of reading difficulties* (3rd ed.). Portsmouth, NH: Heinemann.

Clay, M.M. (1993). *An observation survey of early literacy achievement.* Portsmouth, NH: Heinemann.

Clay, M.M. (1998). *By different paths to common outcomes.* York, ME: Stenhouse.

Cochran-Smith, M., & Lytle, S.L. (1990). Research on teaching and teacher research: The issues that divide. *Educational Researcher, 19,* 2–11.

Cochran-Smith, M., & Lytle, S.L. (1993). *Inside/outside: Teacher research and knowledge.* New York: Teachers College Press.

Cochran-Smith, M., & Lytle, S.L. (1995). Foreword. In S.E. Noffke & R.B. Stevenson (Eds.), *Educational action research: Becoming practically critical* (pp. vii–viii). New York: Teachers College Press.

Coles, G. (1998a, March 11). Letters to the editor. *Education Week,* pp. 3–7. Retrieved February 20, 2000, from http://www.edweek.org/ew/1998/26letter.h17

Coles, G. (1998b). *Reading lessons: The debate over literacy.* New York: Hill and Wang.

Coles, G. (2000). *Misreading reading: The bad science that hurts children.* Portsmouth, NH: Heinemann.

Collinson, V. (1999). Redefining teacher excellence. *Theory-Into-Practice, 48*(1), 4–11.

Colvin, R.L. (1996, May 4). Phonics is best aid for reading, study shows. *Los Angeles Times, Home Edition,* p. A1. Retrieved February 24, 2000, from http://www.latimes.com

Cree, K., & Donaldson, S. (1996). Cooperative learning: Enhancing talking and listening. In P. Jones (Ed.), *Talking to learn* (pp. 66–79). Marrickville, Australia: Primary English Teaching Association.

Creswell, J.W. (1994). *Research design: Qualitative & quantitative approaches.* Thousand Oaks, CA: Sage.

Dahl, K.L., & Farnan, N. (1998). *Children's writing: Perspectives from research.* Newark, DE: International Reading Association; Chicago: National Reading Conference.

Dahl, K.L., Scharer, P.L., Lawson, L.L., & Grogan, P.R. (2001). *Rethinking phonics: Making the best teaching decisions.* Portsmouth, NH: Heinemann.

Darling-Hammond, L. (1997). *The right to learn: A blueprint for creating schools that work.* San Francisco: Jossey-Bass.

Deford, D. (1985). Validating the construct of theoretical orientation in reading instruction. *Reading Research Quarterly, 20,* 351–367.

Delpit, L. (1990). Language diversity and learning. In S. Hynds & D. Rubin (Eds.), *Perspectives on talk and learning* (pp. 247–266). Urbana, IL: National Council of Teachers of English.

Delpit, L. (1991). A conversation with Lisa Delpit. *Language Arts, 68,* 17–19.

Delpit, L. (1994). Seeing color: A review of *White Teacher.* In B. Bigelow, L. Christensen, S. Karp, B. Miner, & B. Peterson (Eds.), *Rethinking our classrooms: Teaching for equity and justice* (pp. 130–132). Milwaukee, WI: Rethinking Schools.

Delpit, L.D. (1988). The silenced dialogue: Power and pedagogy in educating other people's children. *Harvard Educational Review, 58,* 280–298.

Derman-Sparks, L., & Phillips, C.B. (1997). *Teaching/learning anti-racism: A developmental approach.* New York: Teachers College Press.

Dewey, J. (1990). *The school and society* and *The child and the curriculum* (Expanded ed.). Chicago: University of Chicago Press. (Original work published 1900 and 1902)

Dewey, J. (1997). *Experience and education.* New York: Collier. (Original work published 1938)

Dickinson, J. (1993). Children's perspectives on talk: Building a learning community. In K.M. Pierce & C.J. Gilles (Eds.) (with D. Barnes), *Cycles of meaning: Exploring the potential of talk in learning communities* (pp. 99–116). Portsmouth, NH: Heinemann.

Donoahue, Z. (1996). Collaboration, community, and communication: Modes of discourse for teacher research. In Z. Donoahue, M.A. Van Tassell, & L. Patterson (Eds.), *Research in the classroom: Talk, texts, and inquiry* (pp. 91–107). Newark, DE: International Reading Association.

Donoahue, Z., Van Tassell, M.A., & Patterson, L. (1996). *Research in the classroom: Talk, texts, and inquiry.* Newark, DE: International Reading Association.

Dorn, L.J., French, C., & Jones, T. (1998). *Apprenticeship in literacy: Transitions across reading and writing.* York, ME: Stenhouse.

Duckworth, E. (1987). *"The having of wonderful ideas" and other essays on teaching and learning.* New York: Teachers College Press.

Duckworth, E., & the Experienced Teachers Group. (1997). *Teacher to teacher: Learning from each other.* New York: Teachers College Press.

Duffy, G., & Anderson, L. (1984). Teachers' theoretical orientations and the real classroom. *Reading Psychology, 5,* 97–104.

Dyson, A.H. (1986). Transitions and tensions: Interrelationships betv the drawing, talking, and dictating of young children. *Researc Teaching of English, 20,* 379–409.

Dyson, A.H. (1987). Individual differences in beginning composing: *A.* or-chestral vision of learning to compose. *Written Communication, 4,* 411–4 :

Dyson, A.H. (1989). *Multiple worlds of child writers: Friends learnir.* write. New York: Teachers College Press.

Dyson, A.H. (1993). *Social worlds of children learning to write in an urban primary school.* New York: Teachers College Press.

Educational Testing Service. (2001). *Professional assessments for beginning teachers: Principles of learning and teaching* (The Praxis Series). Princeton, NJ: Author.

Edwards, C., Gandini, L., & Forman, G. (Eds.). (1994). *The hundred languages of children: The Reggio Emilia approach to early childhood education* (Rev. ed.). Norwood, NJ: Ablex. (Original work published 1979)

Ehri, L.C. (1991). Development of the ability to read words. In R. Barr, M.L. Kamil, P.B. Mosenthal, & P.D. Pearson (Eds.), *Handbook of reading research* (Vol. 2, pp. 383–417). White Plains, NY: Longman.

Eisner, E. (1981). On the differences between scientific and artistic approaches to qualitative research. *Educational Researcher, 10,* 5–9.

Elbaz, F. (1983). *Teacher thinking: A study of practical knowledge.* London: Croom Helm.

Elliott, J. (1985). Facilitating action research in schools. In R.G. Burgess (Ed.), *Field methods in the study of education* (pp. 235–262). London: Falmer Press.

Erickson, F. (1973). What makes school ethnography "ethnographic"? *CAE Newsletter, 4*(2), 10–19.

Erickson, F. (1986). Qualitative methods in research on teaching. In M.C. Wittrock (Ed.), *Handbook of research on teaching* (3rd ed., pp. 119–161). New York: Macmillan.

Fang, Z. (1996). A review of research on teacher beliefs and practices. *Educational Research, 38,* 47–65.

Farkas, S., Foley, P., Duffett, A., Foleno, T., & Johnson, J. (2001). Just waiting to be asked? A fresh look at attitudes on public engagement. *Public Agenda Research Studies.* Retrieved February 13, 2002, from http://www.publicagenda.org/aboutpa/aboutpa7.htm

Fedele, F. (1996). Building a reflecting classroom. In Z. Donoahue, M.A. Van Tassell, & L. Patterson (Eds.), *Research in the classroom: Talk, texts, and inquiry* (pp. 36–50). Newark, DE: International Reading Association.

Feldman, A., & Atkin, J.M. (1995). Embedding action research in professional practice. In S.E. Noffke & R.B. Stevenson (Eds.), *Educational action research: Becoming practically critical* (pp. 127–137). New York: Teachers College Press.

Feldman, E.B. (1970). *Becoming human through art: Aesthetic experience in the school*. Englewood Cliffs, NJ: Prentice Hall.

Feldman, E.B. (1971). *Varieties of visual experience: Art as image and idea* (2nd ed.). Englewood Cliffs, NJ: Prentice Hall.

Ferreiro, E., & Teberosky, A. (1994). *Literacy before schooling* (K.G. Castro, Trans.). Portsmouth, NH: Heinemann. (Original work published 1979)

Fetterman, D.M. (1989). *Ethnography: Step by step*. Thousand Oaks, CA: Sage.

Fine, M. (1994). *Chartering urban school reform: Reflections on public high schools in the midst of change*. New York: Teachers College Press.

Fisher, B. (1991). *Joyful learning: A whole language kindergarten*. Portsmouth, NH: Heinemann.

Flippo, R.F. (1999). *What do the experts say? Helping children learn to read*. Portsmouth, NH: Heinemann.

Flood, J., Heath, S.B., & Lapp, D. (Eds.). (1997). *Handbook of research on teaching literacy through the communicative and visual arts*. New York: Macmillan.

Foorman, B.R., Francis, D.J., Fletcher, J.M., & Lynn, A. (1996). Relation of phonological and orthographic processing to early reading: Comparing two approaches to regression-based, reading-level-match design. *Journal of Educational Psychology, 88*, 639–652.

Foorman, B.R., Francis, D.J., Fletcher, J.M., & Schatschneider, C. (1998). The role of instruction in learning to read: Preventing reading failure in at-risk children. *Journal of Educational Psychology, 90*, 37–55.

Foorman, B.R., Francis, D.J., Novy, D., & Liberman, D. (1991). How letter-sound instruction mediates progress in first-grade reading and spelling. *Journal of Educational Psychology, 83*, 456–469.

Fosnot, C.T. (1989). *Enquiring teachers, enquiring learners: A constructivist approach to teaching*. New York: Teachers College Press.

Fountas, I.C., & Pinnell, G.S. (1996). *Guided reading: Good first teaching for all children*. Portsmouth, NH: Heinemann.

Francis, D.J., Shaywitz, S.E., Stuebing, K.K., Shaywitz, B.A., & Fletcher, J.M. (1996). Developmental lag versus deficit models of reading disability: A longitudinal, individual growth curves analysis. *Journal of Educational Psychology, 88*, 3–17.

Fraser, J., & Skolnick, D. (1994). *On their way: Celebrating second graders as they read and write*. Portsmouth, NH: Heinemann.

Freedman, S.W. (Ed.). (1985). *The acquisition of written language: Response and revision*. Norwood, NJ: Ablex.

Gambrell, L.B., Morrow, L.M., Neuman, S.B., & Pressley, M. (Eds.). (1999). *Best practices in literacy instruction*. New York: Guilford.

Gandini, L. (1994). Educational and caring spaces. In C. Edwards, L. Gandini, & G. Forman (Eds.), *The hundred languages of children: The*

Reggio Emilia approach to early childhood education (Rev. ed., pp. 135–149). Norwood, NJ: Ablex. (Original work published 1979)

Gee, J.P. (1989). What is literacy? *Journal of Education, 171*, 18–25.

Genishi, C. (1982). Observational research methods for early childhood education. In B. Spodek (Ed.), *Handbook of research in early childhood education* (pp. 564–591). New York: Macmillan.

Genishi, C., Yung-Chan, D., & Stires, S. (2000). Talking their way into print: English language learners in a prekindergarten classroom. In D.S. Strickland & L.M. Morrow (Eds.), *Beginning reading and writing* (pp. 66–80). New York: Teachers College Press; Newark, DE: International Reading Association.

Giacobbe, M.E. (1986). Learning to write and writing to learn in the elementary school. In A.R. Petrosky & D. Bartholomae (Eds.), *The teaching of writing: Eighty-fifth yearbook of the National Society for the Study of Education* (pp. 131–147). Urbana, IL: National Council of Teachers of English.

Glaser, B.G., & Strauss, A.L. (1967). *The discovery of grounded theory: Strategies for qualitative research.* Chicago: Aldine.

Glass, R.D. (2000). Reading Patrick Shannon on reading instruction: Reflections on politics and education. *Reading Research Quarterly, 35*, 284–297.

Goff, S. (1996). Experienced teachers & action research: A model for professional development. In G. Burnaford, J. Fischer, & D. Hobson (Eds.), *Teachers doing research: Practical possibilities* (pp. 155–162). Hillsdale, NJ: Erlbaum.

Goodman, K.S. (1976). Reading: A psycholinguistic guessing game. In H. Singer & R.B. Ruddell (Eds.), *Theoretical models and processes of reading* (2nd ed., pp. 470–496). Newark, DE: International Reading Association.

Goodman, K.S. (1986). *What's whole in whole language?* Richmond Hill, Ontario, Canada: Scholastic.

Goodman, K.S. (1993). *Phonics phacts.* Portsmouth, NH: Heinemann.

Goodman, K.S., Smith, E.B., Meredith, R., & Goodman, Y.M. (1987). *Language and thinking in school: A whole-language curriculum* (3rd ed.). Katonah, NY: Richard C. Owen.

Goodman, Y.M. (1985). Kidwatching: Observing children in the classroom. In A. Jaggar & M.T. Smith-Burke (Eds.), *Observing the language learner* (pp. 9–18). Newark, DE: International Reading Association; Urbana, IL: National Council of Teachers of English.

Goodman, Y.M., & Burke, C. (1980). *Reading strategies: Focus on comprehension.* Katonah, NY: Richard C. Owen.

Goodman, Y.M., Watson, D.J., & Burke, C.L. (1987). *Reading miscue inventory: Alternative procedures.* Katonah, NY: Richard C. Owen.

Goodman, Y.M., & Wilde, S. (Eds.). (1992). *Literacy events in a community of young writers*. New York: Teachers College Press.

Goswami, D., & Stillman, P.R. (Eds.). (1987). *Reclaiming the classroom: Teacher research as an agency for change*. Portsmouth, NH: Boynton/Cook.

Gramsci, A. (1971). The study of philosophy: Some preliminary points of reference. In Q. Hoare & G.N. Smith (Eds. & Trans.), *Selections from the prison notebooks of Antonio Gramsci* (pp. 1–39). New York: International Publishers. Retrieved February 13, 2002, from http://www.colorado college.edu/Dept/PS/Finley/PS425/reading/Gramsc.html

Graves, D. (1978). *Balance the basics: Let them write*. New York: Ford Foundation.

Graves, D.H. (1983). *Writing: Teachers & children at work*. Portsmouth, NH: Heinemann.

Graves, D.H. (1994). *A fresh look at writing*. Portsmouth, NH: Heinemann.

Greene, M. (1973). *Teacher as stranger: Educational philosophy for the modern age*. Belmont, CA: Wadsworth.

Greene, M. (1994). Epistemology and educational research: The influence of recent approaches to knowledge. In L. Darling-Hammond (Ed.), *Review of research in education* (Vol. 20, pp. 423–464). Washington, DC: American Educational Research Association.

Grossen, B. (1998). *30 years of research: What we now know about how children learn to read*. Retrieved October 16, 1998, from http://cftl.org/ 30years/30years.html

Grover, S.P. (1990). The approach of a school system. In C. Kamii (Ed.), *Achievement testing in the early grades: The games grown-ups play* (pp. 49–59). Washington, DC: National Association for the Education of Young Children.

Harste, J.C., & Burke, C.L. (1977). A new hypothesis for reading teacher research: Both the teaching and learning of reading is theoretically based. In P.D. Pearson (Ed.), *Reading: Theory, research and practice* (pp. 32–40). Clemson, SC: National Reading Conference.

Harste, J.C., Woodward, V.A., & Burke, C.L. (1984). *Language stories and literacy lessons*. Portsmouth, NH: Heinemann.

Heath, S.B. (1982). What no bedtime story means: Narrative skills at home and school. *Language in Society, 11*, 49–76.

Heath, S.B. (1983). *Ways with words: Language, life, and work in communities and classrooms*. New York: Cambridge University Press.

Heath, S.B., & Mangiola, L. (1991). *Children of promise: Literate activity in linguistically and culturally diverse classrooms* (S.R. Schecter & G.A. Hull, Eds.). Washington, DC: National Education Association, Center for the Study of Writing and Literacy and American Educational Research Association.

Hill, L., & Weaver, A. (1994). A multicultural curriculum in action: The Walt Disney Magnet School. In M. D'Emidio-Caston, L. Hill, & J. Snyder (Eds.), *Teachers' voices: Reinventing themselves, their profession, and their communities* (pp. 19–29). New York: National Center for Restructuring Education, Schools, and Teaching, Teachers College, Columbia University.

Hoffman, J.V. (1998). When bad things happen to good ideas in literacy education: Professional dilemmas, personal decisions, and political traps. *The Reading Teacher, 52,* 102–112.

Holdaway, D. (1979). *The foundations of literacy.* New York: Ashton Scholastic.

Hubbard, N. (1996). Taking a risk: Learning about physics with young children. In G. Burnaford, J. Fischer, & D. Hobson (Eds.), *Teachers doing research: Practical possibilities* (pp. 109–116). Hillsdale, NJ: Erlbaum.

Hubbard, R.S., & Power, B.M. (1993). *The art of classroom inquiry: A handbook for teacher-researchers.* Portsmouth, NH: Heinemann.

Hubbard, R.S., & Power, B.M. (1999). *Living the questions: A guide for teacher-researchers.* York, ME: Stenhouse.

Huck, C.S., Hepler, S., Hickman, J., & Kiefer, B.Z. (1997). *Children's literature in the elementary school* (6th ed.). Boston: McGraw-Hill.

Hursh, D. (1995). Developing discourses and structures to support action research for educational reform: Working both ends. In S.E. Noffke & R.B. Stevenson (Eds.), *Educational action research: Becoming practically critical* (pp. 141–153). New York: Teachers College Press.

International Reading Association & National Association for the Education of Young Children. (1998). Learning to read and write: Developmentally appropriate practices for young children. *The Reading Teacher, 52,* 193–216.

International Reading Association & National Council of Teachers of English. (1996). *Standards for the English language arts.* Newark, DE: Author; Urbana, IL: Author.

Interstate New Teacher Assessment and Support Consortium. (1992). *Model standards for beginning teacher licensing and development: A resource for state dialogue.* Retrieved August 25, 2001, from http://www.ccsso.org/intaspub.html

Interstate New Teacher Assessment and Support Consortium. (1995). *Next steps: Moving towards performance-based licensing in teaching.* Retrieved February 9, 2002, from http://www.ccsso.org/intaspub.html

Isaacs, S. (1948). *Childhood and after: Some essays and clinical studies.* London: Routledge & Kegan Paul.

Jackson, P.W. (1990). Introduction. In J. Dewey, *The school and society* and *The child and the curriculum* (Expanded ed., pp. ix–xxxvii). Chicago: University of Chicago Press. (Original work published 1900 and 1902)

Jaggar, A. (1985). On observing the language learner: Introduction and overview. In A. Jaggar & M.T. Smith-Burke (Eds.), *Observing the language learner* (pp. 1–7). Newark, DE: International Reading Association; Urbana, IL: National Council of Teachers of English.

Jones, P. (1996a). Language and learning. In P. Jones (Ed.), *Talking to learn* (pp. 1–10). Marrickville, Australia: Primary English Teaching Association.

Jones, P. (1996b). Talk about literacy in the content areas. In P. Jones (Ed.), *Talking to learn* (pp. 126–144). Marrickville, Australia: Primary English Teaching Association.

Juel, C. (1988). Learning to read and write: A longitudinal study of fifty-four children from first through fourth grade. *Journal of Educational Psychology, 80,* 437–447.

Kamii, C. (1979). Piaget's theory, behaviorism, and other theories in education. *Journal of Education, 11,* 13–32.

Kamii, C. (1989). Social interaction and invented spelling. In G. Manning & M. Manning (Eds.), *Whole language: Beliefs and practices, K–8* (pp. 104–114). Washington, DC: National Education Association.

Kamii, C. (1990). *Achievement testing in the early grades: The games grown-ups play.* Washington, DC: National Association for the Education of Young Children.

Katz, L.G., & Chard, S.C. (1979). *Engaging children's minds: The project approach.* Norwood, NJ: Ablex.

Kincheloe, J.L. (1991). *Teachers as researchers: Qualitative inquiry as a path to empowerment.* New York: Falmer.

King, M.L. (1985). Language and language learning for child watchers. In A. Jaggar & M.T. Smith-Burke (Eds.), *Observing the language learner* (pp. 19–38). Newark, DE: International Reading Association; Urbana, IL: National Council of Teachers of English.

Kirk, I. (1996). Voice matters. In P. Jones (Ed.), *Talking to learn* (pp. 114–125). Marrickville, Australia: Primary English Teaching Association.

Knapp, M.S. (Ed.) (with N.E. Adelman, C. Marder, H. McCollum, M.C. Needels, C. Padilla, P.M. Shields, B.J. Turnbull, & A.A. Zucker). (1995). *Teaching for meaning in high-poverty classrooms.* New York: Teachers College Press.

Knapp, M.S., Shields, P.M., & Turnbull, B.J. (1995). Teaching for meaning in high-poverty classrooms. In M.S. Knapp (Ed.) (with N.E. Adelman, C. Marder, H. McCollum, M.C. Needels, C. Padilla, P.M. Shields, B.J. Turnbull, & A.A. Zucker), *Teaching for meaning in high-poverty classrooms* (pp. 183–204). New York: Teachers College Press.

Kuhn, T. (1962). *The structure of scientific revolutions.* Chicago: University of Chicago Press.

Ladson-Billings, G. (1994). *The dreamkeepers: Successful teachers of African American children.* San Francisco: Jossey-Bass.

Lather, P. (1986). Research as praxis. *Harvard Educational Review, 56,* 257–277.

Lemann, N. (1997, November). The reading wars. *The Atlantic Monthly, 280,* 128–134.

Leslie, L., & Caldwell, J. (1990). *Qualitative reading inventory.* New York: HarperCollins.

Lincoln, Y.S., & Guba, E.G. (1985). *Naturalistic inquiry.* Beverly Hills, CA: Sage.

Lovett, M.W., Steinbach, K.A., & Frijters, J.C. (2000). Remediating the core deficits of developmental reading disability: A double-deficit perspective. *Journal of Learning Disabilities, 33,* 334–358.

Luijpen, W.A. (1969). *Existential phenomenology* (Rev. ed., Duquesne Studies: Philosophical Series, Vol. 12). Pittsburgh, PA: Duquesne University Press.

Lyon, G.R. (1996, Spring). Learning disabilities. *The Future of Children, 6,* 54–76.

Lyon, G.R. (1997, Summer/Fall). Language and literacy development. *Early Childhood Update, 6.* [Summary of testimony] Retrieved February 4, 2002, from http://www.ed.gov/offices/OERI/ECI/newsletter/97fall/early 6.html

Lyon, G.R. (1998a, March 11). Letters to the editor. *Education Week, 26,* 3–6. Retrieved February 20, 2000, from http://www.edweek.org/ew/1998/ 26letter.h17

Lyon, G.R. (1998b). Why reading is not a natural process. *Educational Leadership, 55*(66), 1–7. Retrieved February 28, 2000, from http://www. ascd.org/pubs/el/mar98/exylon.htm

MacLean, M.S., & Mohr, M.M. (1999). *Teacher-researchers at work.* Berkeley, CA: The National Writing Project.

Malaguzzi, L. (1994). History, ideas, and basic philosophy: An interview with Lella Gandini (L. Gandini, Trans.). In C. Edwards, L. Gandini, & G. Forman (Eds.), *The hundred languages of children: The Reggio Emilia approach to early childhood education* (Rev. ed., pp. 41–89). Norwood, NJ: Ablex. (Original work published 1979)

Mallory, B.L., & New, R.S. (Eds.). (1994). *Diversity and developmentally appropriate practices: Challenges for early childhood education.* New York: Teachers College Press.

Manning, G. (1991, March). [Course notes. ECE 512, Models of Teaching]. The University of Alabama at Birmingham. Unpublished raw data.

Manning, G., Manning, M., & Long, R. (1989). In the process of becoming process teachers. In G. Manning & M. Manning (Eds.), *Whole language: Beliefs and practices, K–8* (pp. 235–240). Washington, DC: National Education Association.

Manning, M.M., Manning, G.L., Long, R., & Wolfson, B.J. (1987). *Reading and writing in the primary grades*. Washington, DC: National Education Association.

Manzo, K.K. (1997, March 12). Study stresses role of early phonics instruction. *Education Week*, pp. 1–4. Retrieved February 20, 2000, from http://www.edweek.org/ew/1997/24read.h16

Manzo, K.K. (1998, April 29). More states moving to make phonics the law. *Education Week*, pp. 1–5. Retrieved February 20, 2000, from http://www.edweek.org/ed/vol-17/33read.h17

Marzano, R.J., Pickering, D.J., & Pollock, J.E. (2001). *Classroom instruction that works: Research-based strategies for increasing student achievement*. Alexandria, VA: Association for Supervision and Curriculum Development.

Maslow, A.H. (1970). *Motivation and personality* (2nd ed.). New York: Harper & Row.

Mayeroff, M. (1972). *On caring*. New York: Harper & Row.

McCarrier, A., Pinnell, G.S., & Fountas, I.C. (2000). *Interactive writing: How language & literacy come together, K–2*. Portsmouth, NH: Heinemann.

McCollum, H. (1995). Managing academic learning environments. In M.S. Knapp (Ed.) (with N.E. Adelman, C. Marder, H. McCollum, M.C. Needels, C. Padilla, P.M. Shields, B.J. Turnbull, & A.A. Zucker), *Teaching for meaning in high-poverty classrooms* (pp. 11–32). New York: Teachers College Press.

McFarland, K.P., & Stansell, J.C. (1993). Historical perspectives. In L. Patterson, C.M. Santa, K.G. Short, & K. Smith (Eds.), *Teachers are researchers: Reflection and action* (pp. 12–18). Newark, DE: International Reading Association.

McLaren, P. (1989). *Life in schools: An introduction to critical pedagogy in the foundations of education*. White Plains, NY: Longman.

McNiff, J., Lomax, P., & Whitehead, J. (1996). *You and your action research project*. New York: Hyde.

McQuillan, J. (1998). *The literacy crisis: False claims, real solutions*. Portsmouth, NH: Heinemann.

Merriam-Webster's online. (2001). Retrieved June 3, 2001, from http://www.m-w.com

Mohr, M.M. (1987). Teacher-researchers and the study of the writing process. In D. Goswami & P.R. Stillman (Eds.), *Reclaiming the classroom: Teacher research as an agency for change* (pp. 94–107). Portsmouth, NH: Boynton/Cook.

Mohr, M.M. (1996). Wild dreams and sober cautions: The future of teacher research. In Z. Donoahue, M.A. Van Tassell, & L. Patterson (Eds.), *Research in the classroom: Talk, texts, and inquiry* (pp. 117–123). Newark, DE: International Reading Association.

Morrow, L.M., & Smith, J.K. (Eds.). (1990). *Assessment for instruction in early literacy.* Englewood Cliffs, NJ: Prentice Hall.

National Commission on Excellence in Education. (1983). *A nation at risk: The imperative for educational reform.* Washington, DC: U.S. Government Printing Office.

National Council for Accreditation of Teacher Education. (2000, March 7). *National Council for Accreditation of Teacher Education program standards for elementary teacher preparation.* Retrieved February 7, 2002, from http://www.ncate.org/standard/elemstds.pdf

National Council of Teachers of English. (1997). *Teaching reading and literature in early elementary grades: Standards consensus series.* Urbana, IL: Author.

National Institute of Child Health and Human Development. (2000, April 13). *NIH news release: National Reading Panel reports combination of teaching phonics, word sounds, giving feedback on oral reading most effective way to teach reading.* Retrieved May 5, 2001, from http://www.nih.gov/news/pr/apr2000/nichd-13.htm

National Reading Panel. (2000, April 13). *Teaching children to read: An evidence-based assessment of the scientific research literature on reading and its implication for reading instruction.* Retrieved June 19, 2000, from http://www.nationalreadingpanel.org/nrparchive/documents/pr_final report.htm

Nelson, N. (1998). Reading and writing contextualized. In N. Nelson & R.C. Calfee (Eds.), *The reading-writing connection: Ninety-seventh yearbook of the National Society for the Study of Education, Part II* (pp. 266–286). Chicago: The National Society for the Study of Education.

Nelson, N., & Calfee, R.C. (Eds.). (1998). *The reading-writing connection: Ninety-seventh yearbook of the National Society for the Study of Education, Part II.* Chicago: The National Society for the Study of Education.

Neuman, S.B., & Roskos, K.A. (Eds.). (1998). *Children achieving: Best practices in early literacy.* Newark, DE: International Reading Association.

Newkirk, T. (1989). *More than stories: The range of children's writing.* Portsmouth, NH: Heinemann.

Newman, J. (1985). *Whole language: Theory in use.* Portsmouth, NH: Heinemann.

New Standards Primary Literacy Committee. (1999). *Reading & writing grade by grade: Primary literacy standards for kindergarten through third grade.* Washington, DC: National Center on Education and the Economy; Pittsburgh, PA: University of Pittsburgh.

Nussbaum, N., & Puckett, L. (1990). Literacy through interaction. In K.G. Short & K.M. Pierce (Eds.), *Talking about books: Creating literate communities* (pp. 83–101). Portsmouth, NH: Heinemann.

Odell, L. (1987). Planning classroom research. In D. Goswami & P.R. Stillman (Eds.), *Reclaiming the classroom: Teacher research as an agency for change* (pp. 128–160). Portsmouth, NH: Boynton/Cook.

Ogle, D. (2001, August/September). President's message: Celebrating teachers and teaching. *Reading Today, 19*, p. 8.

Ohanian, S. (1999). *One size fits few: The folly of educational standards.* Portsmouth, NH: Heinemann.

Oja, S.N., & Smulyan, L. (1989). *Collaborative action research: A developmental approach.* Philadelphia: Falmer.

Paley, V.G. (1990). *White teacher.* Cambridge, MA: Harvard University Press. (Original work published 1979)

Paley, V.G. (1995). *Kwanzaa and me: A teacher's story.* Cambridge, MA: Harvard University Press.

Paley, V.G. (1997). *The girl with the brown crayon: How children use stories to shape their lives.* Cambridge, MA: Harvard University Press.

Paterson, K. (1988). *The spying heart: More thoughts on reading and writing books for children.* New York: Lodestar.

Patterson, L. (1996). Reliving the learning: Learning from classroom talk and texts. In Z. Donoahue, M.A. Van Tassell, & L. Patterson (Eds.), *Research in the classroom: Talk, texts, and inquiry* (pp. 3–9). Newark, DE: International Reading Association.

Patterson, L., Stansell, J.C., & Lee, S. (1990). *Teacher research: From promise to power.* Katonah, NY: Richard C. Owen.

Pearson, P.D. (Ed.) (with R. Barr, M.L. Kamil, & P. Mosenthal). (1984). *Handbook of reading research.* New York: Longman.

Pearson, P.D. (1993). Teaching and learning to read: A research perspective. *Language Arts, 70*, 502–511.

Peterson, R. (1992). *Life in a crowded place: Making a learning community.* Portsmouth, NH: Heinemann.

Peterson, R., & Eeds, M. (1990). *Grand conversations: Literature groups in action.* New York: Scholastic.

Piaget, J. (1955). *The language and thought of the child.* (M. Gabain, Trans.). New York: World Publishing.

Piaget, J. (1977). *The development of thought: Equilibration of cognitive structures.* New York: Viking.

Pierce, C.M. (1990). A profile of an effective teacher: A microethnography of a seventh-grade social studies classroom (teacher effectiveness). (Doctoral dissertation, University of Alabama, 1990). *Dissertation Abstracts International, 52* (02A), 413.

Pierce, K.M., & Gilles, C.J. (Eds.) (with D. Barnes). (1993). *Cycles of meaning: Exploring the potential of talk in learning communities.* Portsmouth, NH: Heinemann.

Pollard, A. (1985). Opportunities and difficulties of a teacher-ethnographer: A personal account. In R.G. Burgess (Ed.), *Field methods in the study of education* (pp. 217–233). London: Falmer Press.

Pressley, M., Allington, R., Morrow, L.M., Baker, K., Nelson, E., Wharton-McDonald, R., et al. (1998). *The nature of effective first-grade literacy instruction* (CELA Report No. 11007). Retrieved May 15, 2000, from http://cela.albany.edu/1stgradelit/main.html

Purkey, W.W., & Novak, J.M. (1996). *Inviting school success: A self-concept approach to teaching, learning, and democratic practice* (3rd ed.). Belmont, CA: Wadsworth.

Quantz, R.A. (1992). On critical ethnography (with some postmodern considerations). In M.D. LeCompte, W.L. Millroy, & J. Preissle (Eds.), *The handbook of qualitative research in education* (pp. 447–505). New York: Academic Press.

Ravitch, D. (2000). *Left back: A century of failed school reforms.* New York: Simon & Schuster.

Reading Excellence Act of 1999, Pub. L. No. 105-277, § 2252, 5 Stat. 1–2. Retrieved February 22, 2000, from http://www.ed.gov/offices/OLCA/Handbook/publiclaws.html

Rogoff, B. (1990). *Apprenticeship in thinking: Cognitive development in social context.* New York: Oxford University Press.

Rosenblatt, L.M. (1994). The reader, the text, the poem: The transactional theory of the literary work. Carbondale, IL: Southern Illinois University Press. (Original work published 1978)

Routman, R. (1988). *Transitions: From literature to literacy.* Portsmouth, NH: Heinemann.

Routman, R. (1994). *Invitations: Changing as teachers and learners K–12.* Portsmouth, NH: Heinemann.

Routman, R. (1996). *Literacy at the crossroads: Crucial talk about reading, writing, and other teaching dilemmas.* Portsmouth, NH: Heinemann.

Routman, R. (2000). *Conversations: Strategies for teaching, learning, and evaluating.* Portsmouth, NH: Heinemann.

Rubin, B.M. (1997, March 2). Reading wars: Endless squabbles keep kids from getting the help they need. *Chicago Tribune,* pp. B1, B4.

Schon, D. (1983). *The reflective practitioner: How professionals think in action.* New York: Basic Books.

Seidman, I.E. (1991). *Interviewing as qualitative research: A guide for researchers in education and the social sciences.* New York: Teachers College Press.

Share, D.L., & Stanovich, K.E. (1995). Cognitive processes in early reading development: Accommodating individual differences into a model of acquisition. *Issues in Education: Contributions From Educational Psychology, 1,* 1–57.

Shaughnessy, M.P. (1977). *Errors and expectations: A guide for the teacher of basic writing.* New York: Oxford University Press.

Shaywitz, B.A., Shaywitz, S.E., Fletcher, J.M., Pugh, K.R., Gore, J.C., Constable, R., et al. (1997). The Yale Center for the Study of Learning and Attention: Longitudinal and neurobiological studies. *Learning Disabilities, 8,* 21–29.

Shields, P.M. (1995). Engaging children of diverse backgrounds. In M.S. Knapp (Ed.) (with N.E. Adelman, C. Marder, H. McCollum, M.C. Needels, C. Padilla, P.M. Shields, B.J. Turnbull, & A.A. Zucker), *Teaching for meaning in high-poverty classrooms* (pp. 33–46). New York: Teachers College Press.

Shipman, M. (1985). Ethnography and educational policy-making. In R.G. Burgess (Ed.), *Field methods in the study of education* (pp. 273–281). London: Falmer Press.

Short, K.G., & Pierce, K.M. (Eds.). (1990). *Talking about books: Creating literate communities.* Portsmouth, NH: Heinemann.

Short, K.G., Schroeder, J., Laird, J., Kauffman, G., Ferguson, M.J., & Crawford, K.M. (1996). *Learning together through inquiry: From Columbus to integrated curriculum.* York, ME: Stenhouse.

Shulman, L.S. (1986). Those who understand: Knowledge growth in teaching. *Educational Researcher, 15*(2), 4–14.

Shulman, L.S. (1987). Knowledge and teaching: Foundations of the new reform. *Harvard Educational Review, 57*(1), 1–22.

Sinclair, H. (1994, April). *Piaget and Vygotsky on collaboration, argumentation, and coherent reasoning.* Presentation given to the School of Education, University of Alabama at Birmingham.

Smith, B.O. (1980). Pedagogical education: How about reform? *Phi Delta Kappan, 62,* 87–93.

Smith, F. (1971). *Understanding reading: A psycholinguistic analysis of reading and learning to read.* Hillsdale, NJ: Erlbaum.

Smith, F. (Ed.). (1973). *Psycholinguistics and reading.* New York: Holt, Rinehart.

Smith, F. (1975). *Comprehension and learning: A conceptual framework for teachers.* Katonah, NY: Richard C. Owen.

Smith, F. (1978). *Reading.* Cambridge, UK: Cambridge University Press.

Smith, F. (1985). *Reading without nonsense* (2nd ed.). New York: Teachers College Press.

Smith, F. (1999). Why systematic phonics and phonemic awareness instruction constitute an educational hazard. *Language Arts, 77,* 150–155.

Smith, J.K. (1983). Quantitative versus qualitative research: An attempt to clarify the issue. *Educational Researcher, 12,* 6–13.

Snow, C.E., Burns, M.S., & Griffin, P. (Eds.). (1998). *Preventing reading difficulties in young children.* Washington, DC: National Academy Press.

Soltis, J.F. (1992). Inquiry paradigms. In M.C. Alkin (Ed.), *Encyclopedia of Educational Research* (6th ed., Vol. 2, pp. 620–622). New York: Macmillan.

Spradley, J.P. (1980). *Participant observation*. New York: Holt, Rinehart and Winston.

Stanovich, K.E. (1993/1994). Romance and reality. *The Reading Teacher, 47*, 280–291.

Stanovich, K.E., Cunningham, A.E., & Feeman, D.J. (1984). Intelligence, cognitive skills and early reading progress. *Reading Research Quarterly, 19*, 278–303.

Stenhouse, L. (1985). A note on case study and educational practice. In R.G. Burgess (Ed.), *Field methods in the study of education* (pp. 263–271). London: Falmer Press.

Stewart, M.T. (1997). [Field notes from second-grade class]. Unpublished raw data.

Stewart, M.T. (1998). [Field notes from second-grade class]. Unpublished raw data.

Stewart, M.T. (2000). [Interviews with first-year teachers]. Unpublished raw data.

Stewart, M.T. (2001). [Keyword search of the term "best practices" in the Library of Congress Online Catalog]. Unpublished raw data.

Stewart, M.T. (in press). *WRITING: "It's in the bag." Ways to inspire your students to write*. Peterborough, NH: Crystal Springs.

St. Pierre-Hirtle, J. (1996). Technology and reflection: Knowing our world and our work. In Z. Donoahue, M.A. Van Tassell, & L. Patterson (Eds.), *Research in the classroom: Talk, texts, and inquiry* (pp. 81–90). Newark, DE: International Reading Association.

Strickland, D.S. (1998a, June/July). Reading and the media. *Reading Today, 15*, p. 12.

Strickland, D.S. (1998b). *Teaching phonics today: A primer for educators*. Newark, DE: International Reading Association.

Strickland, D.S., & Morrow, L.M. (2000). *Beginning reading and writing*. New York: Teachers College Press; Newark, DE: International Reading Association.

Tafel, L.S., & Fischer, J.C. (1996). Lives of inquiry: Communities of learning and caring. In G. Burnaford, J. Fischer, & D. Hobson (Eds.), *Teachers doing research: Practical possibilities* (pp. 125–136). Hillsdale, NJ: Erlbaum.

Taylor, B. (Ed.). (1990). *Case studies in effective schools research*. Dubuque, IA: Kendall/Hunt.

Taylor, D. (1998). *Beginning to read and the spin doctors of science: The political campaign to change America's mind about how children learn to read*. Urbana, IL: National Council of Teachers of English.

Thomas, R.M. (1992). *Comparing theories of child development* (3rd ed.). Belmont, CA: Wadsworth.

Thompson, A. (1990). Thinking and writing in learning logs. In N. Atwell (Ed.), *Coming to know: Writing to learn in the intermediate grades* (pp. 35–51). Portsmouth, NH: Heinemann.

Toch, T. (1997, October 27). The reading wars continue. *U.S. News and World Report, 123*(16), 77.

Trelease, J. (1979). *The read-aloud handbook.* New York: Penguin.

Trelease, J. (1995). *The new read-aloud handbook* (3rd ed.). New York: Penguin.

Trelease, J. (2001). *The read-aloud handbook* (5th ed.). New York: Penguin.

Tripp, D. (1993). *Critical incidents in teaching: Developing professional judgement.* New York: Routledge.

Vacca, R.T. (1996, October/November). The reading wars: Who will be the winners? Who will be the losers? *Reading Today, 14,* p. 3.

VonDras, J.C. (1993). Empowerment through talk: Creating democratic communities. In K.M. Pierce & C.J. Gilles (Eds.) (with D. Barnes), *Cycles of meaning: Exploring the potential of talk in learning communities* (pp. 59–77). Portsmouth, NH: Heinemann.

Vygotsky, L.S. (1978). Mind in society: The development of higher psychological processes. (M. Cole, V. John-Steiner, S. Scribner, & E. Souberman, Eds. & Trans.). Cambridge, MA: Harvard University Press. (Original work published 1934)

Vygotsky, L.S. (1997). *Thought and language.* (A. Kozulin, Trans., Rev. ed.). Cambridge, MA: MIT Press. (Original work published 1934)

Wagstaff, J.M. (1999). *Teaching reading and writing with word walls: Easy lessons and fresh ideas for creating interactive word walls that build early literacy skills.* New York: Scholastic.

Walker, R., & Wiedel, J. (1985). Using photographs in a discipline of words. In R.G. Burgess (Ed.), *Field methods in the study of education* (pp. 191–216). London: Falmer Press.

Watson, D.J. (1993). Community meaning: Personal knowing within a social place. In K.M. Pierce & C.J. Gilles (Eds.) (with D. Barnes), *Cycles of meaning: Exploring the potential of talk in learning communities* (pp. 3–15). Portsmouth, NH: Heinemann.

Weade, R., & Green, J. (1989). Reading in the instructional context: An interactional sociolinguistic/ethnographic perspective. In C. Emihovich (Ed.), *Locating learning: Ethnographic perspectives on classroom research* (pp. 17–56). Norwood, NJ: Ablex.

Weaver, C. (1994). *Reading process and practice: From socio-psycholinguistics to whole language* (2nd ed.). Portsmouth, NH: Heinemann.

Weaver, C. (1996). *Teaching grammar in context.* Portsmouth, NH: Boynton/ Cook.

Weaver, C. (Ed.). (1998a). *Practicing what we know: Informed reading instruction.* Urbana, IL: National Council of Teachers of English.

Weaver, C. (Ed.). (1998b). *Reconsidering a balanced approach to reading.* Urbana, IL: National Council of Teachers of English.

Wharton-McDonald, R., Pressley, M., & Hampston, J.M. (1998). Literacy instruction in nine first-grade classrooms: Teacher characteristics and student achievement. *The Elementary School Journal, 99,* 101–128.

Whitford, B.L, & Gaus, D.M. (1995). With a little help from their friends: Teachers making change at Wheeler School. In A. Lieberman (Ed.), *The work of restructuring schools: Building from the ground up* (pp. 18–42). New York: Teachers College Press.

Willinsky, J. (1990). *The new literacy: Redefining reading and writing in the schools.* New York: Routledge.

Wolf, S.A., & Heath, S.B. (1992). *The braid of literature: Children's worlds of reading.* Cambridge, MA: Harvard University Press.

Wood, D., Bruner, J., & Ross, G. (1976). The role of tutoring in problem solving. *Journal of Child Psychology and Psychiatry, 17,* 89–100.

Zemelman, S., Daniels, H., & Bizar, M. (1999). Sixty years of reading research—But who's listening? *Phi Delta Kappan, 80,* 513–517.

Zemelman, S., Daniels, H., & Hyde, A.A. (1998). *Best practice: New standards for teaching and learning in America's schools* (2nd ed.). Portsmouth, NH: Heinemann.

Children's Literature Cited

Allard, H. (1978). *The Stupids have a ball.* Ill. J. Marshall. Boston: Houghton Mifflin.

Allard, H. (1981). *The Stupids die.* Ill. J. Marshall. Boston: Houghton Mifflin.

Brett, J. (1992). *Goldilocks and the three bears.* New York: Dodd, Mead.

Brown, M. (1993). *Arthur's pet business.* Boston: Little, Brown.

Kasza, K. (1995). The wolf's chicken stew. In R.C. Farr & D.S. Strickland (Eds.), *Sidewalks sing* (pp. 122–132). Orlando, FL: Harcourt Brace.

Mwalimu. (1995). Awful aardvark. In R.C. Farr & D.S. Strickland (Eds.), *All kinds of friends* (pp. 16–28). Orlando, FL: Harcourt Brace.

Noble, T.H. (1980). *The day Jimmy's boa ate the wash.* Ill. S. Kellogg. New York: Dial.

Resnick, J.P. (1996). *Eyes on nature: Snakes.* Chicago: Kidsbooks.

Silverstein, S. (1974). *Where the sidewalk ends.* New York: HarperCollins.

Silverstein, S. (1981). *A light in the attic.* New York: HarperCollins.

Wright, M. (Producer), & Naderi, H. (Director). (1986). *Mr. Know-It-Owl's video school: All about animals* [videotape]. (Available from Apollo Educational Video, 6901 Woodley Avenue, Van Nuys, CA 91406-4878)

Author Index

A

ADAMS, M.J., 2, 13, 14, 15, 18
ALDRIDGE, J., 11, 16, 191
ALLARD, H., 193
ALLEN, J., 186
ALLEN, R.V., 117
ALLINGTON, R.L., 2, 3, 4, 33, 35, 43, 90, 178, 188
AMAREL, M., 44, 194
ANDERSON, G.L., 4, 61, 62
ANDERSON, L., 45
APPLE, M., 20
ATKIN, J.M., 197
ATWELL, N., 3, 58, 149, 197
AVERY, C.S., 191

B

BAKER, K., 3
BALDWIN, L.E., 191
BANNER, J.M., 129
BARNES, D., 180, 181, 187
BARTON, B., 135
BEATTIE, M., 50
BERLINER, D.C., 36
BIDDLE, B.J., 36
BIGELOW, B., 4
BIKLEN, S.K., 62, 67, 70
BISSEX, G.L., 2, 3, 62, 189
BIZAR, M., 4
BLOCK, C.C., 3
BLOOME, D., 15, 188
BLUMER, H., 62

GREENE, M., 43, 61
GRIFFIN, P., 2, 28, 64
GROGAN, P.R., 2
GROSSEN, B., 13, 14, 29
GROVER, S.P., 197
GUBA, E.G., 19, 20, 62, 68, 69

H

HAMPSTON, J.M., 3
HARSTE, J.C., 3, 45, 187, 194
HEATH, S.B., 2, 50, 55, 91, 109, 110, 114, 152, 153, 177, 187, 188, 191, 192
HEPLER, S., 90
HERR, K., 4, 61, 62
HICKMAN, J., 90
HILL, L., 3
HOFFMAN, J.V., 8–10
HOLDAWAY, D., 4, 15, 50, 90, 189, 192, 193
HUBBARD, N., 4, 68
HUCK, C.S., 90
HURSH, D., 197
HYDE, A.A., 2, 27, 29

I

INTERSTATE NEW TEACHER ASSESSMENT AND SUPPORT CONSORTIUM, 6, 39–40
ISAACS, S., 44

J

JACKSON, P.W., 47
JACOBS, V.A., 191
JAGGAR, A., 129, 181
JOHNSON, J., 25
JONES, P., 181
JONES, T., 53, 54, 55, 91, 180
JUEL, C., 15

K

KAMEENUI, E.J., 13, 14, 15
KAMII, C., 46, 48, 197
KARP, S., 4
KASZA, K., 107, 109, 115

P

PALEY, V.G., 4, 31
PATERSON, K., 59–60
PATTERSON, L., 4, 62, 67, 181, 194
PEARSON, P.D., 4
PETERSON, B., 4
PETERSON, P.L., 45
PETERSON, R., 49, 52, 58, 59, 101, 139, 149, 181, 187, 190, 193
PHILLIPS, C.B., 32, 191
PIAGET, J., 46, 48, 54, 180
PICKERING, D.J., 4
PIERCE, C.M., 68, 70
PIERCE, K.M., 180, 181
PINNELL, G.S., 15
POLLARD, A., 62, 66
POLLOCK, J.E., 4
POWER, B.M., 4
PRESSLEY, M., 2, 3, 4, 178
PUCKETT, L., 187, 191
PUGH, K.R., 14
PURKEY, W.W., 3

Q–R

QUANTZ, R.A., 19
RAVITCH, D., 2
READING EXCELLENCE ACT, 2, 4
RESNICK, J.P., 161, 162
ROGOFF, B., 54, 180
ROSENBLATT, L.M., 15, 50, 194
ROSKOS, K.A., 5
ROSS, G., 54
ROUTMAN, R., 15, 37, 43, 57, 178
RUBIN, B.M., 13

S

ST. PIERRE-HIRTLE, J., 149
SCHARER, P.L., 2
SCHATSCHNEIDER, C., 14, 23
SCHON, D., 20
SCHROEDER, J., 57
SEIDMAN, I.E., 67

Subject Index

Note: Page numbers followed by *f* indicate figures.

A

B

C

tention in, 56–57; semiotics of, 18–19; as social process, 46–49, 54–55, 57–59; taking responsibility for, 142; *See also* literacy instruction

LEARNING COMMUNITIES. *See* community of learners

LEARNING DEFICITS, 32–33

LETTER WRITING, 171–173, 172*f*

LIBERAL PERSPECTIVE: on education, 11–12

LICENSING: standards for, 38–40

LISTENING: active, 59–60, 181

LITERACY CONTEXT, 55–56, 56*f*

LITERACY INSTRUCTION: balancing forms and styles in, 123–128; code-emphasis vs. meaning-emphasis, 13–16, 17–18, 32–33; conceptual frameworks for, 55–56; confusions about, 33–34; consensus standards for, 27–30; culturally relevant, 30–33, 48–49, 51–53, 177, 182–184; entry points for, 105–108; expectations in, 74–75, 77–78, 171–173, 179, 189–190; facilitating success in, 106–115; in high-poverty classrooms, 30–33, 46–49, 48–49, 51–53, 177; holistic approach in, 55–56; interconnected literacy elements in, 188–189; knowledge base for, 41–42, 50–51; learning choices and, 56–57; learning conditions and, 56–57; literacy context in, 55–56; modeling in, 78–79, 149–150; multiple modes of representation in, 116–128; negotiated curriculum for, 57; oral language in, 96–97; organizing vision in, 104–130; philosophy of, 53–61; phonics in, 13–16; polarized positions on, 43; process orientation in, 36–38, 46–47; reciprocity in, 44, 47, 154–156, 179, 192; reflective practice in, 114–116; relevant strategies in, 78–83; requisites for learning in, 56; responsible choice in, 83–85; scaffolding in, 54–55, 81, 90, 91; suggestions for, 33–34; supportive structures in, 89–91; teachable moments in, 81–82; theory-to-practice gap in, 197; *See also* reading; writing

LITERACY LEARNING. *See* learning; literacy instruction

LITERATURE. *See* books; reading

M

MANDATED CURRICULA, 34–35

MEANING-EMPHASIS INSTRUCTION: vs. code-emphasis instruction, 13–16, 17–18; in high-poverty classrooms, 32–33

MEANING MAKING, 136–142, 193–194

MEMBER CHECKS, 69

MIXED RESEARCH METHODOLOGIES, 19

MODELING, 78–79, 149–150

MULTIPLE MODES OF REPRESENTATION, 116–128

N

O

P